DAVID LOUD

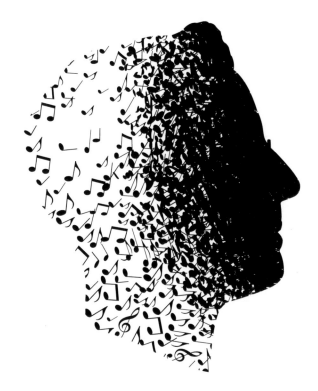

FACING THE MUSIC

A Broadway Memoir

Regan Arts.

For Pedro Porro

. . .

Regan Arts.

Copyright © David Loud, 2022

First Regan Arts trade paperback edition, October 2022

Library of Congress Control: 2021943226

ISBN 978-1-68245-191-5 (hardcover)
ISBN 978-1-68245-213-4 (trade paperback)

Interior design by Beth Kessler, Neuwirth & Associates
Cover design by Richard Ljoenes
Back Cover Photo by Michael Brosilow

Printed in the United States of America

Prelude : 2007

Where the hell is my music?

I was standing at the podium in an orchestra pit, a baton in my right hand, ready to begin. But due to a series of mishaps, there was no music on the music stand in front of me. It was the opening night of a new Broadway musical, *Curtains*, a cheerful murder mystery set in the hectic backstage world of a new Broadway musical.

I was the conductor of the musical, but I was also playing the small role of Sasha, the conductor of the musical-within-the-musical. I was wearing an elaborate set of tails, and my hair had been slicked back, 1950s style, by one of the show's hairdressers. The platform I was standing on was actually a motorized elevator lift, allowing me to rise into the audience's view to perform my lines and my song, then disappear back down into the pit.

I waited, listening to the murmurs of the audience mixing with the sounds of the orchestra warming up. It was disconcerting, staring at the empty wooden podium, where my score usually sat.

Curtains had been in previews for the last four weeks. Countless changes had been made to the show and to the score. Each cut, rewrite, and addition had to be copied into every musician's part and rehearsed. It had been an exhausting month.

That morning, I had asked a young music intern to copy a final set of corrections into my conducting score. Orchestra pits are cramped spaces, so he carried the large manuscript to a table in the orchestra locker room. For the past month, the show's orchestrator had been working at the same table, making his revisions during previews. When the intern finished, he left my score there with the orchestrator's music, intending to return the score to my podium before the performance.

AN HOUR EARLIER, I HAD ARRIVED AT THE STAGE DOOR. MY MOOD WAS BRIGHT. The long path to this particular opening night had been a singularly joyful journey. Bouquets of flowers, colorfully wrapped packages, cards, and telegrams spilled out of the dressing rooms into the narrow backstage hallways and staircases. Dodging clusters of balloons and elegant fruit baskets, I made my way up to my fourth-floor dressing room, where I discovered the young intern, wide-eyed and trembling.

"I can't find your score," he blurted out.

The jubilant opening night soundtrack playing in my brain came to a screeching halt.

"I've been searching for it for half an hour," he added.

Hoping that I had misunderstood him, I asked quietly, "My conducting score?"

He looked frightened. Like he expected me to start throwing things.

My knees felt weak. I sat down. We both knew that there was no backup score.

"I could cobble something together from the rehearsal piano book," he offered wanly.

"It would only confuse me," I said.

None of this made sense. Who would take my score?

"It has to be here somewhere," I said.

I interrogated the young intern and we retraced his every step.

The hallways and tunnels beneath the Martin Beck Theatre are filled with odd angles and mysterious doorways. We searched the pit and examined every nook and cranny we could access, to no avail. Our perplexed sleuthing was made more difficult by the constant stream of opening night gifts, notes from friends, and flowers being delivered to my small dressing room.

I made a decision, in the heat of the moment, not to broadcast my dilemma. A Broadway opening night is special—the culmination of an arduous journey—and I didn't want it to become about me. But my mind was working overtime, alternating between numb resolve and breathless panic.

You know every note of this score, I told myself. *It's going to be fine.*

You've never conducted this show without a score in front of you, I told myself. *It's going to be a disaster.*

When the stage manager announced, "Fifteen minutes. Fifteen minutes to showtime!" over the backstage speaker, I left my fate in the hands of the young intern and concentrated instead on dressing and preparing for the performance.

The woman who dealt with my hair didn't notice that I wasn't listening to her nightly monologue about her mother—I was mentally going through the more complicated sections of the score I was about to conduct. And as I changed into the first of the two crisply starched tuxedo shirts that had been delivered to my dressing room, my fingers inserted the studs and cuff links without the benefit of my brain, which was obsessively cataloguing all the dialogue cues that were written so helpfully in my missing score. Properly combed and costumed, I took my baton from its velvet-lined case and made my way downstairs to the stage. The company was gathering for a special meeting before the performance. The baton's wooden handle felt cool against my hot palm.

We stood onstage in a large circle. The thick red house curtain was down. We could hear the audience buzzing behind it. Our tightly knit *Curtains* company, bound together by years of readings, workshops, and a lengthy out-of-town engagement, had endured the deaths of its original book writer and its original lyricist. Tonight, their ghosts were palpably present. The director showed us how their names had been inscribed discreetly on the backs of two set pieces, visible to the actors, not the audience. He acknowledged how hard we had all worked to reach this night. The number of songs written and discarded exceeded the number of songs in the show. Even the title song, "Curtains," had been tossed. In the *Playbill*, the director had thanked, by name, the fifty-seven actors who had participated in readings of the musical but *hadn't* made it into the opening night cast. As I've learned repeatedly, showbiz is a fickle bitch.

"Break a leg," said the director. We disbanded.

I made my way downstairs to the pit. The stage manager's voice rang through the backstage speakers: "Places! The call is places." My heart skipped and skittered. The show would be starting momentarily, music or no music. Pausing outside the doorway to the pit, listening to the pre-show cacophony of squeaks, blasts, and wheezes from within, I briefly considered running for the hills. Instead, I squeezed through the gathered musicians and stepped up onto the podium. My hands were moist with sweat. The baton's wooden handle felt slippery in my fingers.

I waited.

Where the hell is my music?

From my position at the podium, I saw a small flurry of movement at the back of the pit. The young intern had darted in, handed a note to the French horn player, and dashed out. The horn player passed the folded piece of paper through the woodwind section and up to me. I opened the note.

Operating on a hunch, the intern had located the orchestrator in a bar near the theater. The orchestrator had finished his work on the show. To avoid lugging his heavy manuscript to the opening night performance and party, he had bundled up the music on the table, accidentally including *my* copy of the score, and instructed his driver to take it all back to the orchestrator's home in Connecticut.

When the intern alerted him to the crisis he had caused, the orchestrator called his driver, who had now turned around and was heading back toward New York City with my score. The intern was now driving, in a borrowed car, to a prearranged meeting point at a gas station somewhere in Westchester.

A little red light on my podium flashed twice. I picked up the phone and greeted the stage manager, and I confirmed that the musicians were in place. I told the stage manager that if the young intern came backstage during the performance, he *must* be allowed to come down to the pit to deliver something important. The stage manager was intrigued but had more pressing things to worry about. "Tell me later," she said, "at the party."

I nodded into the camera. I knew the stage manager was watching me on a TV monitor from her station in the stage right wing. She was an old friend, having been the stage manager for *Merrily We Roll Along*, the show in which I had made my Broadway debut twenty-six years earlier.

Soon the red light flashed on again, and this time I raised my baton, gathering the attention of the orchestra. The players were instantly ready. But a hard knot of fear had lodged itself in my stomach.

The musicians stared up at me, trusting and alert, utterly unaware that I would be flying blind.

The red light went out. I took a carefully timed breath, willing the brass and wind players to breathe with me, and I gave the preparatory beat that triggered the overture. Arpeggios and glissandos cascaded around me. A brass fanfare rang out as we charged into battle, a lickety-split rising scale catapulting us into the snappy first tune. As the trumpets blared the melody, the rhythm kicked in, the bass player and drummer laying a foundation on which the other players confidently rode. We sailed into the next melody and the next, seamlessly gliding through the music, building to a snazzy high climactic chord, and ending with a big low plunk—what we in the business call a "button." I turned around, bowed to the audience, acknowledged the orchestra, and turned back around to go on with the show.

The theater vibrated with the extra energy of an opening night performance. The show raced smoothly along. To my surprise, once I got used to it, the experience of conducting without music was freeing. The long weeks of previews had ingrained every eighth note, fermata, and trill into my cerebellum. My body instinctively knew the crucial sequences of cues and cutoffs that made up each musical number, and the extra tingle of danger seemed to oxygenate my brain.

Forty minutes into the first act, something down in the pit caught my eye. It was the young intern, sweaty and bedraggled in his rumpled opening night tuxedo, grinning up at me. He was creeping through the tightly packed musicians with my score. Reaching up, he handed it to me, its pages open to the upcoming song—a rueful ballad called "Coffee Shop Nights." I silently mouthed to him, "Thank you. You saved the show." He beamed with pride. The dialogue cue came from the stage. I started the introduction to the song, and I shifted my focus away from the pit and its dramas, back up to the stage, where the show was barreling forward.

ON MY PODIUM, I AM AT THE FOCAL POINT OF THREE DISTINCT WORLDS. FROM the pit, I look up at the actors, who aim their performances over my head, occasionally glancing down at me to ensure that we are synchronized. I see their shoes, mostly, if they're downstage, close to me, but as they move upstage, I see them clearly, and I hear the rustle of their costumes and the breaths they take to sing.

Below me is the orchestra, packed tightly into the pit, every inch of space a negotiated treaty. The musicians divide their focus between the music on their stands and the baton in my right hand, which tells them when, and how fast, to play. I tell them other things with my left hand and my body. I control their volume so they blend properly. I show them how the notes should be articulated and how to shape the phrases. One of the numbers in *Curtains* has a Western feeling; another has a vaudeville pizzazz; yet another evokes the smooth sheen of a Hollywood movie musical. I try to physically embody the style of the music we are playing, encouraging the players to join me in the spirit of that style.

Behind me, unseen but always felt, is the audience. I feel them on the back of my neck. I sense their attention and their boredom; I hear their laughs and their coughs. I try to watch the show through their new eyes and listen through their fresh ears.

The intersecting energy of these three worlds is heady, intoxicating. The thrill of making music overwhelms me. I am hyper-alert, monitoring conditions in three directions. I have rituals that I repeat at every performance: Eye contact with the actor playing the composer as he launches his high note, a wink at the actress playing the producer when her first joke gets a laugh. A cue I always give to the drummer in a particular way, guaranteeing that he will strike his triangle at the precise moment that the ingénue and the police inspector kiss. I raise my hands high to cue the ensemble for a vocal entrance or to help them cut off precisely. Occasionally, I conduct toward the camera so the stage manager can synchronize her lighting cues with my tempos. I breathe with the singers. The musicians breathe with me. On a good night, we become entwined, lifting each other into effortless flight.

Tonight is a good night.

Two hours later, after the finale and the curtain call and the exit music had all been played, I remained on the podium for a moment. My relief at having successfully led the company through tonight's performance was undercut by another, unexpected feeling. A feeling of dread. My left shoulder hurt in a way that I didn't recognize; the pain was making my left arm stiff. And the forty minutes I had spent conducting without a score had illuminated something else, something I had been willfully ignoring for months.

The left side of my body was off-kilter. A slight tremor had developed in my left hand. Occasionally, at home, I found myself typing using only my right hand. I was also having trouble putting on shirts and jackets, my left arm searching in vain for the opening of the sleeve.

During those first forty minutes, my left hand, usually occupied with the simple task of turning the pages of my score, had hung without expression. I realized that during the four weeks of previews, I had essentially been conducting with my right hand alone. I had been compensating for this in ways I hadn't noticed before. I was giving cues with my eyes and head instead of with my left hand, and I was avoiding large movements in favor of smaller ones, movements that were occasionally difficult for the musicians to see.

Shaken, I climbed down from the podium and made my way back up the stairs to my dressing room, stopping by the stage manager's office to request a physical therapy appointment with someone from the team of specialists that kept the dancers in working order.

My dressing room, already hosting a small crowd of friends, was bursting with merriment, the laughing and hugging overflowing out into the hallway. My father and stepmother had found their way backstage and were pouring champagne. Everyone was celebrating. As a longtime expert at masking my fears, I joined in. It had been a terrific night. But I knew something was wrong. Very wrong.

Chapter One

1967

{**M**}y mother moved slowly down the cramped aisle of the fabric store, examining the prints and patterns. She smiled to herself as she felt the different bolts of fabric, her dark brown shoulder-length hair kept in place, as always, with a black headband.

My mother made all my father's underwear. He liked to wear boxers, and she took a surprising amount of pleasure in searching out the most outrageous fabrics she could find—wild stripes, bright paisleys, neon polka dots. She was a talented and industrious seamstress. What started as a goofy whim turned into a major collection. Shopping trips with my mother usually ended with a trip to one of Cincinnati's fabric stores. It became our family game: find the perfect print for the next pair of boxers. Hawaiian hula dancers? Psychedelic butterflies? Bright yellow daisies?

She kept a swatch of fabric from each pair of underwear she made, and she created a book out of the swatches. The thick cardboard cover of the book had a cutout in the shape of a pair of boxers so you could see the latest print through the cutout.

I was five years old. I stared up at my mother. She was very pretty, her dark eyes dancing as they darted between the wads and twists of cloth. Endlessly patient, she could fix broken zippers and reweave unraveling scarves. Her hands were cool and soft, and she never tired of reading me stories, though she wasn't as good as my father at doing the different character voices that I required.

Suddenly, she laughed out loud. There, stuck in with the checks and plaids, was a print made of Budweiser beer labels.

"Perfect," she announced.

My father liked his beer. A six-pack a day.

When I was older, my mother made the tan corduroy suit that I wore for my high school graduation, and years later, my little sister's wedding dress, a creamy creation dappled with faint autumn leaves. But the boxers were different. They seemed to be a secret that my mother and father shared. He may have looked serious and professional in his jacket and tie, but they knew there was something wilder underneath, hidden away.

MY FATHER TAUGHT ALGEBRA AND CALCULUS AT THE HILLSDALE SCHOOL, AN all-girls high school, in Cincinnati. Ruggedly good-looking with a vaguely military crew cut, he had a dry sense of humor and a rigorous love of mathematics. His first two years at Hillsdale, he was the only male faculty member. There was no men's room in the school, only a tiny W/C labeled "Mr. Loud."

We lived in a small red house on Madison Road, in a quiet neighborhood near the school. Violets grew in a small patch of grass near the back door. We had a cat named Panther and a dog named Fang. Fang, a basset hound, had long drooping ears that hung down on either side of his face. Panther, a gently striped, grey tabby cat, worshipped Fang. She followed him everywhere. My little sister, who loved all animals unconditionally, spoke to them both in a language of purrs and growls and sighs. It was clear that they understood her perfectly.

Our living room, paneled with blond, knotty wood, held a dark green overstuffed couch, a big comfortable chair, a hi-fi stereo, a record cabinet, and a black-and-white television set.

My mother wanted to learn how to play the guitar. She found a television program called *Folk Guitar Plus* that gave lessons. It aired at 6:00 a.m., featuring a stylish lady named Miss Laura Weber. The "Plus" referred to the additional instruments she taught: the soprano recorder and the autoharp. I asked my parents for a recorder. We ordered workbooks from an educational television station in Nebraska.

My mother and I would stumble groggily into the living room and pull the television set close to the couch—me in my pajamas, with my wooden recorder, my mother in her nightgown, with her guitar. I learned how to read a melody line, following the notes as they went by in the workbook. I studied the fingerings, and we played along while Miss Laura Weber sang "Greensleeves" and "My Grandfather's Clock."

One morning, after weeks of struggling with how to cover the holes in the recorder with my little fingers, how to get a clear tone that didn't crack or whistle, and how to coordinate my fingers with my breathing, my mother and I made it through "Jesu, Joy of Man's Desiring" without any mistakes.

We sat in silence for a moment, surprised. I liked hearing how my part fit snugly into the other part; I liked making music with another person.

When I was six, I started piano lessons. My teacher, Miss Corn, old and portly, had gnarled hands. She wore bright red lipstick and had a big black mole on her face. Clear and precise, she began teaching me the fundamentals of music theory and gave me a small book of pieces to learn. She never allowed mistakes to go by uncorrected, usually balancing each criticism with a compliment. "That's an E-flat there, David, not an E-natural," she would say, "but my goodness, your rhythm is exactly right."

My mother and father bought a used, upright piano for $100, and they made the odd choice to put it in their bedroom. On weekends, they liked to sleep late. I've always been an early riser. At 6:00 a.m., I would march into their bedroom and practice.

Miss Corn taught her lessons from a cramped house she shared with her sister, a harpist. Its shelves were stuffed with ancient sheet music, frayed and crumbling. The piano was jammed into a wide doorway between two rooms. The low notes were in the dining room; the high notes were in the vestibule.

One day, while I was playing a minuet I had learned, Miss Corn leaned over and put her surprisingly strong hands over mine.

"David, stop," she said.

Her face was uncomfortably close. The gentle smell of her clinical, lemony perfume wafted over me.

"You play all the right notes, but you play without . . . inquiry. Have you ever asked yourself, 'Why is the next note the next note?'"

I had not.

"You must think about what Mozart was doing when he chose that particular note to be the next note. There are so many other notes he could have chosen! I want you to think about each note before you play it, as you play it, and after you play it."

She let my hands go. Settling back into her chair, she looked down at her lap, then up at me. Her dark, watery eyes gleamed.

"Music has consequences," she said.

Somehow, I understood what she was saying.

I tried to put it into practice.

SCHOOL WAS A BEWILDERING SEESAW OF TRIUMPHS AND FAILURES. I WON SPELLING contests and aced math tests, but I couldn't throw or catch a baseball. When I played "The Mountain Gnome" at a recital, everyone applauded. At football practice, I sat on the bench—sweating, miserable, petrified—wearing the oversized shoulder pads, jersey, and plastic mouthguard that had cost my parents seventeen dollars.

The record collection housed in our living room cabinet included a dozen or so original cast recordings of Broadway musicals: *My Fair Lady*; *Brigadoon*; *Bye Bye Birdie*; *Bells Are Ringing*; *The Music Man*; *Guys and Dolls*; *Hello, Dolly!*; *Fiddler on the Roof*; *Fiorello!*; *West Side Story*; *Kiss Me, Kate, Carousel*; and *Oklahoma!* Entranced, I played them over and over on our hi-fi stereo.

My parents kept strict control over the black-and-white television set. My sister and I were occasionally allowed to watch, but our viewing had to be planned in advance. Saturday morning cartoons were strictly rationed. Our neighbors, the Glovers, had a large color TV, which we were *never* allowed to watch. One spring evening, however, my mother worked out a secret plan with Mrs. Glover.

After an early dinner, my mother casually suggested that we go next door. Mrs. Glover invited us into her parlor. She had baked chocolate chip cookies, and she sat us down with delicate china plates in our laps, in front of the large console TV.

A movie started. It was in black and white. I was disappointed. Why would we come over here, I wondered, to watch a black-and-white movie? A mean lady on a bicycle was trying to take a girl's dog. The girl sang a sad song about wanting to be somewhere else. There was a scary storm, and her house blew up into the sky. When it landed, she opened the door, and I saw both color TV and the Land of Oz for the first time. It was the best day of my life so far.

At that time, *The Wizard of Oz* was broadcast annually, nationwide, each spring. Starting that year, I never missed a viewing. I thought about Oz a lot. At six years old, I already knew, inside, that I needed to be somewhere else, far away from this world in which I already felt, for reasons I didn't understand, like an outsider.

When I read the book *The Wonderful Wizard of Oz*, I discovered, at the end, that Dorothy Gale's trip to that magical land *hadn't* been a dream. That "dream" was Hollywood's cruel invention. I took comfort in the knowledge that there really was an Oz, after all. I just had to figure out how to get there.

The Hillsdale School had an ambitious theater teacher, Mr. Emerson. Tall and thoughtful, his dark brown hair was a bit longer than I was used to seeing on a man. He lived in our neighborhood. Noticing my interest in the theater, he started putting me in the high school plays when they needed a little boy. My first appearance onstage was as a dead child, in a multimedia show Mr. Emerson created about the horror of war. I had to stay completely still, as if I weren't breathing, in the arms of a high school junior, who was playing my mother. Apparently, I was convincing.

When I was in the second grade, Mr. Emerson directed a production of Samuel Beckett's *Waiting for Godot*, in which I played the Boy. The role of Vladimir was played by a high school senior girl. She was white, and Mr. Emerson had her wear blackface. Estragon, played by another senior girl, who was black, wore whiteface. I don't know what the significance of this was, but it was the '60s and I'm sure it meant something important to Mr. Emerson.

I had to memorize lots of lines for *Waiting for Godot*. After dinner, I would sit on my father's lap in the big comfortable chair in our living room, while he ran my lines with me. When the show was over, I was sad that our evening ritual wouldn't continue.

The following year, I was in Mr. Emerson's adaptation of *Alice's Adventures in Wonderland*. I played the Knave of Hearts. I had a red velvet costume with an elaborate crown and a long monologue, which I delivered alone onstage. It began, "I *did* steal the tarts," which got a big laugh.

I waited for the laughter to crest before saying my next line. I felt safe on that stage. I was in Wonderland.

At moments of celebration, like the night after my third and final performance as the Knave of Hearts, my mother and father would gather my sister and me into a tight circle, our arms wrapped around each other, and we would hug each other as tightly as we could.

I thought we had the happiest family in the world.

WHEN I WAS EIGHT YEARS OLD, MY FATHER ANNOUNCED AT DINNER THAT HE HAD been offered a position as assistant headmaster at North Country School, a progressive institution in the Adirondack Mountains, near Lake Placid, New York. We would be moving there permanently. It was the job my father had always wanted. He had grown up in New York City, but he had spent his summers at Camp Treetops in the Adirondacks, and he loved hiking and climbing. He felt at home in the mountains. My parents had met and fallen in love at Camp Treetops in the summer of 1959, when they had both been counselors there. North Country School operated on the camp property during the school year.

My mother told us that North Country School was a boarding school for a hundred students, fourth grade through eighth grade. The school was on an organic farm.

I packed my books and clothes into cardboard boxes.

Miss Corn wrote me a note telling me to keep practicing. Mrs. Glover came from next door to say goodbye; she hugged my mother tightly. Mr. Emerson waved from his porch as we drove away. Everything we owned was in a Mayflower moving van that drove behind us.

My sister and I sat in the back seat. We held hands. I looked out the window at the small red house, wondering if I would ever see it again. Tears streamed down my face, but I didn't make a sound.

Chapter Two

1970

{ "*H*allo*. My name is Chris Nicholson." The sandy-haired boy, taller than me, was to be my roommate for the year. He had light blue eyes that crinkled when he flashed his ready smile. I shook his hand and wondered about his accent. British? Australian? It turned out that his family lived on the island of Antigua, in the West Indies, and Chris's refined, clipped way of speaking came from spending time at country clubs and yachting regattas. I helped him move his things into the room that had both our names on the door. There were two beds, two desks, two chairs, and two lamps.

My family had moved into Cascade House, a residence located up the hill from North Country School's main building. Cascade House was designed to accomodate a faculty couple and ten students. The picture window in the communal living room framed a perfect view of Cascade Mountain. I was going into the fourth grade, so I was assigned a room in the student section. My parents and my sister occupied the faculty apartment. My sister started second grade at the public school in Lake Placid, seven miles away.

I had been dreading having an assigned roommate, but Chris's decent spirit was instantly apparent, and I soon lowered my guard. His older sister had been a student at North Country School, so he was a good source of information.

"Did you know," he asked me, when we were alone, "that candy is forbidden at North Country School? I'm going to tell you a secret now. My sister gave me some Hershey Bars before I left. She said to keep them in my dress shoes until I found a better hiding place. You're not going to tell your parents, are you?"

I swore that I would not.

"Did you know," he asked me, "that we all have to have jobs?"

Walter Clark, who had founded the school in 1938, believed that children needed to connect to the earth. Students planted, tended, and harvested the gardens, and they took care of the many animals who lived in the big wooden barn. The jobs rotated every two weeks. Walter encouraged his students to "be rugged, be resourceful, be resilient."

Mostly, I was bewildered and anxious.

My first job at North Country School was shoveling horse manure.

On the first day of school, I woke at six thirty, got dressed, and walked a half-mile in the chilly dawn air to the barn for "barn chores." The campus was startlingly beautiful. Fields glistened with heavy dew, gently stroked by dawn's first light. I walked by clusters of silver-white birches and through spacious groves of tall pines. The garden was bursting with rows of fall vegetables, their leaves a riot of shapes and hues. Vines laden with pea pods raced up chicken-wire trellises. The dirt roads were lined with grey split-rail fences. Mountains loomed in the distance.

Chores began at seven. Other students fed the horses hay and oats, tended the pigs in the pigsty, gave kitchen scraps to the goats, or gathered eggs in the henhouse. My job: muck out the horse stalls.

Fifteen horses lived in the barn. Their stalls backed onto a corridor. An iron track ran along the ceiling of the corridor, and a heavy iron trough, known as the "honey wagon," hung from the track, supported by iron chains. You could push the trough from stall to stall the whole length of the barn. Once the horses were out in the pasture for the day, I was required to shovel all the nice fresh horse manure from each of the stalls into the honey wagon, then slide it to the end of the corridor and out the door. Then, using a complicated series of chains and pulleys, I was supposed to flip the honey wagon, dumping the wagonload of horse manure onto the compost pile. I was eight years old, asthmatic, and small for my age. Nobody showed the slightest bit of concern.

The shovel was enormous. It had a heavy steel blade and a thick wooden handle. I picked it up and tried as hard as I could to push it under the big horse turds strewn around the first of the fifteen stalls. Hoisting it up, I turned around, aiming the shovel up toward the wagon, but my foot slipped, and I fell, the shovel clattering, the dung rolling helter-skelter all around me. Defeated, I sat in the filth, wondering how I could possibly survive this.

Tsu Hansen, a tall, broad, and imposing faculty member with close-cropped hair, supervised barn chores. She appeared from the corridor, concerned that the noise I was making might spook the animals. Dressed entirely in denim, she looked like a big blueberry. I looked up at her as she explained, matter-of-factly, that running a school on a working organic farm required many essential, interdependent steps. If I failed to remove the manure from the stalls, not only would the horses be standing in their own poop that evening, but the compost pile would go unnourished, meaning that next year's crops, which had to be fertilized with this year's compost, would suffer. This would result in less food for the community.

I got myself up off the floor of the stall, found a smaller shovel, and went to work, lifting the manure up into the foul-smelling trough. I needed help pushing the heavy shit-caked wagon to the next stall, and I was useless at operating the arcane system of rusty iron levers and springs that would, finally, release the precious cargo onto the steaming compost pile.

Breakfast was at eight in the school dining room. I didn't make it on time once in those first two weeks. Straggling in late, red-faced and sweaty, smelling of horse manure and inadequacy, I'm sure I made a wonderful first impression on the other students.

• • •

WE ATE AT WOODEN TABLES—FIVE STUDENTS AND ONE FACULTY MEMBER AT each one—in an airy room with big windows that looked out over the fields. Breakfast consisted of fruit (stewed rhubarb from the garden, or prunes) and a daunting thick bran cereal known as "Sawdust." Each table received a large bowl of the hot porridge. I could make it edible with enough honey and milk, but even then, it was a formidable opponent. The adults expected us to finish our Sawdust before going to class. Fierce battles of will ensued between sullen students and stern faculty over what exactly constituted an empty bowl.

Then it was classes, lunch, more classes, time outside playing or hiking or working on the farm, study time, dinner, and up the hill to Cascade House. Bedtime was 9:00 p.m. Chris Nicholson and I would whisper in the dark. He told me about growing up at Pigeon Point, Antigua, where his parents had built a house facing the Caribbean, and how much he loved sailing. I told him about the small red house on Madison Road, which, in comparison, didn't seem very interesting.

Chris asked me once if I missed Cincinnati. To my surprise, I didn't. As unfamiliar as this new world was, my schedule was so jam-packed—who had the time? Chris liked North Country School but got terribly homesick. The only fight we ever had was when he angrily, tearfully explained to me that I could never understand what he was feeling because my parents lived right down the hall. He was right; my position was unique. We usually fell asleep pretty quickly. It always felt like mere seconds had elapsed before I was being shaken awake again. The honey wagon wasn't going to fill itself.

I STARTED TAKING PIANO LESSONS FROM DON RAND, THE SCHOOL'S MUSIC teacher. He was erudite, witty, and an accomplished classical pianist. Don's lessons were different from the nurturing sessions I'd had with

Miss Corn. Don expected me to practice every single day: scales, exercises, and études. If I didn't, he could always tell. He never got angry, just disappointed in the gap between where I was and where I might have been. Which was, of course, devastating. He forced me to take responsibility for my playing, and when I followed his demands to the letter, I could feel the improvement in my technique.

Don was responsible for the big theatrical production of the year—the Thanksgiving play. All the parents visited the school for Thanksgiving. Each year, after a turkey dinner served with potatoes and vegetables grown in the garden, Don presented a musical. The musical was staged in the Quonset Hut, which was the school's basketball court. Don directed, wrote the script, composed the songs, designed the set, and accompanied the performance on the piano. This became the event that I cared most about at North Country School. I wanted a part in the Thanksgiving play. I wanted lines to memorize and solo songs to sing. Instead, I was assigned to the alto part in the chorus.

The shows that Don created were amazing.

That first year, when I was in fourth grade, he did Egyptian Gods and Goddesses, with songs about Osiris and Anubis. The Quonset hut was decorated with Egyptian hieroglyphics and images of the pyramids. A girl with a pretty voice reminded him of Cleopatra, so he wrote his own version of the Caesar/Cleopatra/Mark Antony story. Don composed heartbreaking, romantic music for the lovers and a fast, tricky "patter song" for Ftatateeta, Cleopatra's maid. The following year it was Greek Myths and Legends with a harrowing retelling of the Medusa fable. One year, inspired by two students who were identical twins, Katie and Noni, he presented a musical version of *Cinderella.*

When the fairy godmother waved her wand at Katie, who was playing dirty, downtrodden Cinderella, dressed in rags, she ran behind a tree and instantly reappeared, resplendent in a sparkling ball gown, face scrubbed, hair lustrous. Of course, it wasn't Katie, it was Noni. She had been pre-set behind the cardboard tree for twenty-five minutes. We knew it was Noni, but, as one does in the theater, we suspended our disbelief. The effect was magical.

My favorite was an oratorio he composed. It was a *serioso* composition, with recitatives, choruses, and arias, that told the story of *Little Red Riding Hood*. It had an unusual ending.

The traditional conclusion of the story, you may recall, involves the unexpected appearance of a Huntsman. He slices open the wolf, which has eaten the girl and her grandmother. They escape alive, the wolf having not even chewed them. This was not the resolution that Don wanted for his oratorio. Instead, after the Wolf devoured Little Red and Granny, Don had the choir turn directly to the audience. And in a subtle tribute to the guiding spirit of the school, founder Walter Clark, we sang this chorale:

> *We here refute the theology*
> *That brands the Wolf a sinner.*
> *We here salute ecology,*
> *Wherein the Wolf's a winner!*
> *His appetite of great renown*
> *Keeps the population down.*
> *Nor is it to his detriment*
> *His conscientious use of excrement!*
> *So, as through the woodlands you go,*
> *Think of Gran and Child, helping trees to grow.*
> *Ah, Wolf,*
> *Ah, Wolf!*

I sang my part fervently. Don had set the words "Ah, Wolf" so they fooled the audience into thinking we would be singing "Amen." I remember the parents' astonished faces and also the thrill I felt at the audacity of "Ah, Wolf," with its rejection of traditional religion and its clear-eyed embrace of the dark truth about the natural life cycle.

I took it for granted then, but we were under the uncompromising guidance of a genuine artist. Don was a shining example of a precept that took me a long time to learn: being your own quirky self is invariably more interesting than doing what people expect you to do.

My last year, I finally landed a leading role in Don's Thanksgiving production, a revival of the Caesar/Cleopatra opus. My joy at being given the part of Mark Antony, who sang the big love song, was only slightly diminished by the fact that I had to sing it to my sister, who was playing Cleopatra.

ONE CHILLY, MID-OCTOBER DAY, OUR HEADMASTER STOOD UP AT BREAKFAST AND solemnly announced that the day's classes were canceled. Jubilation! Then he told us why.

"It's Chicken Plucking Day," he said.

For some students, this was a great holiday; for others, it was the most disgusting of North Country School's traditions. A few of the more bloodthirsty senior boys—eighth-graders—were chosen to go to the chicken coop with ponchos, gloves, and knives. There were quick, humane ways to kill the chickens, but, inevitably, there would also be the riveting demonstration of the phrase "running around like a chicken with its head cut off." In my five years at North Country School, I only saw it once. It involved an ax, a chopping block, and a freshly decapitated chicken forced into a standing position. Horrible.

The students divided into two teams: plucking and gutting. Everyone was required to participate, and that first year, having no idea what I was doing, I chose plucking. When the freshly slaughtered chickens arrived from the henhouse, we plunged them into vats of boiling water, which loosened their feathers. The chickens had to be removed from the hot water immediately, before the meat started to cook. We hung the chickens by their feet from ropes attached to the rafters. The stench of boiled feathers was revolting.

Using rubber gloves, I yanked the steaming feathers off the birds. We had to pluck the feathers as quickly as possible, while the skin was still hot. The feathers came off unwillingly, three or four at a time. Hot droplets of water flew from the larger feathers as they sprang from the chicken's skin, spraying my face and hair. If I didn't pull them firmly, the feathers could break off at the point where they entered the skin, leaving the tip of the quill embedded inside. Broken quills had to be dug out by hand, which meant taking off my gloves. The awful smell lingered on my fingers for days.

The next year, I tried gutting. This meant reaching into the warm cavity to remove the innards, but *anything* was better than grappling with those hot, wet feathers. I pulled out the organs and sorted them, saving the hearts, gizzards, and livers, being careful not to rupture the bile duct, and discarding the other intestines.

I also gently harvested the eggs that hadn't been laid yet. This was fascinating. Tomorrow's egg would be almost fully formed, with a soft shell, and sometimes there would be three or four other eggs-in-waiting, in decreasing levels of evolution. These eggs-to-be, without shells, formed a gently fading palette, from bright orange to pale yellow. Most students preferred plucking, but from then on, I opted for gutting.

After Chicken Plucking Day, Chris and I announced, solemnly, that we were converting to vegetarianism. The vow only lasted a few days, but the urge behind it was genuine. I've never eaten chicken since without recalling each step it took to get that meat onto my plate.

WINTERS IN THE ADIRONDACKS WERE AN INTIMIDATING SUCCESSION OF SNOW-storms; temperatures were bone-chilling. I was serious about playing the piano, and the best piano at school was in the Music Room, which had enormous glass windows. It also had, I can testify, a heating system that did not work between 1970 and 1975. In winter, it was the coldest place in America. I tried to practice at least an hour each day, breathing on my fingers to warm them or jamming them under my armpits. I played Beethoven sonatas, Chopin waltzes, and Bach inventions. Often, I could see my breath in front of me as I played.

At the end of the semester, the other students climbed into a chartered bus to New York City for Christmas vacation. The desolate stillness they left behind was tangible. Wind howled and snow blew in every direction, forming massive drifts. Going outside meant long underwear, two pairs of socks, boots, a parka, hat, mittens. Better to stay inside and read.

A title on my parents' bookshelf caught my eye: *Act One*. A paperback, with a black cover. The author had the unlikely name of Moss Hart. Standing at the bookshelf, I read the first two paragraphs. Then I curled up by the fire with the book. Three weeks later, when I put it down, I had read it twice, and it had changed my life. That book should come with a warning label. Parents who don't want their children throwing their lives away in show business should avoid having such a dangerous recruitment tract in their homes. As I lingered over the ending, for the second time, tears in my eyes, I could feel that an ember had been lit inside me.

I needed to be living in New York City, working in the theater.

Chapter Three

1972

{In the barn, morning sunlight streamed through cracks in the walls, slicing through the dim air in thin dusty beams. I sat on a low wooden stool, milking a big brown cow. My forehead rested gently against her stomach. I had rotated through many jobs in the two years since we had arrived at North Country School, but this was my first stint on milking duty. I squeezed the cow's small udders (sized perfectly for a ten-year-old's hands) from top to bottom. When I started milking, only a few drops dribbled out per squeeze, but as my hands found their rhythm on the teats, the sprays got longer and fuller until the warm milk streamed into the tin bucket. The sound changed as the bucket filled. The hollow, metallic reverberation of milk against tin blurred into a softer splash of milk on milk.

There was a brown cow and a black one. They paid no attention to me, concentrating only on eating their breakfast. Both cows seemed resigned to their fate: their mammary glands would be handled by a never-ending parade of novice children learning how to milk a cow.

The barn cats, usually antisocial, gathered around me, hoping for a charity spritz. If I aimed the udder anywhere near them and squeezed, they positioned their mouths, with voracious expertise, in the perfect spot to catch every drop of the warm liquid. Though it was against the rules, I occasionally sprayed the raw milk into my mouth as well. It had a musky tang. If I sipped the milk that had accumulated in the bucket, even just a few moments later, that particular taste was not present.

I lost track of time and place, spiraling down into the simple act of squeezing and releasing. The cow's udders warmed my hands. She towered over me, patient and docile. I was intoxicated by the pungent odor of the animal, a powerful smell that obliterated the background scents of the barn—hay, horses, manure.

After milking both cows, I poured the warm, frothy liquid from my tin pail into a large milk can. I patted the rump of the brown cow goodbye. She ignored me.

Tsu Hansen helped me load the heavy milk can into the school Jeep. She drove the milk, along with the morning's egg collection, to the kitchen. I rode in the back of the Jeep, bouncing jerkily on the bumpy dirt road, the wind blowing my hair, ravenous for breakfast. The school wasn't allowed to serve unpasteurized milk directly to the students, but Bea, who ran the kitchen, discreetly cooked with it, so it was a contribution to the community.

Later, at evening barn chores, the cows would need to be milked again. Occasionally, when I looked in the mirror before going to bed, I'd see a few cow hairs stuck to my forehead.

CHRIS AND I BECAME FRIENDS WITH ANOTHER BOY, MITCHELL. MITCHELL RARELY spoke, but when he did, it was to say something interesting, like, "That goat has been eating your history book for the last twenty minutes," or, "When we were living in South Africa, there was a beach for white people and a beach for black people."

The three of us were soon inseparable. One warm Saturday afternoon, late fall, we were out exploring in the woods, following the stream that ran through the campus up toward its source, hoping to find a swimming hole.

"Chris! David!"

Mitchell, who never shouted, or displayed any emotion at all, was shouting excitedly, thirty yards behind us. Chris and I walked back to him.

A huge birch had fallen, and its roots had come out of the ground, forming a large natural cave inside the newly exposed tentacles of the tree's massive root system. Intrigued, we wiggled our way in through a gap in the roots, hoping not to find too many snakes or spiders. Inside, it was spacious and dry. There were a few spots where rain might leak through, but otherwise, it was surprisingly well protected from the elements. Chris, a natural leader, organized our efforts. He set about patching the holes with birchbark. I found piles of freshly fallen leaves and carpeted the cave with a soft layer of autumn color—orange and red. Mitchell widened the entryway and inspected for animal life. We worked on our secret fort for the next two weeks whenever we could sneak away. We spoke of it only in code, calling it "BB" for Birch Bungalow.

We wanted to spend a night there, so the following weekend, at 9:15 p.m., we snuck out of our dorms. Carrying sleeping bags and flashlights, Chris and I crawled quietly out the window of our room and down the fire escape. We met Mitchell by the fire escape from his room, and together we ventured into the woods.

It was an altogether different trip by night. The landmarks we depended on to find our way through the forest during the day were unrecognizable in the dim moonlight. The thin beams of our flashlights cast looming shadows, revealing intimidating spider webs. Large, pale moths flitted in and out of the dancing beams.

After some wrong turns in the dark woods, we arrived at Birch Bungalow. Outside, the moon cast a silver luminescence; inside, it was dark, dry, and soft. We inspected for forest creatures, unpacked our sleeping bags, and nestled into the leaves. Chris had smuggled along an entire unopened Hershey Bar, which we carefully divided and shared. Mitchell insisted that we turn off our flashlights, lest they attract the attention of a bear. The smell of dried leaves, the aroma of forest dirt, and the gentle scent of birchbark mingled together into an intoxicating primeval slumber potion. It was like sleeping in the womb of Mother Earth.

When the glow of dawn started peeping through the birchbark patches, I woke up first. I lay there for a bit, enjoying the peaceful strangeness of our forest cocoon. The enormous roots laced together above our heads, the twittery flutters of birdsong reverberating outside. After a few minutes, I nudged the others awake. We packed our gear and hiked quietly back to our houses, sneaking inside and into our beds, just in time to be "woken up."

EVERY SO OFTEN, THERE WOULD BE A SATURDAY NIGHT SQUARE DANCE IN THE Quonset hut. Don Rand played the piano. Ever-modulating choruses of "Red River Valley" and "Honolulu Baby" cascaded from his tireless hands. My father was an expert caller, shouting out instructions for the dances: "Do-si-do and Allemande Left," "Swing your partner 'round and 'round."

I was a good square dancer, in great demand as a partner, and particularly skilled in the Adirondack-style swing. It involved getting a firm grip on your partner's torso, then leaning back and pivoting around a center point, your feet paddling you quickly around. If I locked my gaze on my partner's eyes, I could swing for a long time without getting dizzy.

I danced every dance, relishing the unusual feeling of excelling at something physical. I carefully avoided team sports. Baseball and soccer were just opportunities to be shamed and ridiculed. But I could square dance. I darted from girl to girl like a bumblebee in a thistle patch. I could swing my partner 'round and 'round as fast as anyone at school, and I confidently led the other couples through the intricate patterns. Out of breath, my cheeks flushed bright red, I didn't want it to end. The graham crackers and fruit punch, served in the dining room afterward, always tasted miraculously good.

● ● ●

ONE SPRING, A TOURING COMPANY OF *H.M.S. PINAFORE*, THE GILBERT AND Sullivan operetta, played Lake Placid. As I left the theater, I was laughing at the clever wordplay, and hours later, the buoyant melodies were still careening around my brain. I approached Tsu Hansen, who had also attended the performance, and suggested that we put on a version of *Pinafore* ourselves. To my surprise, she agreed, and the two of us started cajoling other students and faculty members into joining us. Three weeks later, the *N.C.S. Pinafore* set sail. I was at the piano, and Tsu was an enormous Little Buttercup. It was a rollicking success.

ONCE THE SCHOOL YEAR ENDED, MY FATHER RESUMED HIS REAL LIFE'S WORK: taking his son mountain climbing. My summers were a forced march of day trips and overnight hikes. There seemed to be no way out of it. My father couldn't imagine a world in which mountain climbing wasn't the preferred daily activity. And there were strict rules of behavior in that world—no complaining, ever. Only weaklings and sissies cried if the trail was too steep, the backpack was too heavy, or the rain was too cold. I quickly learned to hide my feelings around him.

There are forty-six "high peaks" in the Adirondacks—mountains over four thousand feet high. If you climb them all you become a "46-er," and you get to join a club with the other idiots who've climbed them all. It's called the "Adirondack 46-ers Club." When you join, you get a number. When my father started climbing as a boy, most of the mountains didn't have trails; the ascents required extensive map and compass work. Trips that only take half a day now took three days then. My father is #125 in the club, which means he became a 46-er back when men were men.

Through no desire of my own, I became a 46-er when I was twelve years old. Chris and Mitchell, both of whom enjoyed mountain climbing far more than I did, joined us on the climactic trip. Three days of trudging through freezing April rain, sleeping in sodden tents, and bushwhacking through scrappy trees—capped by a dreary party on the densely wooded summit of Santanoni—gave me my forty-sixth high peak. My father cheerfully checked the final box on my 46-er application form and eagerly sent it off to club headquarters. I am #876. Even our dog, Tigger, became a 46-er: #954.

Gradually, I learned the secret to mountain climbing: if you keep putting one foot in front of the other, you will eventually reach the top.

I was also expected to attend Camp Treetops, which occupied the school campus every summer. For the months of June and July, I lived in a canvas tent. The tents held four beds, each covered by a mosquito-netting coffin. Campers went barefoot most of the time, except when we worked in the barn or rode the horses. I swam in the lake, I went canoeing, I made lanyards, and I weeded the garden. I gathered raspberries and blackberries from thorny bushes. I also played mumblety-peg, which I'm startled to remember, involved throwing a pocketknife up in the air in various ways, hoping it would land with the blade in the ground and not in my foot or my eye.

It all felt like a detour to me. I had to fight for time to practice the piano, and I could feel my hard-won technique slipping away. After three summers of this, armed with a brochure I had found in the school library, I knocked on my parents' door one night as they were getting ready for bed. I announced that *next* summer, I would be attending the New York State Music Camp in Oneonta. This proclamation surprised my parents, who had no counterarguments ready. The following summer, to our collective astonishment, I went away to music camp.

It was very different. There were no animals, we wore shoes, and Sawdust was not on the menu. At breakfast in the cafeteria, confronted with the choice between Froot Loops and Lucky Charms, I wondered if I had accidentally landed on Mars. But soon, I was playing chamber music and accompanying recitals. I had landed, I discovered, in the peculiar world of the music nerd, an under-socialized subset of humanity that spends its childhood in practice rooms, not playing sports, and not going to the mall with friends. I felt instantly at home.

It was the first step in my escape from the Adirondacks.

THE LAKE PLACID COMMUNITY THEATER DID A PRODUCTION OF *SHOW BOAT.* I read in the program that the show was based on Edna Ferber's novel of the same name. Miraculously, the tiny Lake Placid Library had a copy. I devoured it. Comparing the musical to its source material was fascinating. Lake Placid High School put on *My Fair Lady,* and then *The Pajama Game*; I raced through Shaw's *Pygmalion* and tracked down a copy of Richard Bissell's *7½ Cents.* I read T.H. White's *The Once and Future King* and the script for *Camelot; Romeo and Juliet* and the libretto for *West Side Story*; Thornton Wilder's *The Matchmaker* and *Hello, Dolly!*.

But the colorful world that was opening up to me, through books and recordings, seemed impossibly distant—as far as Oz had been from that farm in Kansas. I wanted Broadway shows, pit orchestras, tap-dancing choruses, brassy leading ladies, and shyster producers. My story—growing up in the mountains, longing for New York City—is the exact opposite of my father's.

Mucking out stalls and plucking chickens was not going to get me to Broadway.

My escape plan needed work.

Chapter Four

1974

{I} had a surplus of grandmothers. Three, to be precise: Doddy, Grandmommy, and Grandma. But only two grandfathers.

My father's parents divorced when he was little. His mother lived alone in New York City. We called her "Doddy." A formidable woman —short and solid—she had a bit of a hunch to her back and a German lilt to the way she pronounced her Rs. Doddy had a bright smile and blue-green eyes that twinkled around her children and grandchildren. She also had a knack for sharp, critical barbs, perfectly aimed. She wore black horn-rimmed cat's-eye glasses, which gave her a half-madcap, half-studious look. She loved the theater, having taught drama in the 1930s and '40s at the Brearley School in Manhattan.

One Christmas, we traveled to New York City to visit her. She lived on East Sixty-Sixth Street. The elderly doorman directed us to the elevator, where the ancient elevator man took us up to the fourth floor. Doddy was waiting in the hallway with plastic bags for our shoes. She had recently installed expensive burnt orange wall-to-wall carpeting, and she was determined to keep it spotless. Only after our shoes were bagged and lined up next to the welcome mat did she let us into her meticulously arranged, one-bedroom apartment. Elegant, understated wreaths hung on the walls, and there were several trays of paper-thin Christmas cookies. Doddy smiled nervously and told us to make ourselves comfortable. It felt like four rhinoceroses had accidentally been set loose in a dollhouse. Our family of four somehow slept on the one pull-out couch in her living room.

Christmas morning, she presented us with tickets to a Broadway show. Finally, I was going to see my first Broadway musical! *The Magic Show*. The tickets were for the following night. I was quivering with excitement but also, instantly, a little nervous. What if it didn't live up to my expectations? Something about the title sounded iffy to me. Was some guy going to stand onstage, pull a rabbit out of a hat, and try to pass himself off as a Broadway musical?

We arrived at the Cort Theatre on Forty-Eighth Street, gave our tickets to the uniformed usher, and received *Playbill* programs in exchange. We clambered up to the mezzanine. I put my program away, to devour later. Wide-eyed, I took in the rococo architecture, the decorative murals, and the gilded carvings that decorated the boxes and balconies. I had never seen anything like it, but it was everything I had hoped a Broadway theater would be. The house lights dimmed. My doubts evaporated, and I could feel my heart pounding excitedly in my chest.

I remember every second of *The Magic Show*. The cast was zany and talented, the songs were catchy and smart, the magic tricks . . . astounding. What I loved most was how magic, story, and song intersected. Cal, a drab magician's assistant, sang, "I want to be a lion tamer," with so much emotion in her voice that I yearned for her to be a lion tamer, too. Everyone in the theater did. Plain Cal was jealous of hot Charmin, a sexpot who the magician conjured up, so after the magician sawed Charmin in half, Cal, spitefully, stole her legs. Charmin spent the rest of the show wheeling her torso around, trying to get her legs back. I thought this was hilarious. And at the end, when the magician produced an actual Bengal tiger (where someone had been standing just seconds before), the realization that Cal's dream of being a lion tamer was going to come true after all was immensely satisfying.

I was transported—every sense, thought, and feeling absorbed in the story. That sensation of losing myself, of entering another world and living there for a time, was violently addictive. I began saving any money I could, so that once a year I'd be able to take the Trailways bus to New York City to sleep on Doddy's pull-out couch for a few days. She would meet me, bravely, at Port Authority, holding my hand tightly as we walked past the beggars and bums. We would see as many shows as we could. We stayed up late. She would sip a glass of bourbon while we discussed what we had seen. Occasionally, she would treat me to dinner at Sardi's in the theater district.

New York City, the diametric antithesis of an organic farm, was electrifying to me. Dirty and dangerous, yes, but it contained a universe of possibility. During the day, Doddy and I often rode the bus together. I would look at the other passengers, wondering if any of them, so ordinary on the outside, might, in fact, be actors who would be on Broadway that very evening—making audiences laugh, breaking people's hearts, singing, and dancing—before turning back into ordinary people, wearing drab coats, clutching purses, reading newspapers, and riding buses.

The Broadway actress Marian Seldes had been a student of Doddy's and remained a devoted friend. Marian was appearing in *Equus*, the play by Peter Shaffer. One January, during my stay, Doddy secured matinée tickets and arranged a trip backstage after the performance. The play was exceptional, but I was even more excited about visiting a Broadway star's glamorous dressing room.

We made our way up the aisle amid the departing throng. Doddy seemed to know where she was going; I followed her as she turned into one of the rows, and we scooted sideways past the velvet cushions to one side of the theater. An usher escorted us through a pass door hidden behind a heavy, brocaded curtain.

The backstage of the Plymouth Theatre was not remotely what I had imagined. The air was freezing cold, the walls pockmarked with peeling paint. Bare bulbs cast harsh shadows. Members of the crew lumbered around. One of them opened the door to an alley; an arctic gust of wind blew in. Doddy pulled her old fur coat tightly around her shoulders, grimacing. A bald man with a purple stain on his face pointed us toward a dark alcove. We climbed to the third floor on a treacherously steep iron staircase.

A rusty sink stood outside each dressing room door. Marian Seldes was washing her face in the tiny basin, swearing because there was no hot water. She wore a ripped lavender kimono and fuzzy purple slippers. She was tall, with long, expressive arms.

Seeing us approaching, she gestured dramatically at the sink.

"Ice water," she intoned, with the expertise of a tragedienne.

Then a gasp.

"Oh, but how silly of me! You're not the plumber. You must be David!"

Was that a tear in her eye?

She turned toward Doddy.

Humbly, piously, the actress whispered, "Thank you."

She turned back to me, placing her large right hand on my cheek. Leaning down, she stared into my eyes, makeup from the matinée still caked on her wet face.

"Welcome," she said in her grand, theatrical voice. "Welcome!"

I stared back at her, wondering how to respond.

Removing her hand from my cheek, she pointed to her throat. Her face assumed a mask of profound sorrow. She backed into her dressing room, elaborately pantomiming her deep regret at not being able to say more. The door closed after her.

I thought this eccentric performance might provoke a sarcastic roll of the eyes or a tart one-liner from Doddy, but she remained poker-faced, with a pleasant smile that said, "All is as it should be." We carefully made our way down the stairway and out onto Forty-Fifth Street.

My sister and I called my mother's mother "Grandmommy." Smart, liberal, and opinionated, Grandmommy had a superb eye for interior design and a deep love of a good dirty joke. She had a hug that could solve every problem and a lap that could quiet any fear.

Grandmommy and Granddaddy seemed like best friends. Early pictures of their marriage show Grandmommy as shorter than her husband, but Granddaddy got smaller and smaller every year, and eventually, she towered over him. He worked as a traveling salesman, selling paint and varnish for the Cloverleaf Paint Company. His territory was the entirety of New York State, so Grandmommy and Granddaddy reluctantly left New York City, where they had both grown up, to live more centrally.

They found a comfortable house in Syracuse and filled it with antiques and fine furniture, all scavenged from tag sales and flea markets. They enjoyed a martini every day at 5:00 p.m., accompanied by homemade cheese crackers, big black olives, and thinly sliced carrot sticks. Grandmommy would carry a tray into her comfortable living room, where Granddaddy would be pouring cocktails. One martini each was enough. Two would be "verging on alcoholism." Paintings gathered from their travels crowded the walls. Pale-green grasscloth wallpaper reflected a golden sheen over the room.

When my sister and I were little, Grandmommy and Granddaddy also had a summer house on Martha's Vineyard. We would visit at the end of summer, driving to Woods Hole, Massachusetts, then taking the ferry to the island. Granddaddy had a daily ritual—a pre-breakfast swim in the Atlantic—and I loved joining him. My sister and I slept in teeny rooms in the attic. At 6:30 a.m., Granddaddy would quietly call up the stairs, ready to go.

"David? Are you awake?"

Carrying my towel, I would tiptoe down the steep stairs in my bathing suit, and he would drive us in his Cadillac to the beach, a mile away, which was usually deserted at that time. We would swim for ten minutes, then, freezing cold, dry off and bundle up in sweatshirts for the ride back. Granddaddy loved trying to identify whatever classical music was playing on the car radio.

"It's Schubert!" he would say decisively.

Then, a few moments later, "But it could be Mendelssohn . . ."

We would wait for the announcer to tell us who it was.

"Schumann!" he would gasp, stunned. "Of course."

"You must listen to opera, symphonies, chamber music," he would say to me. "How lucky you are to have your whole education in front of you!"

Granddaddy had been fourteen years old when his father died, and he dropped out of school that year to get a job. He became a self-educated expert on the Italian Renaissance, and for the last forty years of his long life, he was writing a book on quantum mechanics. He would sit on the toilet for hours every morning, covering index cards with his spidery handwriting. Grandmommy typed the cards up at the end of each week, looking up the obscure mathematical terms in her enormous Merriam-Webster dictionary.

Grandmommy played the piano by ear, entirely for her own pleasure, occasionally singing along in a breathy whisper. She loved the American songbook, but not indiscriminately, preferring Rodgers & Hart to Rodgers & Hammerstein and Cole Porter to Irving Berlin. She had dabbled in songwriting herself as a young woman, and she enjoyed attending musicals. She had seen the original company of *My Fair Lady* on Broadway, then caught another performance two years later. Disappointed by a few things in that second viewing, she wrote a concerned letter to the director, addressing it to the Mark Hellinger Theatre.

Once, when I was looking through the music that Grandmommy stored inside her piano bench, I found an envelope, carefully preserved in an acid-free folder. I asked her what it was. She said she would show me.

We sat together at her kitchen table. She gently opened the envelope and carefully took out the letter: a respectful response, on thick, creamy notepaper, thanking her for taking the time to write.

"I'll hold a brush-up rehearsal soon," it said.

The letter was signed, "Yours, Moss Hart."

Awestruck, I touched the expensive-looking stationery. Somehow, my dreams of Broadway seemed nearer.

Whenever Grandmommy and Granddaddy spent a weekend in New York City, they went to a musical. In 1974, they saw *A Little Night Music*. Grandmommy bought two copies of the original cast album and sent one of them to me with a note asking if I'd ever heard of Stephen Sondheim, who had written both the music and the lyrics.

I listened to the record for hours, sitting on the Cascade House living room couch, following the printed lyrics and staring at the album cover. At first, it looked like an ordinary drawing of a tree, but if I stared at it long enough, I could see, hidden in the branches, erotic sketches of nude men and women.

The waltz-strewn score of *A Little Night Music* wrapped me in its deliriously scented musk. I particularly liked a sequence where three characters sing successive solos, titled "Now," "Soon," and "Later." Musically, the songs couldn't be more different, appropriately tailored to the three individual characters. Then, unexpectedly, the three songs are sung simultaneously, in counterpoint, intertwining in ways that bring out their contrasts and their similarities, building to a jaw-dropping climax, the three titles echoing back and forth between the voices.

Who was this Stephen Sondheim? I wanted more.

MY THIRD GRANDMOTHER, "GRANDMA," WAS A MODERN WOMAN. IN 1939, when she was twenty-two, she had worked at the World's Fair in Flushing Meadows, Queens, demonstrating radiators for the Standard Heating Company. Tall and buxom, she lived with two roommates on the Lower East Side, girls who also worked at the fair. They would take the early train out to the fairgrounds, ahead of the tourist crowds, and stroll to work past the Trylon and the Perisphere in the World of Tomorrow.

Grandma worked as the office manager of a pricey real estate firm in the Pan Am building on Park Avenue. Gently curled dark blonde hair surrounded her broad, genteel face. She ruled the secretaries and office staff with an iron fist concealed in a velvet glove. Her coworkers loved telling the story of a summer day when the air-conditioning broke and the office was an oven. Grandma marched into the executive suite and inquired if the secretaries could go home. The answer was no. That afternoon, she was seen working at her desk in just her skirt and a lacy brassiere. Her blouse had been hung, in pointed protest, from the useless thermostat.

When she met my father's father, who was tall and freshly divorced from Doddy, she knew she had found her permanent dance partner. She doted on him. As the breadwinner in the family, she supported him, saying it was "an honor."

By all reports, they were a charismatic, fun couple. Unfortunately, by the time I got to know them, their marriage had deteriorated to a bitter battle of wills over his smoking. Her nagging was tenacious. His acid retorts were usually delivered sotto voce after she had left the room, often while quickly lighting up again. Crushed half-packs of Lucky Strikes were hidden in every chair in their apartment.

"Yappy bitch," he'd mutter, flicking his silver lighter.

Late in his life, Grandpa was chosen by Woody Allen to play the older version of a character in Allen's faux documentary, *Zelig*. Jowly and rumpled, wearing his own clothing, he's a natural on-screen. He looks and acts exactly as I remember him from childhood visits to their New York apartment. Grandma made a big fuss over his geriatric movie stardom, hosting celebratory viewing parties when *Zelig* came out on videotape.

GRANDMA AND GRANDPA SLEPT IN A KING-SIZE BED. THEIR BEDROOM WAS shockingly untidy, sheets and pillows tossed everywhere. Grandmommy and Granddaddy slept in separate twin beds, always crisply tucked in, a spare blanket neatly folded at the foot. Doddy slept, presumably alone, in a full-size bed, occasionally made. If these were the options that the World of Tomorrow was offering, why couldn't I see myself in any of them?

The sleeping arrangements at home were getting confusing as well. My father's continuing enjoyment of large amounts of beer, while never impeding his work at the school, was a growing challenge for my mother. I noticed, occasionally, if I wandered into the faculty apartment, that she had chosen to sleep in the guest room. This was never discussed.

The night before I graduated from North Country School, my eighth-grade class performed our senior play. I had convinced my classmates to do *The Man Who Came to Dinner* by George S. Kaufman and Moss Hart. I played Beverly Carlton, a composer modeled on Noël Coward. I had lots of funny lines, and I delivered them in what I was convinced was a cracking British accent. Accompanying myself at the piano, I also sang an overwrought song by Cole Porter, written as a parody of a Noël Coward ballad.

Grandmommy and Granddaddy loved the play.

Grandma and Grandpa praised my performance.

Doddy took me aside, deeply concerned.

"You spoke too quickly, darling," she said. "You were very difficult to understand."

I'm sure she was right, but it stung.

I HAD BEEN ACCEPTED, WITH A LARGE SCHOLARSHIP, AT PHILLIPS EXETER ACADEMY, a prestigious prep school in New Hampshire. Maybe there I would learn what the World of Tomorrow held in store for me.

Interlude : 2007

Five months after opening night, I stood at the podium, conducting *Curtains*. The reviews had been good; the show was a hit. Debra Monk and David Hyde Pierce were onstage, singing heartily, leading the company through a number called "Show People," a tongue-in-cheek toe-tapper celebrating the hoary adage "The show must go on." I watched the two of them split to opposite sides of the stage as other members of the company joined the number.

As I did at each performance, I watched as the two actors looked at each other. He raised an eyebrow; she pursed her lips. It was a private moment, shared in the most public place imaginable, a brightly lit Broadway stage. Confident that the audience's attention was momentarily elsewhere, they took that brief, precious second to connect. The connection gave them a charge—fuel to continue. The moment passed, and the number churned on to its high-kicking ending.

David Hyde Pierce had clearly made it his mission to make *Curtains* the best possible experience for everyone involved. He gave gifts. He threw parties. He remembered people's birthdays and wrote witty poems. This one appeared on my forty-sixth:

> *Roses are red,*
> *Homos are proud.*
> *No matter the volume,*
> *The best music's Loud!*
> *—DHP*

His devotion to the show inspired the rest of the company. It was the happiest place I ever worked.

But, after five months of physical therapy, my left shoulder wasn't feeling any better. Ed, my physical therapist, was as frustrated as I was. Our weekly sessions helped alleviate the stiffness, allowing me to continue conducting, but he couldn't locate the underlying cause of the pain. Exercises with pulleys and elastic bands hadn't helped. Cortisone shots didn't work. Ed had recently given me the name of another specialist he thought I should see.

Nor had my other symptoms abated: the occasional numbness in my fingers, the slight tremor, my instinctive tendency to avoid left-handed tasks. More alarmingly, my piano technique was declining. Pieces I had played perfectly were now speckled with small mistakes. The equation I lived by—*[New piece of music] x [Number of hours spent practicing] = [Noticeable improvement]*—was suddenly false. I did not improve. It was mystifying.

I mentioned none of this to anybody.

Instead, I buried myself, quite happily, in work.

Conducting a Broadway musical is the best job in the world. Days and nights swirl by, and the success of *Curtains* means life is full and busy. The performances, eight per week, are a laugh-filled pleasure. Standing at the podium, caught between worlds, I am the beating heart of a complex, living organism whose sole purpose is to tell a story.

Playing the same music over and over quickly becomes a surreal exercise in consistency and variation, made more challenging by the shockingly cramped quarters of Broadway orchestra pits and the surprisingly large egos of those who make their living there. Temperament is everything in a pit musician. One jerk with an easily triggered temper, an unkind tongue, poor personal hygiene, or a weakness for petty theft can destroy an entire orchestra.

Knowing when to lead and knowing when to follow is the crucial balancing act that the conductor of a musical performs. I move between those two modes of operation—at times responding to the singers' instincts, at times insisting on my own.

As I conduct, I make hundreds of decisions. The actress playing the ingenue seems tired tonight; do I help her by increasing the tempo of her song? The actor playing the composer took a breath in a different spot than he usually does and is now behind the beat; do I ever-so-slightly slow down to accommodate him, or do I keep the tempo steady and let him catch up? The woodwind countermelody in the second verse of Debra Monk's number "It's a Business" has been too soft for the last few performances. I give a strong cue to the flautist, and I make eye contact with the clarinet player, encouraging them both to play more fully. There's a passage coming up where the melody is low for David Hyde Pierce's voice. If the trombones are too loud, they will drown him out. As we approach the spot, I turn to face them, clearly showing them the palm of my hand, forcing the trombonists to play more delicately. The first trumpet player is obviously drunk; do I let him struggle through, or should I call a substitute musician in to replace him as soon as possible?

Singers breathe, and the air passes through their lungs and their vocal cords, causing the vibration of song. French horn players in the pit breathe, and the air vibrates through their pursed lips, entering the brass coils of their instruments, creating the resonance of tone. Violinists don't use breath to create tone, but we mark their musical phrases with slurs, so their bow strokes synchronize with the breathing of the other instruments. String players also create "vibrato" with their fingers to match the natural vibrato of voices and wind instruments.

If they all place their artistry and their faith in the hands of the conductor, if they all breathe with me, we can perform the miracle that is music.

We fuse. We are "together."

• • •

THERE ARE, OF COURSE, NIGHTS WHEN NOTHING WORKS, NOTHING GELS. Thankfully, these performances are the exception, at least at *Curtains*. But tonight was one of them—squeaks from the clarinets, trumpet splats on the buttons, and a substitute drummer. I exited the theater through the stage door, frustrated that the orchestra's performance had been so sloppy.

The August night air on West Forty-Fifth Street was warm and hazy. Departing theatergoers blocked the street traffic. A crush of people gathered around the stage door. To my surprise, I saw a familiar face. Ed, my physical therapist, who, for the last five months, had been trying to solve the riddle of my shoulder injury, waved hello. I made my way through the crowd to where he stood.

"I was walking my dog," he said, "and I thought I'd catch you as you left the theater." He had something to give me. A business card. His eyes looked serious as he handed it to me.

"Here is the card of that doctor I recommended to you," he said. "The neurologist."

The neurologist?

"Thanks," I say, staggered that he had taken the trouble to coordinate his dog walk with the precise moment that *Curtains* came down. Why was he treating this with such urgency?

"Call him," he said.

I thanked him, put the card in my pocket, and headed to the subway.

Chapter Five

1975

{S}tanding with my hands in my pockets, I watched my parents drive away. The Phillips Exeter Academy campus looked impossibly tidy, its grass lawns and stone walkways immaculate in the late-afternoon sun. The early September air smelled clear and fresh, with faint traces of stone and brick baking in the sunlight.

As our blue Dodge van was about to disappear around the corner, my mother turned and waved one last time. She looked worried, her lips tightly pursed. It was a five-hour drive from Exeter, New Hampshire, back up to Lake Placid, and road trips with my father hadn't been much fun lately. He rarely spoke to her, and when he did, he was annoyed and patronizing. A six-pack a day can do that to a marriage.

I turned to go back into the big brick dormitory where we had just dropped off my suitcases and boxes when, without the slightest warning, a football slammed into my head. I stumbled and fell down, my glasses skidding across the pavement. My hand was bleeding. A swarthy older boy walked toward me to retrieve the ball. "Prep faggot," he snarled. The boy walked away.

Shit, I thought. *Now what have I gotten myself into?*

Thankfully, my glasses hadn't broken. I got up, retrieved them, and went into the dorm. Its name, DUNBAR HALL, was etched into the stone lintel above the doorway. Dark green ivy swarmed over every bit of brick; the tendrils seemed to be searching for cracks in the stonework, trying to get inside. I climbed the stairs to the fourth floor.

ACADEMY NINTH GRADERS WERE CALLED "PREPS." I HAD BEEN ASSIGNED MY OWN small room, but I had to walk through another Prep's room to get to mine. His room was filled with lacrosse sticks and baseball bats. Gauntly muscular, with dark curly hair, acne, and a surly sneer, he rarely looked up from his desk when I went by. I thought it unlikely that we would become friends.

I made my bed, unpacked my portable record player, and set it up on the nightstand. I played my recording of *Gilbert and Sullivan Overtures*. Looking in the mirror, I saw a bruise forming next to my right eye, where the football had smacked me. I skipped the orientation dinner that night and unpacked my clothes and music. Later that night, listening to *The Carpenters' Greatest Hits*, I heard a pounding on my door and a menacing, "Turn that shit off." I did. The room was warm. I lay on top of my bed, unable to sleep, wondering what I was doing in this place.

Classes started the next morning. We wore jackets and ties; mine were secondhand. I went to breakfast in the dining hall and sat alone, trying to hide my bruised temple. I was gripped with a fear that if I spoke to anyone, they would instantly know how unqualified I was to attend this rarified institution. Breathing deeply, I tried to quell the panic surging up inside me. I couldn't eat anything. Eventually, I picked up the campus map I had been issued and set off to find my first class—English, with Mr. Kane.

The Exeter campus glowed with resplendent tranquility.

The red brick Georgian academic buildings, gathered in formal quartets, created majestic quadrangles, teeming with crisscrossing students for the ten minutes between each class period, then standing austerely empty for the other fifty minutes of the hour. The venerable Academy Building, where we met for Assembly each morning, with its tolling bell tower, marble steps, and worm-eaten wood paneling, had these words inscribed in granite over its front entrance:

HUC VENITE PUERI UT VIRI SITIS
Come here, boys, that you may be made men.

Exeter had gone co-ed in 1970, five years before I arrived, but in keeping with its traditionally glacial rate of change, that motto wasn't modified until 1996. The young women in my class, who also had to pass under those words each day, just kept their heads down and took their chances.

I LOCATED PHILLIPS HALL AND WOUND MY WAY UP THE MARBLE STAIRWAY. I WAS early. The classroom door was slightly ajar, so I pushed it open and went inside.

There it was. One of the crown jewels of the Exeter educational system: a Harkness table. Constructed of massively solid wood, oval in shape, Harkness tables were built to seat twelve students and one teacher.

In 1930, Edward Harkness gave the Academy $5.8 million. Every classroom at Exeter contains a Harkness table, which means that every class is limited to twelve students. Everyone has an equal spot at the table, including the teacher. There is no hiding in the back row, hoping to go unnoticed. Classes at Exeter are conversations, often traveling in unexpected directions.

Exeter's commitment to the Harkness method is complete and practically irreversible. The tables are so big they don't fit through the doors of the classrooms. Each one was constructed in the room in which it stands. To remove it, you would have to destroy it.

Mr. Kane stood, his back to the door, looking out the window at the bustling chaos in the quadrangle below. I wasn't sure if he'd heard me enter. I took a seat at the table. One by one, other students entered. We sat in anxious silence.

Finally, Mr. Kane turned around, revealing a kind smile, tired eyes, and the perfect costume for a New England prep-school teacher: wire-rimmed spectacles, a brown tweed jacket with patches on the elbows, the obligatory rep tie, and penny loafers. He looked at us, stretching the moment out dramatically, then spoke:

> *Something there is that doesn't love a wall,*
> *That sends the frozen-ground-swell under it,*
> *And spills the upper boulders in the sun;*
> *And makes gaps even two can pass abreast.*

Slowly, eloquently, he recited the poem—"Mending Wall," by Robert Frost—bringing it to life in an urgent, careful manner. Then, looking around the table, he asked for our thoughts. After patiently hearing our initial reactions, he guided us through a line-by-line examination of the poem, questioning the author's precise meaning at every turn. He made observations on Frost's choice of words and punctuation, filling his remarks with details from the poet's life. Frost had lived and worked on New Hampshire farms. This particular poem, published in 1914, had been written while he was living in Derry, less than thirty miles from Exeter.

Mr. Kane, along with every other teacher at Exeter, assigned us a bone-crushing amount of homework. I struggled to meet the demands, staying up late writing essay after essay. I appreciated the high expectations, and I didn't mind wearing a tie every day. But one aspect of life at Exeter I found unbearable.

The Prep class was sentenced to two hours of mandatory athletics each weekday. The coaches divided us into groups ranked by athletic ability. I ended up in the lowest-scoring group. We were then rotated through every sport played at the Academy. After two weeks of track and field, we had two weeks of soccer, then two weeks of lacrosse, and on through the Nine Circles of Hell. The coaches treated our group with disdain. Nothing had prepared me for the humiliation we were expected to endure for having the audacity to be bad at squash, water polo, or the long jump.

The only positive results of the program were the relationships I formed within this Athletic Losers Group, our bonds forged in the torrents of abuse we inspired from the sadistic athletic instructors.

The first friend I made at Exeter, Steve, was a dryly sarcastic science nerd who loved languages and Russian literature. One grey fall day we were jogging next to each other, gradually falling behind the other runners. Leaves crunched under our feet.

"Pansy weaklings!" shouted one of the assistant coaches.

Steve rolled his eyes at me and mimed a quick suicide by revolver.

I laughed, careful not to draw the coach's attention.

"Pansy weakling" became a term of respect between us.

I survived the yearlong smorgasbord of torture only by discovering that I genuinely didn't care what they thought of me. I doubt that was the lesson I was supposed to be learning on those magnificently maintained playing fields, but each extra set of laps I was forced to run, each punishing push-up I performed, only strengthened my indifference. If I had the slowest time, so what? The only real leverage the coaches had over me was my attendance. Three unexcused absences meant I could be brought before the faculty and expelled. I showed up every day. Somebody had to have the slowest time.

To earn my financial scholarship, I worked three days a week in the Exeter Library, where I was assigned to work for two librarians. They were both named Mrs. Thomas. Mrs. Thomas #1, the head librarian, was tall, elegant, and aloof, with pale blonde hair and a razor-sharp, forward-thinking ambition. Mrs. Thomas #2, always in muted earth tones, was mousy and maternal, instinctively kind but unnaturally timid. They fascinated me. The yin-yang nature of their personalities created a tension that kept their underlings hopping.

The Exeter Library took pride in the breadth of its collection. Its carefully curated holdings included medieval illuminated parchments, a prized Shakespeare Second Folio, and original manuscripts from alumni writers such as John Knowles, author of *A Separate Peace*, and Peter Benchley, author of *Jaws*. The Academy clearly had the means to purchase any item it deemed worthy of acquisition. So why, I wondered, did their collection of musical theater recordings . . . suck?

After working there for a month, I asked the question to Mrs. Thomas #2. Her whispered response: "That's not the sort of thing we focus on in this library, dear. We are a serious educational institution."

The next day I gathered my courage and approached Mrs. Thomas #1. She listened to me coolly and responded sharply, "Highly unlikely. But have a proposed list of titles on my desk Friday morning. Perhaps we could investigate requisitioning the necessary funds."

Excited, I jotted down the complete works of Stephen Sondheim, Frank Loesser, Jerry Herman, and Jule Styne. From there, I built a list of twenty-five shows, filling it in with titles from my parents' record collection. I showed the list to Mrs. Thomas #2. "Oh dear," she fretted. "No—it's much too much. Start with just a few titles and see how it goes. She'll never agree to this."

Back in my dorm room, ignoring her advice, I doubled the list, going back to *Show Boat* and adding every historical title I could think of. Then I tripled it, appending all the contemporary titles I could muster.

Friday morning, before classes started, I knocked on Mrs. Thomas #1's office door and presented her with the finished document. Surprised, she examined it, then looked down at me, eying me as if she were trying to decide whether to flick me off her plate or spear me with a fork and eat me. I could hear what she was thinking: *Why is this fourteen-year-old twerp telling me how to run my library?*

Finally, she spoke. "It's too much. Cut it in half."

I swallowed hard. "Why would Exeter want to have an incomplete collection?" I asked, my voice wavering only slightly.

A frosty pallor spread across her cheeks.

"Let me finish," she said icily. "Cut it in half. We'll order the rest of the titles next semester." Walking back to her desk, she said, "It's a good list. But you left off *The Most Happy Fella*. I would like *The Most Happy Fella* to be on the list."

She paused. "If you agree."

When I emerged from the head librarian's office, Mrs. Thomas #2 looked surprised to see me, as if she expected me to have been incinerated. I gave her a thumbs-up and ran to my calculus class.

HALFWAY THROUGH MY FIRST SEMESTER, AFTER A PARTICULARLY AWFUL SESSION of enforced sports, I spotted a flyer on a bulletin board. Students who played the recorder were needed for a production of Shakespeare's *Henry IV, Part 1*, in the Fisher Theatre.

I telepathically thanked Miss Laura Weber for her early morning televised lessons.

I dug out my soprano recorder and called the number on the flyer.

Two weeks later, as the house lights dimmed, I sat nervously at a music stand in the stage left wing of the Fisher Theatre, my recorder in my hands. There were five of us in the band, three on various-sized recorders, one strumming a lute, another playing a *viola da gamba*. We had been practicing feverishly, trying to perfect a suite of Renaissance-style motets that one of the senior boys had written to accompany *Henry IV, Part 1*. It was opening night. We would be playing between scenes and during the battles. The wafting smells of makeup and spirit-gum floated in the air, mixing with the odor of dusty colored gels overheating in bright lights.

A stage manager cued us, and we started the prelude, a spirited saraband. Upperclassmen whirled past in capes and leggings as they entered and exited, carousing their way through the story of Prince Hal outgrowing his youthful folly and maturing into a sober prince worthy of his father's crown. I watched from the dark wing, looking out at the stage, reveling in the shared energy and the almost sacred feeling of being part of something larger than myself.

It hit me suddenly, with a force that left me breathless. I knew what I was doing at Exeter. I belonged in this theater. The wooden recorder in my hands had been my ticket into a place where I was valued and welcome. Something inside me, which had been tensely coiled for years, started to relax. I belonged here.

And that feeling of belonging would never leave me.

Chapter Six

1976

{T}he following Christmas, during my sophomore year at Exeter, Doddy's present to me came in an envelope decorated with a long row of gingerbread men, each kicking up one leg. The envelope contained tickets for the two of us to see *A Chorus Line*. It was the hottest show in town, and Doddy wanted mezzanine seats, front row, dead center. I pictured her trying to charm the box office staff, telling them about her talented grandson, *anything* for a better location. The tickets were for July, an interminable seven months away.

It was worth the wait.

As we entered the Shubert Theatre, the empty stage was visible. We sat in our perfect seats. The house lights dimmed. In the blackout, a brief piano fanfare—six notes—followed by a voice in the dark:

Da-da da-da da da. "Again!"

The lights snapped on, and the stage was crowded with dancers. They were in the middle of a grueling dance audition.

It was a stunning effect.

MANY YEARS LATER, AS *A CHORUS LINE* WAS APPROACHING THE END OF ITS sixteen-year Broadway run, I bought a standing room ticket. A friend of mine had taken over the role of Diana Morales, and I was looking forward to watching her performance. I had seen *A Chorus Line* a few more times over the years but never standing at the back of the theater. The matronly ushers bustled around, handing out programs. As the house lights dimmed, I noticed that several of the ushers bent down, using the programs they were holding to cover the little lights that gently illuminated the aisles.

Da-da da-da da da. "Again!"

The show started.

After the performance, I asked one of the ushers why she had done that.

"Oh, sweetie," she said. "We've been doing that since the beginning. Michael Bennett asked all us ushers to do it. It makes the blackout a little bit darker, so the dancers can get onstage without nobody seeing."

A CHORUS LINE TOOK HOLD OF ME LIKE A FEVER. I DREAMED THAT I WAS WATCHING it again, that I was in it, that I was an understudy, that I was the rehearsal pianist. I loved how the lighting magically let the audience know when the characters were speaking out loud and when they were singing their inner thoughts. Plus, it was so sexy. Women singing about tits and ass. Men talking about being gay. Exeter's cast recording collection was taking forever to get started, so I bought a copy of the album for myself. I couldn't listen to it without getting a throbbing erection.

But don't think about that.

It was difficult not to think about that.

It was in the Exeter Library, a few weeks later, that the thought first occurred to me. It felt like a giant bell ringing in the center of my skull.

Am I gay?

Don't think about that.

But what if I'm gay?

My habit of avoiding dangerous topics by ignoring them was already second nature. Since I was six years old, various unkind contemporaries had called me names.

Sissy. Fairy.

As soon as they identified me as a boy who took piano lessons, wanted to be in musicals, and didn't want to play baseball, they somehow knew something about me that I didn't yet know. And what they saw in me made me feel ashamed. Shame that burned my cheeks and made me want to disappear.

There was nobody I felt I could talk to.

Furtively, I looked in the library card catalog for books on sex. Exeter did have the world's largest collection of Revolutionary War handbills and broadsides, but on the subject I sought, there was only one title: *Oh! Sex Education!* The author had the you-couldn't-possibly-make-this-up name of Mary Breasted. I was too embarrassed to check it out at the front desk, so I read it while hiding in one of the library's study rooms. The book was not helpful.

Continuing my habit, I kept my fears to myself. I entered a four-year period of bifurcated thinking. My mind effectively split in half. Part of me thought I might be gay; part of me decided I wasn't.

In the locker rooms at the Exeter gym, I tried not to stare at the muscular, handsome upperclassmen as they changed back and forth from their preppy academic attire to their athletic gear. Stealing quick glances was all I ever allowed myself, and I avoided showering there.

I also managed to have a serious crush on a girl my junior year, followed by an actual girlfriend my senior year. No sex, though, on either side of the great divide. Not yet. Exeter put great effort into making it difficult for a boy and a girl to be alone together. That was fine with me. We kissed a lot. My feelings for her were real, albeit not sexual.

It was very confusing.

AFTER MY TANTALIZING EXPERIENCE PLAYING THE RECORDER IN THE WINGS, I TOOK every theater course Exeter offered. The Fisher Theatre was tucked out of sight behind the music building, and for good reason. Its industrial-style corrugated steel walls were wrapped with bright orange exterior pipes and ducts. Inside, there wasn't a Harkness table in sight. Classes were held in a purple-carpeted amphitheater with no seats. We sat on the purple-carpeted steps and stretched out on the purple-carpeted floor. The building housed a modern theater with a big stage, and a smaller "black box" workshop space for student productions. The modern construction, so out of step with the other campus architecture, seemed to demand experimentation.

The theater professor, Mr. Marriott, was as offbeat as the building he presided over. Tall and thin, his hair and beard dyed an odd yellow, he looked like a demented giraffe. Strutting around the campus, usually in a plaid suit topped with a deerstalker hat, he was a garishly mod iconoclast in a sea of preppy conformity. Inside the Fisher Theatre, he was a mesmerizing teacher and an inspiring director. He treated the students in his plays as if we were trained professionals, demanding complete commitment from everyone involved.

Mr. Marriott's acting classes were a combination of theater games and scene study. With a clarity that eluded the over-testosteroned Neanderthals at the gymnasium, he taught that theater was, in the best way, a team sport. I loved doing trust exercises, falling back into other students' arms, and mirror work to heighten our observation of each other. I learned to improvise in ways that provided opportunities for other actors. We held hands and felt energy pass between us. We staged scenes on stairways, in dressing rooms, and outside windows. We mined our memories for feelings of fear and loss and love, to use onstage like chemistry experiments. We learned that each of us was only a part of the whole and that the whole couldn't function without all its contributing parts. This concept was familiar to me, forever tied to a pungent memory of a little boy shoveling manure.

MY EFFORTS AS UNOFFICIAL CURATOR OF THE PREVIOUSLY SUCKY MUSICAL THEATER recording collection started to produce results. Unwrapping each day's shipment was my favorite part of the job. Stephen Sondheim's

Company arrived, the bright purple and orange cover radiating contemporary urban energy. It was all I could do not to grab the album, run to my dorm room, and jam it on my turntable. Somehow, I was able to patiently assign it a library code, register it carefully in the catalog, calmly check it out of the library, attend my late-afternoon American history class, and *then* run to my room.

Alone at last, I turned on my record player and removed the vinyl record from the cardboard album cover. I slid the black disk out of its crisp white paper sleeve. Trying not to get any fingerprints on the pristine disk, I slid it onto the spindle and swung the over-arm out to hold it in place. I flicked the speed selector, set to 33, and the spindle clicked, gently dropping the disk onto the now slowly rotating turntable. The tonearm made its short, precise trip to the outermost edge of the disk and lowered itself down. The needle engaged with the widely spaced grooves, then the familiar scratches and hisses gave way to a new sound: an orchestra playing an angular, percussive vamp. Gentle voices, singing "Bobby, Bobby" over and over, filled my dorm room. The voices were soft, seductive, detached. Mesmerized, I imagined myself sitting in a theater, the house lights dimming around me. The prelude finished, and the show began.

The album of *Follies*, also by Stephen Sondheim, arrived at the library a week later. When I played that one on my stereo, theatrical ghosts seemed to emerge mistily from the speakers.

I didn't know anything about Sondheim's *Pacific Overtures*. It turned out to be a musical about the westernization of Japan. It was austere, intimate, and funny. I forced my friend Steve (proud member of the Athletic Losers Group) to listen to the whole album with me. His reaction was a bewildered "Huh?" so I made him listen to it a few more times. I don't think he ever found the intense, haiku-like songs as powerful as I did, but he was a good sport.

I read and reread all the albums' liner notes. Clearly, Sondheim could do anything he set his mind to and do it more brilliantly than anyone else could have imagined. I started saving money to buy the published sheet music from his shows. I practiced Sondheim's

challenging vamps and accompaniment figures much more enthusiastically than I had ever practiced my sonatas and études.

ONE OF MY ENGLISH TEACHERS, MR. PLOEGSTRA, STARTED BEING VERY FRIENDLY.
Tall and owl-like, with white hair, a shiny bald spot, and a piercing wit,
he was a renowned Shakespearean scholar and a gifted teacher, rigorous and exacting. He occasionally requested that I stay after class.
He would praise a paper I had written or elaborate on his answer to
a question I had asked. It was quite flattering.

One Saturday night, he invited me to go to a concert; the Boston
Symphony Orchestra was playing Beethoven's Ninth at Symphony
Hall in Boston. On the drive there, he asked me questions about
my childhood. I found myself talking about Miss Corn and Mr.
Emerson and how much they had influenced me. Things I hadn't
thought about in years came tumbling out. He seemed genuinely
interested.

During the concert, at the hair-raising moment when the chorus,
which had been sitting silently for three movements, suddenly stood
up and began singing, Mr. Ploegstra put his hand on my knee for a
few long seconds, caressing it. He did this two more times before the
end of the performance. *He certainly feels strongly about this music,* I
thought nervously.

On the drive back to Exeter, he casually put his hand further up
on my thigh and left it there.

This, I couldn't explain away.

The thought of what he wanted from me made me nauseous.

I had no idea what to do.

I stayed still, pretending it wasn't happening. I tried thinking
about the concert we had just heard, my homework assignments,
anything.

Eventually, he removed his hand.

We rode in silence.

He dropped me off at my dorm. Relieved that he hadn't attempted anything further, I thanked him for taking me to the concert and tried to put the whole night out of my mind.

In contrast to the high-energy zip and zoom of the Fisher Theatre, the music department at Exeter was calm and dignified. I entered the Piano Concerto Competition and won a spot in the end-of-year concert, playing Mozart's *Piano Concerto in C minor* with the symphony orchestra. I had never had an opportunity like this before. I was excited. I had always wondered what it would be like—playing the piano with a full orchestra supporting me. Maybe this would lead to other opportunities, to a life in classical music!

The concert was presented in Phillips Church, a tranquil stone chapel with good acoustics. I was the final performer on the program.

I waited in the minister's office, surrounded by ecclesiastical robes and vestments. I had practiced religiously, but I was nervous about the memorization. The office was warm and smelled of incense, making my stomach a little sick. As I waited, my queasiness increased. When it was finally my turn, it took everything I had not to throw up on the liturgical wear.

At the last minute, I decided to take my music out onstage with me. I sat down on the piano bench and placed the music at my feet. I needed the security of having it close, though the logistics of actually consulting it during the concert would have been ghastly. The cold air in the church was a relief after the stuffiness of the office. My hands were clammy; I wiped my sweaty palms on my pants. The orchestra started to play. Moments before my first entrance, I thought about making a quick lunge for the music. I talked myself out of it.

I played the first phrase. The right notes came out, but my hands were generating moisture at an alarming rate. The keys seemed to be slipping out from under me.

To my dismay, I found myself abandoning the fingerings I had so carefully practiced. Instead, I was grabbing at notes with whatever finger was closest. I tried to focus on the music, but my brain wouldn't cooperate, judging every passage as I played it while simultaneously worrying about the challenges to come. The agony stretched on forever. I was playing the right notes at the right time, but with none of the musicality, the dynamics, or the phrasing that I had spent hours preparing. When I gratefully reached the final measures, I remember thinking, *This is definitely not what I want to do with my life.*

ON AN EARLY MARCH DAY, AFTER CLASS, MR. PLOEGSTRA ASKED ME WHAT MY plans were for the upcoming spring vacation. I told him I would be taking the Greyhound bus to Albany, where my father would meet me to drive me to Lake Placid. Mr. Ploegstra offered to drive me to Albany himself. I was surprised. It was a four-hour trip.

"I have to head that way for something anyway," he said vaguely.

I was torn. The car ride from Boston had certainly been uncomfortable, but he hadn't put me in an awkward position since then . . . and I hated riding the bus.

I accepted his invitation.

It was a classic New England spring day, brisk and bright. We stopped for lunch at a picturesque country inn. He treated me to an expensive meal, and he told me how much I reminded him of a favorite former student of his. The boy had been a true friend, he said, staring at me.

"He was sensitive and thoughtful," said Mr. Ploegstra, "like you."

When we got back in his car, he leaned over and tried to kiss me. His chin slid along my cheek as I turned my head away from him. He was breathing heavily, and he reached his arm toward me. I batted it away, and he retreated. I couldn't look at him. EMERGENCY, my brain was screaming. We sat in the car for a while, not speaking. Every muscle in my body wanted to open the car door and run, but I couldn't. Where would I go? I was trapped.

How had I let myself get in this position? I was completely dependent on him to drive me to Albany. Why had I stupidly assumed it wouldn't happen again?

The silence continued. His breathing was quieter. I wondered if Mr. Ploegstra would give me a bad grade in his class.

Luckily, he seemed to have gotten the message.

He started the car, and we continued our trip.

EXETER, AT THAT TIME, HAD NO MECHANISM IN PLACE TO DEAL WITH SITUATIONS like this, no office I could visit to report his actions. So I just made sure I never got into a car with him again.

Occasionally, when I was at my job in the library, I thought about confiding in Mrs. Thomas #2. She had been at Exeter a long time and seemed to have a genuine fondness for me—maybe she would have an idea about what I could do. Once, I even sat down in the chair next to her desk. She looked at me and smiled.

I didn't know what to say. It would have been such a relief to talk to her about it, but I wondered if I had somehow brought the whole mess on myself.

"Something on your mind?" she asked.

I looked at her kind face.

Just say it, I thought.

I didn't say anything.

I couldn't. Talking about him would have meant talking about me.

Mr. Ploegstra chose his boys carefully. As long as I was held captive by my shame, I was no threat to him whatsoever.

I CONCENTRATED ON OTHER THINGS.

I directed *The Fantasticks* in the experimental theater. I convinced Steve to help me with the set and the props, which though simple, had to be perfect. The budget for these shows was exactly zero. Steve and I stealthily cased the campus, searching for items we could discreetly borrow. We went dumpster diving behind the art department; I emerged with some only slightly soiled construction paper that we used to make leaves and rain and snow. Steve rescued some half-empty paint cans with enough sky-blue paint to repaint the scuffed black platforms that were used in every student production. I taught the music, blocked the scenes, staged the numbers, coached the pianist, demanded that the lighting designer differentiate between moonlight and sunlight, bullied the costume designer, helped Steve paint those platforms, and generally micromanaged everybody into submission.

While rehearsing *The Fantasticks*, I discovered that the show held a profound message, despite its let's-put-on-a-play-with-a-ladder-and-a-stick simplicity. As the harshness of winter is necessary to produce the tender growth of spring, suffering is inevitably required to produce the ability to love. Before the first performance, I gathered the cast in a circle. We held hands. Steve, in charge of the props, lingered in the corner. I motioned for him to join the circle.

We stood on the freshly painted sky-blue platforms, and I thanked the other students for their hard work. I told them that I had grown up on an organic farm and how much the show meant to me, with its use of the changing seasons as a metaphor and its emphasis on the natural life cycle: birth, growth, death, and renewal. I told them to honor the text and make sure the audience could understand every word. I reminded them how lucky we were to have such beautiful music in our lives and what a privilege it was to share that music with other people. We stood in silence for a few moments, concentrating our energy, and then the cast gave an astonishing performance, playing each scene as if their lives depended on the outcome.

The principal of the Academy, Mr. Kurtz, came backstage afterward and tearfully thanked me. This surprised me, as he was generally quite reserved and rarely attended student productions. As he left the theater, alone, it looked like he was still weeping.

Later, as Steve and I sat in the empty theater, he said, "I wish the Science Department had hand-holding inspirational circles before conducting big experiments."

WE RECEIVED OUR MAIL AT EXETER IN SILVER-COLORED, METALLIC MAILBOXES THAT had little glass windows. Mine was right at eye level, and the light shone through it in such a way that I could spot from far away if I had mail. I loved getting mail. Doddy sent notes, telling me about plays she'd seen. Grandmommy wrote interesting letters, always neatly typewritten. Grandma occasionally scrawled something quickly, sometimes tucking a ten-dollar bill into the letter, along with the admonition, "Don't tell Grandpa."

One day, in my junior year, walking by the post office, I saw, through the open door, the telltale diagonal shadow across the window of my mailbox. I retrieved the envelope and slid my finger under the flap to open it. My father had written me a brief letter containing the incomprehensible news that Chris Nicholson, my roommate from North Country School, had died while climbing Mount Cook, in New Zealand.

I stood in the post office lobby, holding the letter in one hand and the envelope in the other.

How could this be?

Numb, I remained there, unable to move, for I don't know how long.

Students hurried by me in the frantic blur of Exeter's between-class rush.

The rush quieted; the post office was empty.

I needed to get to my English class, but I couldn't move.

Confused, I put the letter back in its envelope, unable to process the information it contained.

Somehow, I started walking. Eventually, my body figured out where I was supposed to be going.

• • •

MY SENIOR YEAR, WHILE FINISHING MY ACADEMIC REQUIREMENTS AND APPLYING
to colleges, I took Exeter's advanced theater course. It was called,
reverently, "The Acting Project." We also called it, less reverently,
"Touchy-Feely-for-Credit." We played a lot of theater games. As part
of this course, Mr. Marriott organized a trip to New York City to see
Stephen Sondheim's new musical, *Sweeney Todd*, which had just
opened on Broadway.

Finally, I would experience a new Sondheim musical in the theater, instead of on my record player! It was a complicated undertak-
ing, involving buses from New Hampshire to New York, parental
permission slips, and an overnight stay in the city. I reserved Doddy's
couch. My anticipation was so intense it hurt. On the ride to New
York, I kept shifting around in my seat—unable to read or study.

As we entered the Uris Theatre, the set was mostly visible. The
director, Harold Prince, had staged the show in an immense factory.
A broadcloth hung in front of the set, painted with "The Beehive"—an
illustration of the British class system. A spectral organist played a
grim prelude. Two gravediggers tore down "The Beehive." The lights
dimmed, a deafening factory whistle shrieked, and "The Ballad of
Sweeney Todd" began, with its hypnotic vamp and eerie dissonances.

I lost myself in the world that appeared on that vast stage.

At the end of the first act, Sweeney Todd and Mrs. Lovett devise
a plan to dispose of bodies by baking them into pies. They sing a
beer-soaked waltz, imagining how each pie made from a different
person might taste. The grotesque subject matter, the buoyant,
tattered music, and the insanely clever lyrics, combined with the
go-for-the-jugular performances of Len Cariou and Angela Lansbury,
created a theatrical experience so unexpected, so satisfying, that I
never wanted it to end. When Lovett's rolling pin and Todd's razor
stabbed the air on the final dissonant "button," I burst into tears. To
this day, I consider that duet the apotheosis of what it is possible to
achieve in musical theater.

Over the next year, I stalked the production. Whenever I could scrape thirty dollars together and get to New York, I would buy a ticket. Each time, I noticed new, previously unseen, details. The way certain chorus members would linger, eavesdropping on scenes. How Len Cariou sang the word "naïve" in the first act—gently, sadly, with the interval of a second—and the way he sang it in the second act—as if it was coming up from the depths of his damaged soul, with the leap of an entire octave.

I was heartbroken when the show closed after its sixteen-month run.

What, I wondered, would Sondheim and Prince do next?

THAT SPRING, MY FINAL SEMESTER AT EXETER, THE LILAC TREES BLOOMED WITH their usual abundance; their perfume filled the campus. I asked both Mrs. Thomases if I could stage a Gilbert and Sullivan concert in the library atrium. They graciously agreed. Mrs Thomas #2 decorated the atrium with lilac boughs. Mrs. Thomas #1 volunteered to host a nonalcoholic party for the cast in the bookbinding room.

A few days later, as I approached the Exeter post office, I saw auspicious, diagonal shadows across the window of my mailbox. There were several letters inside, including a thick one from Yale University. I tore it open. I had been accepted. Ecstatic, I put the other mail in my book bag to read later. Yale had been my first choice, and their generous "need-blind" scholarship policy meant that I could afford to go.

It wasn't until much later in the day, back in my dorm room, that I looked at the other letters I had received that morning. One was from my father. After twenty years of marriage, my mother had decided to leave him. His letter was short and factual, with a minimum of emotion.

I was crushed. A divorce. My parents.

I hadn't seen it coming, though there had certainly been clues. How, over the four years I had been away at prep school, could I have gotten so disconnected from them?

I stretched out on my bed, looking at the ceiling. Cracks in the layers of white paint formed a grim mosaic above me. Finally, I relaxed, letting my mind wander.

An image from my childhood in Cincinnati slowly came into focus.

I FELT GENTLE SUNLIGHT ON MY CHEEKS AND SOFT GRASS UNDER MY BARE FEET. I was playing in the backyard with Fang, our basset hound. A sunny spring day. My father was leaving the house, walking out the back door on his way to teach at Hillsdale. My mother came out the door after him, smiling, throwing her arms around him and giggling, wanting to kiss him goodbye. He laughed, and kissed her, then went on his way. My mother sat down on the little step by the back door. Absentmindedly, she reached down and picked a few violets from the patch of grass by the step, making a little bouquet that she held in her fingers. She motioned to me to bring the dog back into the house. Fang and I followed her inside. I noticed that she had put the violets in a tiny glass vase in the window by the kitchen sink.

I SAT UP ON MY BED.

That part of their marriage seemed ancient.

They hadn't been that happy around each other in years. *Maybe this is for the best,* I thought miserably.

The letter from Yale, on my desk, caught my eye. The pride I had felt that morning now felt like a sin for which I was being punished. I had been so self-involved, I hadn't noticed my family falling apart.

MY LAST FEW WEEKS AT EXETER SPUN BY IN A BLUR. I DIDN'T WANT TO SPEND THE summer at home. On a whim, I wrote to the venerable entertainment business newspaper *Variety*, in New York City, inquiring if they had summer work.

Graduation was excruciating because of the impending divorce. My parents weren't speaking. My sister looked shell-shocked. All five grandparents arrived for the weekend, their rivalries and resentments keenly focused on the situation. They all stayed at the Exeter Inn, a stuffy, dignified hotel near campus. We had made our reservations years before. On commencement morning, we gathered there for an awkward breakfast. I watched my parents performing the stately gavotte of divorce, calculatedly ignoring each other. They seemed absent, each just trying to survive the day. I know their willingness to endure that horrible meal was a clear sign of how much they loved me, but at the time, it seemed a brutal punishment.

The day grew uncomfortably warm. I wore the tan corduroy suit that my mother had made. The campus lawns and walkways looked as ridiculously pristine as they had the day I had arrived, four years before.

Quite unexpectedly, I won the Williams Cup, which was given to a student who *"has brought distinction to Phillips Exeter."* Principal Kurtz presented me with a giant silver cup, three feet high. I was also handed a polite, typewritten explanation that I was welcome to be photographed with the cup for the next thirty minutes but then it would be locked back into its dusty display case in the Academy Building. My name would be inscribed on a plaque somewhere.

We gathered on the lawn after the ceremony. For a few moments, a cease-fire seemed to have been declared. Pictures were taken of me, the silver cup, my parents, and grandparents.

Mr. Marriott made a point of coming over to meet my family. Sweating profusely in the sun, he was wearing a peculiar orange suit with wide brown lapels. I tried to express to him how much he and the theater department had meant to me, but I'm afraid I stammered through most of what I wanted to say. I do remember the strange sight of Doddy, in her horn-rimmed cat's-eye glasses, taking his arm and smiling coquettishly up at him. She led him away from the rest of us, presumably for some theatrical shoptalk, one professional to another.

One by one, they all asked me what I would be doing that summer. Luckily, I had an answer. To my surprise, Norma Nannini, secretary to the publisher of *Variety*, had written me back, offering me a summer job as a messenger. And Doddy had said yes when I asked if her couch was available for the next three months.

One of the custodians appeared to gently repossess the enormous cup.

My splintered family said their goodbyes and retreated to their respective corners.

Chapter Seven

1980

{L}eaving the chilly lobby of the Majestic Theatre, I turned left and walked briskly down West Forty-Fourth Street, darting between pedestrians, dodging hot-dog carts and Jews for Jesus. The morning sun splashed down on the sidewalks and streets, glancing brightly off windows and cars. By noon, the soggy heat from the August sun would be unbearable, but for the next hour or so I could still do my aggressive "messenger trot"—a fast walk that put me ahead of most people and signaled others to stay out of my way. I passed the St. James Theatre on my right, the Broadhurst and the Shubert on my left. I took the shortcut through Shubert Alley, crossed Forty-Fifth Street, dodging cars, and turned right, passing the Minskoff on my right, and the Bijou and the Morosco on my left. In Duffy Square, I checked the time on the big clock over the TKTS booth and turned onto Forty-Sixth Street. I had finished two messenger runs, and it wasn't even 10:00 a.m. Maybe I could make some extra money today.

The *Variety* building was painted a dark kelly green. A mere six stories high, it was surrounded by enormous office towers that stretched up to the heavens, dwarfing the little building. Walking through the old wooden door was like entering another time.

Inside, rows of ancient desks filled the dingy rooms, each desk a character study in how to stack telexes, memorandums, back issues, and cigarette butts. A noticeable afternoon smell settled in like fog after the three-martini lunches. One of my tasks was updating the "morgue" of old reviews, clipped and mounted on stiff paper, which filled rows of rickety dark kelly green filing cabinets.

Presiding over everything was bouffant-coiffed Norma Nannini, the redheaded secretary to the publisher. Norma had a rusty laser of a voice, an uncanny ability to hear conversations three floors away, and a habit of dispensing each small paycheck with a large dollop of personal advice.

The messenger job itself was a dead-end, having nothing to do with the creative side of musical theater. The work was unchallenging; the pay was lousy. There were three of us: Van, Rasheed, and me. We spent our days dashing around the Theater District, dropping off house-seat orders, doing errands for the grumpy old reporters and critics, delivering copy, picking up advertising artwork, and running up and down the creaky stairs of the seriously ramshackle building.

But the job meant I could live in New York, seeing shows. Free tickets to plays and musicals occasionally made their way down to the messengers' table on the ground floor. And I loved rattling around the Theater District, learning the arcane geography of the Broadway theaters, their stage doors, box offices, and alleys.

The trick to making extra money as a messenger was to focus on the medium-length runs. We earned subway fare for any trip over eight blocks; if I did that trip on foot, I could pocket the reimbursement. Subway fare was sixty cents, so each round trip on foot netted a dollar twenty, which could add up over a busy day. But you had to know your breaking point. If a trip was forty blocks, the amount of time it took to walk those blocks, both ways, wasn't worth the lousy dollar twenty. Unless you were super-fast.

Van was super-fast. Six feet tall, plus another five inches of Afro, he had long skinny arms and legs. Sitting in a chair, he looked like a huge origami grasshopper, all folded up. Van wore a brown velour track suit every day, rain or shine, and he knew every shortcut, alley, and restaurant with a back door in Midtown and beyond. He showed me a few parking garages and hotels that had entrances on two different blocks and could be dashed speedily through, but mostly he was too fast for me to follow for very long. If I made an extra ten or twelve dollars at the end of a busy day, Van would usually pocket twenty or even thirty.

Rasheed wasn't interested in extra subway fare. All he wanted to do was write screenplays about aliens and disasters and Nazis and prisons. He wore a ratty green turban and carried multiple notebooks, which he would scribble in whenever he had a few seconds to sit. He was convinced that the job at *Variety* was his ticket to Hollywood riches, but he was too shy to show anyone his screenplays.

The stairs squeaked as I climbed up to Norma Nannini's office on the third floor. I stopped for a moment in the hallway, gathering my strength. You never quite knew where you stood with Norma. I knocked on her door.

"You know you don't have to knock," she shouted.

I walked in and put the house-seat orders I had collected on her desk.

"Thanks, kiddo," she said, looking up at me.

Her voice rasped, a victim of too many whiskey sours.

I smiled at her, turning to leave, but out of the blue, she harpooned me with a question.

"Why do you spend so much time covering up your feelings?"

I didn't respond. I must have looked surprised.

"I don't mean any harm, kiddo," she said. "But you gotta let a little air out of the balloon now and then."

She laughed, not unkindly, and motioned for me to go about my business, her red-lacquered fingernails glistening in the dim light of her office.

I walked back down the stairs to the first floor.

I thought about her question. I didn't know the answer.

Van was out on a trip; Rasheed was hunched over, writing. I knew better than to look over his shoulder.

"You should ask one of the critics if they would read one of your screenplays," I said, not for the first time.

He stared at me for a moment, then went back into his fantasy world.

There were two tickets for *Talley's Folly*, a play by Lanford Wilson, on the table.

I knew that Van had no interest in the theater. He had worked at *Variety* for five years. I don't think he'd ever seen a play.

"Rasheed—do you want those tickets?" I asked. As the newest, I was at the bottom of the totem pole.

He looked up. "What's it about?" he said.

"It's a man and a woman talking in a boathouse," I said, making it sound as boring as possible.

Rasheed rolled his eyes. The tickets were mine.

I was perfectly content, spending my days in this alternate universe. Content enough that after my freshman year at Yale, I re-upped for a second summer in Messengerland. And the job did come with one perk: a free, year-round subscription to *Variety*.

SO THAT IS WHY "THE BIBLE OF SHOW BUSINESS" APPEARED, TIGHTLY ROLLED, IN my Yale post office box every week. I looked forward to its arrival in a half-interested way. I would read the reviews, check to see which of the elderly reporters had died, maybe glance at the casting notices . . . and one day, there it was.

Young people, ages fourteen to twenty, were needed for a new Broadway musical, *Merrily We Roll Along*, by Stephen Sondheim and George Furth, directed by Harold Prince. An open call audition was being held at the Minskoff rehearsal studios on October 2nd. No union membership required.

If the universe operated predictably, I would never have seen that casting notice. I was not pursuing a career as an actor. I was a sophomore at Yale, and I was happy there. But I had made the inexplicable choice to spend two summers working as a messenger at *Variety*, and . . . well, how could I *not* go to that audition? I was eighteen, the show was based on a play by Moss Hart and George S. Kaufman, and the people I respected most in the world were creating it. Plus, one of the smaller parts required an actor who played the piano.

When the day arrived, I took an early train into New York from New Haven. In Grand Central Station, I found a photo booth and snapped a four-inch-by-four-inch picture of myself, which I paper-clipped to the back of the résumé I had typed up the night before. My credits included Linus in *You're a Good Man, Charlie Brown*, and Giles Corey in *The Crucible*. Obviously, I was going to be cast in a Broadway show.

My heart sank as I approached the Minskoff building. Chaos. Every actor in New York from the age of fourteen to seventy-five was there. It was only eight thirty in the morning and already the line of hopefuls snaked out of the building, winding through Shubert Alley. From a distance, it looked like a line of teenagers. Up close, it looked like a lot of middle-aged actors trying to appear younger. I found the end of the line and spent the day wondering what the hell I was doing.

The line inched forward. I wasn't the only one who had never been to a professional audition. The two girls in front of me had come by bus from Alpharetta, Georgia. Neither had ever been north of the Mason-Dixon Line. We held each other's places when we ran to the Howard Johnson's on Forty-Sixth Street to use the bathroom. Our section of the line got chattier as the afternoon stretched on. By five we were best friends, and we had made it inside the Minskoff building. At six, the line stopped moving.

There were only about thirty people in front of me, but the open call was over. As it became clear that I wasn't going to be seen that day, I felt both fiercely disappointed and profoundly relieved. But I was unsure of what to do. Nobody left, so I didn't either. Finally, a kindly assistant appeared and collected pictures and résumés from those of us who had waited. *Well, that's that,* I thought.

A week later, to my dumbfounded surprise, I received a call in my dorm room at Yale from Joanna Merlin, Harold Prince's casting director. She politely asked if I would like to audition for the role of Ted, the piano player, in *Merrily We Roll Along*.

I said I would like that very much.

I hung up the phone and sat for a moment on the edge of my bed.

I knew next to nothing about "the business," but I did know that I was being given an extraordinary opportunity.

Two months of auditions followed. I would take the train into New York, sing my song, "Tonight at Eight," then go to the piano and accompany myself singing another song, "Opus One." Mr. Prince would smile and ask me a question or two, and then I would return to Yale, where Joanna Merlin would call me with another appointment to do it all again, two weeks later.

Sometimes the auditions were on the set of *Evita*, Mr. Prince's show at the Broadway Theatre. The first time I auditioned there, just walking in the stage door was a once-in-a-lifetime rush. Inside, it was dark and calm. Hooks, mirrors, and hanging costumes covered every inch of wallspace. A few other young actors waited in the stairwell. There was none of the camaraderie that had percolated along the line at the open call. Instead, we waited in silence, concentrating on the task ahead. Eventually, Joanna Merlin called my name and showed me where to go. Walking out onto the stage was disorienting. Treacherous light boxes lined the floor, and worse, the set was built on a tilt. Wherever I stepped, my foot seemed to land at an unexpected angle. I was sure I was going to trip and tumble down into the orchestra pit.

I sang my songs, played the piano, Mr. Prince smiled, and I went back to Yale.

I told only a few close friends about my string of callbacks. Mostly, it was a secret. I felt special, removed, privileged. I tried desperately not to fantasize about being in a Broadway show. I focused on the next step, the next audition.

Finally, ninety of us were called at ten in the morning to the Minskoff rehearsal studios. It became clear that we would be spending the entire day running a grueling musical theater triathlon. We sang for Paul Gemignani, the music director, and he taught us music from the score. Ron Field, the choreographer, showed us a dance combination; we read scenes for Mr. Prince. Stephen Sondheim and George Furth watched intently.

We danced, we read, we sang. Then we waited, jammed together in the crowded hallway until Joanna Merlin emerged from the studio, holding a clipboard. She read off some names; the thirty people she called were excused.

We read, we sang, we danced. Chatting in small groups spread out in the hallway, we nervously compared notes on what they'd said to us. Joanna Merlin appeared with her clipboard of doom. Another thirty people disappeared.

We sang, we danced, we read. We sat by ourselves, exhausted and tense, in the spacious hallway.

At five thirty, Joanna Merlin let a few more people go; then she called the twenty-three of us who remained into the studio, a large room with mirrored walls. We stood in a semicircle facing Mr. Prince. He was wearing an expensive-looking blue sweater over a white button-down shirt, and his glasses were perched on top of his head. He looked just like Hal Prince.

"I've got some good news and some bad news," he said. "The show has been cast, and you are it."

I wanted to jump up and down and scream, but nobody else did anything. I figured they were all more professional than me, and this was how one behaved. Then twenty-three giddy teenagers jumped up and down, screaming at the top of their lungs, including me.

Chapter Eight

1980

{I} couldn't comprehend my good fortune. Had I really just been cast in the next Stephen Sondheim/Hal Prince Broadway musical? It didn't make sense, but it seemed to be true. They had offered me the role of Ted, who played the piano in various scenes throughout the show. The train ride back to New Haven was, undoubtedly, the longest two hours of my life. I wanted to announce my extraordinary news to everyone I had ever known, but I was surrounded by strangers and couldn't tell a soul.

The train was packed. I was jammed against a window beside a burly woman. I leaned my head against the glass, thinking back on the scene in the rehearsal studio.

After the screaming and hugging and weeping had subsided, Mr. Prince gave us the bad news. The show was postponed for nine months—we wouldn't be starting rehearsals until September. This was good news for me. I could complete my sophomore year at Yale, move to New York over the summer, and be ready for fall rehearsals. Contracts, Mr. Prince said, would be issued soon. Then he dismissed us.

I hurried to Grand Central Station, stopping at a pay phone on the way to explain that I would be hours late for the student production of *Sweet Charity* for which I was supposed to be playing the piano.

That morning, I had known what the future held for me. Now, I had nothing but questions. My parents, trying to reconstruct their own lives in the aftermath of their divorce, were absentmindedly agreeable to the idea of their firstborn dropping out of college to join the circus. Yale agreed to give me the next year off. I explained to the uninterested registrar that it might even be *two* years. "It's Sondheim and Prince's follow-up to *Sweeney Todd*," I added significantly.

But how could I possibly wait until the fall? The weeks crawled by.

Ron Field, concerned about our obvious lack of dance training, volunteered to give the entire cast "optional" dance classes. Everyone attended. I got very familiar with the Metro-North trains between Connecticut and New York. One cast member, David Shine, published a monthly newsletter (the *Merrily Press*) to keep us in touch, and he organized parties and trips to see each other's shows. Shows that we were doing while we waited. And worried.

We were the luckiest group of people in the world, but it was all so intangible. Concrete information was scarce. And disconcertingly, auditions continued. Hal Prince had told us the show was cast, but the truth turned out to be slightly different. James Weissenbach and Lonny Price had been selected as the two male leads, Frank and Charley, but Joanna Merlin was still searching for the perfect actress to play Mary, the female lead. Mr. Prince was being picky, we heard.

Several of my future castmates trekked to New Haven to see a revue I created of songs by Tom Jones & Harvey Schmidt, the writers of *The Fantasticks*. I directed, orchestrated, and conducted the performances from an old upright piano. The piano teetered precariously on the cramped balcony of a former squash court that had been repurposed as a little theater. Yale sported several of these petite playhouses, scattered throughout its many colleges. They were ideal places to do musicals—no amplification necessary.

The first person to audition had been a dazzling junior from Dallas, Texas, named Victoria Clark. Gifted with a beautiful soprano voice, she could be hilarious one moment and heartbreaking the next.

By the time she finished singing her two songs, I decided I never wanted to do a musical without her for the rest of my life.

Grandmommy and Granddaddy also journeyed to New Haven to see the revue. For years afterward, they would ask about "That girl—from your little show in the squash court—is she a Broadway star yet?" Granddaddy was especially insistent.

"She has what it takes!" he would say, as if I didn't agree with him, which I did.

I wish Grandmommy and Granddaddy had lived long enough to see Vicki's masterful performance in *The Light in the Piazza*, and that I could have heard them crow, "We told you!" when she won the Tony Award for Best Actress in a Musical.

I fell madly in love with Vicki's talent and her hilariously sweet personality, confusing it with romantic love. We took long walks, discussing music, theater, and our dreams. She had studied singing in Vienna and had a broader view of the world than I did. She could make any story into a boisterously funny showstopper, then touch your soul with a kind word and a squeeze of the hand. I loved hanging out in her room. We were so crazy for each other that Vicki broke up with her then-boyfriend. We cuddled and kissed, entering into an unconsummated relationship that proved to be the final months of my bifurcated "I'm-not-gay / am-I-gay?" cerebral gymnastics.

Smitten as I was with Vicki, the fervid desires that had been swirling through my brain, unmet for the last four years, were becoming impossible to ignore. Over pizza, in a New Haven restaurant, I confessed to her that I had a crush on a man. His name was Dan. Her eyes teared up as we held hands. The sun was going down. Dusky light from the window warmed her face. She told me that she'd had her suspicions. Then she sadly revealed that I was the second guy who had figured out that he was gay while dating her.

Dan was a freshman, also in the cast of the Jones & Schmidt revue. He was earnest and adorable with a big smile and a distinctive bouncy walk, pale skin, and black hair. We started spending time together. I was too unsure to flirt. Was he feeling what I was feeling? I couldn't tell.

One night, we caught a movie, then went out for a glass of wine. I walked him back to the Old Campus, where the freshmen lived. He had his own room in a suite he shared with three roommates. They were all out. It was quiet.

We talked and talked, teasing out the evening, postponing whatever it was that seemed about to happen. He sat on his bed. I sat next to him.

Our knees grazed against each other. Every now and then I touched his arm.

We kept talking.

Finally, I leaned in closer and kissed him. We stopped talking.

It felt so natural.

After four years of contortions, my brain relaxed.

I am gay, I thought.

How wonderful.

LATER, WE LAY IN HIS NARROW BED, MY HEAD ON HIS CHEST. I DIDN'T WANT THE night to end. I traced my finger along his stomach, feeling his ribs, how they connected to his neck. I ran my finger around his shoulder, then back to his neck, and down his chest to his belly button. He sleepily took my hand in his and rolled over, pulling me up against his bare backside.

WALKING BACK TO MY ROOM, EARLY IN THE MORNING, IT WAS ALL I COULD DO not to dance along the stone walkways. I looked at the first rays of sunlight hitting the Gothic spires of Yale's venerable towers and crenelated walls as if I had never seen sunlight before.

Dan and I only lasted a few months, but he was a good first boyfriend. We were both inexperienced and excited to be venturing into this new world. I remember how clean he always smelled and the unexpected charge of kissing a mouth with a bit of stubble around it.

Vicki and I managed to remain friends.

At the end of the semester, I packed my things and moved to New York.

Chapter Nine

1981

{I realize now that I took a leave from college and relocated my life without having received a contract or even a letter of intent. I went entirely on faith. It never occurred to me not to. It made for a nerve-wracking summer—fervently hoping each day that an envelope from Hal Prince's office would appear in my mailbox.

My back couldn't take one more night on Doddy's couch. I found a sublet way west on Fifty-Fourth Street, stuffing my belongings into the already crowded home of an opera singer who was jetting to Europe for the next few months. I worked at *Variety* as a messenger for yet another summer, barely able to make ends meet. I became an expert guide to supermarkets that gave out free food samples.

I also perfected the art of "second-acting"—blending in with the audience of a play or musical as they returned from intermission into the theater, quickly scoping out which seats were empty and sliding into one of them just as the house lights dimmed for the second act. *Woman of the Year*, starring Lauren Bacall, was playing at the Palace. I saw the first act once and the second act five times.

• • •

Early in July, sipping morning coffee in my tiny sublet, I read an article in the *New York Times* about a "rare cancer" that was killing gay men. As the summer wore on, a new fear became attached to the idea of two men together. Except for those few spring weeks that Dan and I had in New Haven, that danger has been present my whole life as a gay man.

Ah, Wolf.

ONE NIGHT, A BUNCH OF THE *MERRILY* KIDS ATTENDED AN OFF-BROADWAY SHOW. There was a new face in our group. Hal Prince had finally cast the pivotal role of Mary. Enter Annie Morrison, with a zany warmth that lit up a room and a great voice that mixed two parts honey with three parts carbolic acid. Annie told hilarious stories about touring the country with her former boyfriend's Korean pop band, her hair dyed black, her face heavily made up, trying to pass herself off as "Ah-nee," a Korean vocalist. She was clearly wonderful. We were complete!

The first day of rehearsal was suddenly approaching.

My contract arrived!

I had my first good night's sleep in months.

Then I read the contract.

In addition to playing the role of Ted, Mr. Prince asked if I would understudy Lonny Price in the role of Charley. Well, why not? I thought. Lonny seemed fairly healthy. I signed it and returned it by hand to Mr. Prince's office. I then had to join Actors' Equity, which meant paying a $525.00 initiation fee.

Because I would be playing the piano onstage, I was also required to join Local 802, the Musicians Union. My phone rang one morning; a gruff voice started giving orders.

"Loud. Gemignani. Fifty-Second Street. Broadway. Corner. Noon. Today."

I appeared on the required corner at the appointed time and Paul Gemignani himself escorted me to the Local 802 membership office, located above the Roseland Ballroom on West Fifty-Second Street.

I tried hard to hide my nervousness around him. Big and bearlike, wearing his cool-cat sunglasses, he led me through a dark, dusty warren of black-carpeted hallways and dimly lit cubicles. Populated by a withered band of yesteryear's musicians, the atmosphere was more Mafia Social Club than Labor Bureau.

Paul strode through the smoky maze of offices, greeting everyone by nickname. At the membership desk, he whipped out a thick wad of twenties and peeled off fifteen of them. Generous Hal Prince had decided that the show would pay my Musicians Union membership fee, since I had paid the Equity fee myself. No forms were filled out; no ID was required. I was with Paul Gemignani. My union card appeared promptly, no questions asked.

THE MORNING OF THE FIRST REHEARSAL, I WOKE UP AT 5:00 A.M., CONVINCED that I would be late or wouldn't be able to find the building, which was down near Union Square. The sidewalks, damp from an overnight squall, glistened in the pale sunlight; the heat of August had surrendered to the cool of September.

Arriving painfully early, I met Beverley Randolph, our stage manager, in the elevator. Beverley was tall, with long brown hair. Businesslike and intimidating, she had an unexpectedly kind smile and a shockingly loud laugh. She wore a string of pearls around her neck, and she favored long brown skirts and leather boots. Even years later, when she was the stage manager for *Curtains*, Beverley usually looked like she was going to a Vermont barn dance.

Stage managers generally arrive an hour and a half before the actors are called. I introduced myself and told her I was in the cast. Beverley looked at me like I was unhinged and told me to stay out of the way while her crew prepared the rooms.

We were rehearsing in the building that Michael Bennett purchased after his success with *A Chorus Line*—890 Broadway. It held several floors of rehearsal studios. *Merrily We Roll Along* had taken possession of three spacious studios on the fourth floor, plus several small offices.

I parked myself unobtrusively behind a piano in the largest studio and watched the meticulous pre-rehearsal countdown. Beverley commanded a small squad of assistant stage managers and interns. In an atmosphere of quiet concentration, they updated scripts with the latest rewrites and arranged chairs for the first read-through, during which the cast was going to read the scenes while Mr. Sondheim performed the songs. Simultaneously, the stage managers organized rehearsal props and assembled a tier of bleachers that was the centerpiece of Eugene Lee's set. Eugene Lee had designed the scenery for *Sweeney Todd*. I wondered what miracles he had in store for us.

The early morning calm in the rehearsal studio was soon interrupted, as people started entering through the large set of double doors.

Ruth Mitchell, Mr. Prince's associate producer, appeared wearing, of all things, a cape. A tough little woman with a short sharp haircut, she took one look at the room and demanded that everything move clockwise ninety degrees. She didn't want the sun in Mr. Prince's eyes while he was directing. Beverley mobilized her battalion.

Judith Dolan, the costume designer—wild hair and an artsy smock—dashed in, laden with costume sketches. She started putting drawings up on the walls.

Elderly Mathilde Pincus, the music copyist, arrived toting boxes of music. The score was hand-copied on thick white eleven-by-thirteen paper, each song printed accordion-style, the pages meticulously taped together. Unfortunately, the printing process involved some intense chemicals, and the music smelled overwhelmingly of ammonia. Mathilde started unpacking. Beverley, charging across the room, the heels of her boots clicking crisply under her thick skirt, banished the copyist and her boxes to another, smaller room. There, the harsh odor from the music would be even more intense, but Mr. Prince wouldn't smell it.

Jonathan Tunick, the orchestrator of the five previous Sondheim/ Prince musicals, trotted in, urgently discussing something with Paul Gemignani.

Ron Field (cheekbones and sunglasses), and his assistant, John (trim beard and sunglasses), glided through the doors, surveyed the room, and flounced out.

British, unkempt David Hersey, the lighting designer, and dapper, bow-tied Eugene Lee knocked timidly, wondering if they were in the right place.

A flight of well-dressed producers strolled in, businesslike and dignified, herded by roly-poly Mary Bryant, Our Lady of Press and Publicity.

The cast arrived, one by one, bubbling with excitement, hugging each other frantically. The noise level in the room climbed exponentially.

Stephen Sondheim and George Furth entered quietly, looking disheveled and harried.

At three minutes to ten, the doors flew open one last time. The Prince family appeared, all smiles and love: Hal and Judy, glamorous and fun, and their daughter Daisy, who had also been cast in the show.

I looked around the room, trying to grasp that I was actually a part of this astonishing assemblage of artists. The wait was over. Rehearsals were starting.

What could possibly go wrong?

Chapter Ten

1981

{ T } he central conceit of Kaufman and Hart's play *Merrily We Roll Along* is that the story is told backward. Each scene moves forward, but the scenes are performed in reverse chronological order, starting when the characters are in their forties, in 1934, and going back to their high school graduation day in 1916. The pretentious, bitter alcoholics we meet at the beginning of the play gradually become less jaded and more idealistic, until we finally see the almost unrecognizably optimistic teenagers from which they sprang.

George Furth and Stephen Sondheim's adaptation preserves the structure of the original play, but updates the time period so that it moves from 1976 back to 1957. Hal Prince's concept, using actors who were the age of the characters at the end of the play, sounded brilliant. We would gradually become our true, younger selves, and the ending could be played honestly, without the artifice of older actors pretending to be sixteen.

Rehearsals were exciting and tense and hard. Hal directed the scenes, staging the show meticulously, beat by beat, always making it clear where the audience's focus should be. He loved creating swirls of movement that caught the eye, directing the viewer's attention to the next dramatic event. He preferred to work on large group scenes in the mornings when everyone was energized. As the day progressed, we divided into smaller groups. Hal rehearsed with the principals, and the rest of us worked on the choreographed transitions with Ron Field. Beverley Randolph kept us moving between studios with military efficiency.

When Hal was directing, he kept the core members of his team close, so he could work with the actors and simultaneously discuss the technical elements of the show. The set design included a large turntable built into the stage floor. During rehearsals, without the turntable, Ruth Mitchell was always on Hal's right, taking notes on how the set would move and helping him visualize how the turntable's rotations would affect the rest of the scenery. He shouted ideas for lighting cues to David Hersey. He conferred with George Furth about rewrites. His work with the actors was meticulous but rarely involved text analysis or character discussion. He preferred to leave that "acting school stuff" to the actors.

890 BROADWAY TEEMED WITH THEATRICAL LIFE. IN ADDITION TO REHEARSAL studios, it housed the offices and workrooms of various scenic, lighting, and costume designers. Michael Bennett had envisioned a self-contained theatrical universe, where collaborators were instantly available. For instance, Barbara Matera was building the costumes for *Merrily*. Her workshop occupied the sixth floor. Instead of the usual scheduling of rehearsals around lengthy trips across town for costume fittings, we simply dashed upstairs.

Every few days, we would show Hal the dance routines. Hal would scratch his beard and he and Ron would confer. Then Ron would start from the beginning again in the other room. This process repeated itself over and over. We could feel Ron's mounting frustration over our lack of dance experience. One day, with the full company in the room, he referred to us disdainfully as "the amateur-hour dancers."

Now and then, Stephen Sondheim would bring in a new section of a song or a refined lyric. These were the red-letter days in my diary. I was hopelessly starstruck and shy in his presence, but every now and then we would exchange a few words, and I eventually started to relax around him. He was unfailingly kind.

One day, when we were working on "Rich and Happy," he was sitting near the piano, a small upright, that I played during rehearsals. I had to play a particularly hard passage again and again while Hal was working out the staging. I certainly didn't mind, but Steve thought it was hilariously cruel.

After the rehearsal, as he was packing up his music, he said, "You play that section very well. Better than I ever could. My technique . . ."

He broke off, sadly, shaking his head.

I thanked him, but what I was thinking was that if I died that evening it would be fine with me because my every dream had just come true.

I wish I had been able to relax more around him. I thought his score for *Merrily* was fantastic—tender and bouncy and cleverly constructed. I was in music nerd heaven, and I would have loved to ask him hundreds of questions.

I had noticed that he used the same intervals for the opening melodies of six of the songs. The rhythms were different, and the songs were all stylistically varied. Why had he used the same intervals?

I figured out the answer on my own, and it made clever sense. Frank, the lead character in the show, was a composer, and each song his character composed was based on the same melodic intervals. Sondheim was subtly informing the audience that these songs were related.

I also realized that he wasn't developing his thematic material in the traditional way. Because the show progressed backward, he was exploring and varying the music in reverse as well, using "pre-prises" rather than the usual reprises.

Paul Gemignani taught us the music. We learned it eagerly, and we sounded good when we sang. Paul was strict and demanding, allowing us only occasional glimpses of his dark, dry wit. Gruff and unreadable, he rarely smiled. We adored him and wanted only to please him.

Paul liked to audition the solo lines before assigning them, a nerve-wracking procedure.

"You try it," he might say, pointing his finger at me.

I would try it.

"Now, you try it," he would say, pointing at someone else.

This would go on and on.

Eventually, the line would find its rightful owner.

RON AND HAL HAD COLLABORATED SUCCESSFULLY ON THE ORIGINAL PRODUCTION of *Cabaret*, but Hal continued to reject most of what Ron choreographed for *Merrily*. For us, this meant hours of waiting while Ron tried to figure out exactly what Hal hadn't liked. Ron's assistant, John, was always dramatically outraged on his behalf. John's "notes" to us grew lengthier, more personal, and more vicious. Some days, Ron would have us sing the transitions over and over while he and John danced around, trying to come up with steps they thought we could do. Other days, they would kick us out of the studio so they could choreograph privately. This usually happened after a greasy, leering man arrived with small plastic bags of . . . we knew not what, but we had a pretty good idea. Neither Ron nor John ever learned my name.

John's acid-tongued tirades were particularly hard on the girls. When we were working on the dance break in "Now You Know," John inexplicably singled out Daisy Prince for ridicule. She may not have been the best dancer in the world, but she was certainly no worse than the rest of us. Daisy took his sarcastic harangue stoically, refusing to cry in rehearsal.

Later that day, on the way to a costume fitting, I found myself alone with her in the stairwell. I told her how unfair I thought John had been. Tears started pouring down her face. I held her hand till she calmed down.

"You know," I said, "for five years, I went to a school where my father was the assistant headmaster. I think you're handling your situation here really well. I know how hard it can be." Her tears welled up again.

"I would offer to help you with the dance steps," I said, "but I have no idea what they are, and I can't do them anyway. You can always join me in the back. I'm usually behind a pole, trying hard not to be noticed."

She smiled as she dried her eyes.

I thought about how different her life had been from mine—growing up with luxurious family homes in New York, Mallorca, and Switzerland, artistic royalty popping in and out from dawn to dusk.

Yet here we were, huddled in the same dark stairwell.

Daisy let go of my hand and took a deep breath. We hurried to our fittings.

DESPITE MY CONSTANT, LOW-GRADE FEAR THAT HAL WOULD WAKE ONE MORNING, realize he'd made a mistake, and fire me, I was having a great time. The cast was filled with quirky, interesting, talented people. And I had a nice little part.

My character, Ted, played the piano throughout the opening party scene. During Frank's song "Rich and Happy," the smaller roles each had vignettes that quickly sketched their characters and showed their relationship to him. This was Ted's:

> *RU: (a Hollywood actor, looking around)*
> *WHO'S THE REAL BRIGHT ONE?*

> *TED: (playing the piano)*
> *ASK YOUR EMPLOYER.*

> *RU:*
> *WHO'S THE UPTIGHT ONE?*

> *TED:*
> *THAT ONE'S HIS LAWYER.*
> *AND THAT ONE'S HIS AGENT.*

AND THAT ONE'S HIS BANKER.
AND THAT ONE'S HIS PRESS MAN
WHO HANDLES HIS PRESS.
AND THEN THERE'S HIS YES-MAN,
NOW WHERE IS HIS YES-MAN?
OH, YES . . .

RU:
You makin' money?

TED:
Sure.

RU:
Then shut up.

ALL:
PARTY!!

My favorite number in the show was "Opening Doors." It told many stories simultaneously, whirling through the triumphs and the setbacks of the three young writers as they started out in New York. Jason Alexander was terrific as Joe Josephson, the producer. The song was filled with personal details from Sondheim's past, even poking fun at his reputation for writing "un-hummable" melodies. The sequence shimmered with a truth that elevated it from the rest of the show. I appeared as an audition pianist, playing for the actresses trying out for a showcase the writers were presenting.

Near the end of the number, Sondheim had dramatized the moment that Ted was first hired by Frank:

FRANK:
YOU! DO YOU WANT TO PLAY SECOND PIANO?

TED:

ALL RIGHT, BUT I HAVE TO HAVE ALL OF THE MUSIC,
AND SATURDAY I HAVE TO PLAY A BAR MITZVAH.
SAY, WAIT A SEC, I'VE GOT A COUPLE OF NUMBERS . . .

ALL:

WE'LL WORRY ABOUT IT ON SUNDAY.
WE'RE OPENING DOORS,
SINGING, "HERE WE ARE . . ."

I loved being in the ending. During the final chorus, we marched in a big circle, pushing typewriters and chairs and (in my case) a piano, forming a joyful parade.

"The turntable will be turning as well," Hal told us. "It should feel like your energy is making the whole world spin a little faster."

I ALSO APPEARED IN THE GREENWICH VILLAGE NIGHTCLUB SCENE, PLAYING THE piano for two numbers: "Bobby and Jackie and Jack," a revue-style Irish jig that satirized the Kennedys, and "Thank You for Coming," a vaudeville chaser that followed it.

One day, at the end of a full company music rehearsal, Paul Gemignani pointed at me. "Loud," he said.

He pointed to the corner. I went to the corner.

"Had an idea," he said, joining me. "Kennedy number. Your character, Ted, isn't just the pianist. You know how these things work. Ted is Frank's music director. You probably had to teach 'em all the music and the cutoffs and deal with the Boston accents and figure out how to pronounce all those goddamn names. So, I think you should teach the number to the other actors."

He walked away.

I was surprised to learn that he had that much faith in me. He had never given me any indication of how he thought I was doing.

I taught the music to the other three actors. I worked with them on their diction and on how to pronounce all those goddamn names. Ron and John staged it quickly one afternoon, and we performed it for Hal.

"Swell!" said Hal.

It's one of the only numbers that never changed during previews.

I ALSO APPEARED IN THE TRANSCENDENT FINAL ANTHEM, "OUR TIME," AND THE ever-changing transitions, which threaded through the show. The transitions were filled with topical references, intended to let the audience know which year the story was going back to for the next scene. Many of the references were obscure: "Altamont," "Weathermen," "Mister Ellsberg." I had no idea what they meant.

SINCE I WAS UNDERSTUDYING LONNY PRICE IN THE ROLE OF CHARLEY, I WAS occasionally allowed to attend the smaller, more private rehearsals with Hal and the principals. Beverley explained sternly that this was a privilege. I was to be silent. Invisible. I sat inconspicuously by the piano with Eddie Strauss, one of the rehearsal pianists, absorbing everything I could.

Eddie was mischievous and gossipy. He was a merciless master at prying information out of innocent actors, and I soon learned to be very careful around him. He would duck down behind his piano and wheedle me for news from the other rooms.

"Tell me everything," he would say, his eyes gleaming.

He knew just how loudly he could talk without incurring Beverley's wrath, and he had the professional rehearsal pianist's all-important seventh sense: an infallible knowledge of exactly when and where to start playing.

While seemingly deep in conversation with me, part of Eddie's brain was carefully attuned to everything the director or choreographer was saying. He could be in the middle of a word—his hands would suddenly fly to the piano keys, and he'd be completely focused on the rehearsal. Then he would come right back to whatever word he hadn't finished. Eddie was intrigued by the growing tension between Ron and Hal. But mostly, he wanted to know who was gay and who was sleeping with whom. I was pretty useless to him on that front.

ON THE FIRST DAY OF REHEARSAL, WHEN THE CAST READ THROUGH THE SHOW, there was one song that Sondheim hadn't yet written. It was for Lonny Price, as Charley. Hal referred to it as "the TV studio song." We rehearsed around the empty spot. Sondheim kept promising, apologetically, that he would finish it soon. I was consumed with curiosity.

Hal assured Lonny it would definitely be completed by the second week of rehearsal.

The second week came and went.

At the end of the third week, Sondheim stumbled into rehearsal looking like he hadn't slept for days. The song was finished! Well, a third of the song was finished. The rest would be coming soon, he muttered testily. He pulled his original, handwritten manuscript out of his satchel. There hadn't been time to send it to the music copyist. He grabbed Lonny and Eddie and the three of them disappeared into a studio. It was all I could do not to put my ear to the keyhole.

The song turned out to be a diabolical nervous breakdown called "Franklin Shepard, Inc." The lyrics went lickety-split. Charley had to imitate his writing partner, Frank, on the phone, plus the sounds of telephones ringing and buzzers buzzing, secretaries calling on the intercom, and, at one point, a pig snorting as it grabbed all the money it could.

The rest of the song dribbled in, section by section. Lonny rehearsed it twenty-four hours a day, rattling through the lyrics like a crazy person in subways, on sidewalks, and, I'm sure, in his sleep. He started to lose his voice. As his understudy, this turned my bowels to mush and made my heart race in terror. I begged Beverley for a copy of the music. I started rehearsing it twenty-four hours a day, rattling through the lyrics like the understudy to a crazy person, in my apartment, on elevators, and in my sleep. Liz Callaway, who understudied the role of Mary, offered to rehearse with me. Whenever we could grab Eddie, we would race through as much of our material as we could. The three of us had a ball together. Eddie could play any musical theater song you could think of. In your key. Liz was warm and funny, and she had a lustrous, seamless voice like nobody else on the planet.

HAL PRINCE'S MENTOR, GEORGE ABBOTT, CAME TO AN EARLY RUN-THROUGH. HE was ninety-four at the time and would live another thirteen years. Mr. Abbott didn't smile once. Hal made some cuts in a few of the scenes.

Late in the fourth week of rehearsals, we were working on what must have been the sixteenth version of the First Transition. Ron Field was in a foul mood. We ran through the new routine for him, which was pretty much indistinguishable from the prior fifteen routines we had learned, and he threw a tantrum. The pressure of the last few weeks—Hal rejecting everything he choreographed—was making him insane. He started screaming at Paul Gemignani, saying that the dance music was shit shit shit, and he had the contractual right to use his own damn dance arranger, and he wanted his own damn dance arranger now.

Whenever Ron stopped to take a breath, John would chime in, repeating whatever Ron had just said. It went on and on. Paul stared back at them, inscrutable as stone. A few of us cowered in the corner.

The next day, there were new faces in the dance studio—a slick, chubby guy had been flown in from Las Vegas to write new dance arrangements, along with a drummer, who never took off his black leather jacket or mirrored sunglasses. We waited while they worked on the dance music, adding drum accents and cymbal splashes, arguing, and muttering. Then they banished the cast from the room, so we waited in the hallway. After a while, Beverley sent us to an early lunch.

Over the next few days, the better dancers were invited back into the studio to learn new choreography. I was not among them.

We did our final run-through in the rehearsal studio. It felt awkward performing Ron's unfinished choreography when we knew Hal was unhappy with it. Michael Bennett attended. He looked confused.

That afternoon, Hal had scheduled a costume parade. We presented Judith Dolan's designs, going scene by scene, changing in and out of the many elaborate, custom-built pieces. I thought the costumes were amazingly creative. Every character's sequence of outfits meticulously indicated the backward progression of time. And each character's clothes were linked together in some interesting way. Tonya Pinkins was always in some variety of leopard skin. Donna Marie Elio's clothes were covered with butterflies. Mine all had clocks on them. The tie I wore at the beginning was embroidered with two clocks. The pajamas I wore at the end had a variety of clocks printed up and down the sleeves.

But as the afternoon wore on, Hal got increasingly anxious.

"I cast kids for a reason," he fretted. "They don't look like kids in these costumes."

When we arrived at the second act Greenwich Village nightclub scene, Frank, Beth, Charley, and I were dressed in sweatshirts with our characters' names written on them. It was the only time Hal smiled that entire day.

"Now they look like kids," he said, pointing at us. "The whole show should look like that."

He meant it. Judith's entire original costume design was thrown out, never to be worn onstage.

THE NEXT DAY, THE WHOLE CAST SQUEEZED INTO A NOT-VERY-CLEAN REHEARSAL studio on a creepy block in the shadow of the Port Authority Bus Terminal. The orchestra had been rehearsing. We were gathered for the *sitzprobe*—the first time the cast hears the orchestra play the score. Jonathan Tunick had come up with a bright, exciting sound for the show, heavy on the brass, with some quirks. For instance, the string section consisted only of cellos—he didn't use any violins or violas in the orchestration. Another oddity: the rip-roaring overture featured, at its center, a touching ballad, "Good Thing Going." Instead of assigning the melody to the woodwinds or trumpets, Tunick tossed it to the tuba.

I had heard the entire score many times, of course, but only on piano. Hearing the music played by twenty-three musicians was life-changing. Paul conducted a hand-picked orchestra of Broadway's best players. Sondheim sat nearby, giving the occasional note or suggestion.

Chords shimmered in unexpected ways. Instrumental counter-lines echoed the voices, creating drama, humor, and a sense of conversation between the orchestra and the singers. "Not a Day Goes By" throbbed with emotion as the cellos soared and the muted brass created gentle pillows of supportive bedding. Eddie Strauss played the finger-cramping chromatic sixteenth notes that snaked through Charley's new song, "Franklin Shepard, Inc.," on the synthesizer, evoking a nightmarish, mechanized harpsichord. In the final two choruses of "Opening Doors," Sondheim used the melody of "Old Friends" as the bass line. Tunick's orchestration of that moment was electrifying. The trombones began the melody, and soon the whole brass section was strutting along on "Old Friends" while the singers and the rest of the band were doing "Opening Doors."

We sang through the entire score with the orchestra. It was an overwhelming experience, like swimming in an ocean of sound, music, and color, trying not to be pulled under by the strong currents and the powerful swells. By the end, I was in a giddy, goose-bumped daze, exhausted and blissfully overstimulated.

I finally got here, I thought, remembering the night in Cincinnati when I had first glimpsed the colorful land of Oz on Mrs. Glover's TV set.

Broadway was better than I could ever have dreamed. And a lot more complicated.

Chapter Eleven

1981

{T}he next morning, we reported to our new home, the Alvin Theatre on West Fifty-Second Street, where *Company* had premiered. Seeing the words *Merrily We Roll Along* up in lights on the marquee made my heart almost burst. A feeling of monumental pride enveloped me when I entered the theater through the stage door as a professional actor in a Broadway show. I ordered myself to savor the moment. It might never happen again.

Backstage, the Alvin was crowded, cold, chaotic, and cluttered. We moved into our assigned dressing rooms. I shared a fourth-floor room the size of a coat closet with the acerbically opinionated Paul Hyams.

"Darling," he said to me that first day. "I wouldn't spend a lot of time getting settled in here. Thanksgiving isn't for weeks, but I smell turkey."

The walls were beige; the carpeting was brown, with strange, ancient stains. I couldn't help it—I thought it was wonderful. *And look,* I said to myself, thinking of poor Marian Seldes and her stockings, *a sink—right in the room!* I took a few things out of my bag and put them on my half of the counter. Floating outside our dressing room window was the enormous "L" in the perpendicular ALVIN sign that clung to the theater. Beverley's voice crackled out of a speaker in the hallway: we were to gather onstage to see the set for the first time.

AT NORTH COUNTRY SCHOOL, THERE WAS ALWAYS A MORNING, A FEW DAYS before Thanksgiving, when we woke to discover that the Quonset hut had been transformed, overnight, into a theater. Wooden platforms had been dragged in; folding chairs had been set up. Don Rand and Tsu Hansen would have stayed up late, painting and hammering. I loved seeing it all for the first time. Scenery was constructed from cardboard and basic art supplies. Old, frayed sheets were dyed and shaped to form clouds or hills. Brown paper, crumpled in big swaths, became tree trunks and branches. The absence of a budget required inventive solutions—one year, bushel baskets borrowed from the gardening shed were cleverly transformed into ocean waves carrying a ship; another, we fought an energetic battle using rakes and trowels, instead of broadswords and rapiers. It was my favorite day of the year.

SEEING *MERRILY*'S SET FOR THE FIRST TIME WAS . . . NOT LIKE THAT.

Mostly, it was confusing. Constructed of metal slats and wooden panels, the set looked blandly contemporary. Its bleachers and lockers evoked a generic high school, but it did nothing to move the story backward in time. And it was extraordinarily awkward to climb on.

We changed into our new costumes: colorful T-shirts and sweatshirts with our characters' names printed on our chests. Mine said "TED" or "HIS YES-MAN." At first, I assumed that the shirts were just inexpensive placeholders, while the real costumes were being made. This turned out not to be the case.

We started technical rehearsals, which mostly meant learning how not to fall down when the turntable started spinning. These rehearsals went very slowly. Rather than waiting in my dressing room, I preferred sitting inconspicuously in the dark theater, soaking up everything I could. The tension had quadrupled. Rehearsals

careened from crisis to crisis. There were unending problems with
the turntable; its rotations had to be precisely timed so that the scenery would swing properly into place. Set pieces jammed or slid out
of control. Staircases appeared for no reason, or weren't anywhere to
be found when needed. The actors were in the wrong place, or in the
wrong frame of mind, or in the wrong T-shirts.

Whenever anything went awry, Hal would shout "RUTHIE!!" at
the top of his lungs. Ruth Mitchell would instantly appear, hurtling
down the aisle like a missile aimed at whatever the problem was. She
was impressive. And completely terrifying.

One afternoon, when I was sitting near the back of the theater, the
bleachers got stuck in the stage left wing and the rehearsal ground
to a halt. I felt a firm tap on my shoulder. It was Ruth Mitchell. My
heart skipped two beats. She beckoned to me silently. I followed her
downstairs to the lower lobby, which had been cleared of people,
except for Eddie, who waited at the piano.

Her smile was bright and menacing.

"I want to see you do Lonny's new number," she said.

No warning.

Eddie started to play, and I sang the number for Ruth. Somehow,
the words were all in my brain, in the right order, and I gave a reasonable facsimile of Lonny's performance.

Ruth stared at me impassively.

When I finished, she turned around and left. A few minutes later,
she returned with Hal.

I sang the song again, repeating what I had just done.

As I finished, Hal gave me a big smile.

"Swell!" he said. Then he turned around and left.

I have wondered for forty years what exactly was happening
that day.

ONE EVENING, THE FULL COMPANY WAS ONSTAGE REHEARSING THE OPENING
party sequence, set in Frank's Hollywood mansion. The scene

escalated into a catfight between Frank's wife, Gussie, and his mistress, Meg, ending with Meg pushing Gussie into a swimming pool. The swimming pool surface was made of pale blue construction paper, designed to rip as Gussie fell through it. Mattresses were piled below to catch Terry Finn, who played Gussie. Beverley Randolph, concerned for Terry's safety, had practiced the fall many times herself, and when we got to the fight, she stopped the rehearsal and joined us onstage. She demonstrated how Terry could fall safely into the pool, launching herself backward, ripping the paper as planned, and landing securely on the mattresses. Beverly stood up, smiling, saying, "See how easy?" which was reassuring, except that blood was pouring out of the back of her head. She had slammed into one of the poles that supported the stage. Those of us who could see the blood started yelling, which confused Beverley, who was unaware of her injury. The stage crew summoned an ambulance and strapped her to a stretcher.

"I'm fine," she shouted valiantly. "Stop fussing!"

As they wheeled her out the stage door—blood matted in her hair and running down her face—I heard her calling, "I'll be back in a few minutes. Keep rehearsing."

We kept rehearsing. Ruth Mitchell sprang into action and doggedly started calling cues. It was a grim night. Later, in our dressing room, Paul Hyams said out loud what I had been trying not to think.

"Listen," he said, "if it takes poor Beverley going to the hospital to get them to cut that ridiculous construction-paper-ripping nightmare, it will be blood well spent. I've never seen anything so ludicrous in my life."

It was, indeed, a dreadful moment, and it occurred just when the story had to make its first lurch backward, instead of forward. It was difficult to believe that the people responsible for the extraordinary theatrical effects in *Sweeney Todd* had come up with this one. However, I was confident it would be changed before the first preview.

Beverley was back the next day with a small bandage and a big headache. The crew had spent the morning wrapping every support post in the building with thick foam. Terry couldn't have hurt herself if she tried.

ON OCTOBER 8TH, WE PERFORMED OUR FIRST PREVIEW. TWENTY-ONE OF US MADE our Broadway debuts that night. Tense and nervous, we gathered onstage, the curtain down, wearing our opening costumes—black graduation robes—over our T-shirts. We could hear the excited burble of the audience on the other side of the curtain. Then the burble went quiet, and the band started playing the overture. My feet could feel the vibrations from the pit coming up through the stage floor. The musical transition into "Old Friends" received a burst of applause from the audience. The overture climbed to its pinnacle, the timpani thundering and the trumpets screaming the high notes. The curtain rose.

And I was on Broadway.

WE SANG THE GRADUATION HYMN, "THE HILLS OF TOMORROW." JAMES Weissenbach, as Frank, gave his speech to the graduates. He stumbled over a word or two. We sang "Merrily We Roll Along." As the vamp to "Rich and Happy" started, we took off our graduation robes and became fifty-year-old Hollywood sophisticates. Except we were wearing cheap T-shirts with our names printed on our chests. James Weissenbach seemed uncomfortable singing the song; it dragged on forever, as all the minor characters were introduced.

The audience's reaction to the construction-paper-ripping pool plunge was a smothered, shocked giggle. It became apparent that people in the balcony could see the crew helping Terry off the mattresses. The show lumbered awkwardly along. Every scene felt endless. Obvious laugh lines were met with stony silence; the musical numbers were rewarded with polite applause.

A few days later, Hal cut the pool plunge. It turned out to be the least of our worries. Previewing in New York City, without the benefit of an out-of-town tryout, was brutal. Those first New York audiences hated the show with a disdain I have never since encountered. The backward structure was confusing; the set looked unfinished; the T-shirts were ugly and impossible to read past the tenth row. Moreover, since we started the evening playing mature adults, and we were, literally, teenagers, the acting at the beginning was strained and unconvincing. The final forty minutes of the show were better, because we were playing our real ages, but by then, we had lost the audience.

I mean actually, physically, lost them. We could see people leaving during the first act, storming up the aisles, muttering angrily. In the second act, during the song "Good Thing Going," I was positioned looking straight out at the audience. For the first few weeks of previews, I wondered why the EXIT signs at the back of the theater would always blink during this number. One dismal matinée, I realized it was the heads of the audience members who were leaving, crossing in front of the lit signs.

As exciting as it was to be on Broadway, to be originating a role, to be playing the piano and singing a score I loved, the unvaryingly tepid response from the audience was bewildering and disappointing. I tried not to focus on it, but those first few weeks were a tough slog.

Hal worked tirelessly. He gave notes after every performance; we rehearsed every afternoon. He restaged numbers, re-blocked scenes, and added projections telling the audience what year it was. George Furth rewrote the dialogue, cutting and clarifying. Hal fired James Weissenbach and replaced him with Jim Walton, who had been playing a smaller role, graphically confirming for me just how disposable we all were. Hal hired an older actor to play Frank in the graduation scene. He postponed the opening a week to do more surgery on the show. He asked us, twice, to voluntarily rehearse on our day off. We all said yes, of course.

One afternoon, we gathered in the house, sitting in the plush red seats of the Alvin. I could see Hal and Ruth huddled down by the orchestra pit, talking intently. When Beverley confirmed that we were all present, Hal addressed the company.

He smiled.

"I wanted to let you know what's happened," he said, chuckling a little, "before you read it in the papers."

"I realized," he said, "that Ron Field and I weren't collaborating well. We were telling different stories. Completely my fault. I met with him yesterday, and we decided to part ways on this one."

I was surprised. I had been convinced that if there were more firings, it would be some of the "amateur-hour dancers."

"Please welcome Larry Fuller," he continued, "our new choreographer. Larry worked with me on *Evita* and *On the Twentieth Century*. He's family, and he's going to be terrific. One more thing: I've postponed the opening *another* week to give Larry time to do his work."

Larry Fuller took over the downstairs lobby of the Alvin. He started by re-choreographing the transitions. Sondheim was rewriting them, one by one, eliminating the arcane period references and replacing them with reprises of the catchy opening number, "Merrily We Roll Along."

Songs were cut; songs got better endings. "Not a Day Goes By," initially written for the character of Beth, was suddenly given to the character of Frank. Minor roles were pared down, focusing the show on Frank, Charley, and Mary.

My nice little part didn't last. After a few previews, Hal gathered us onstage and read out a long list of cuts. My introductory vignette in "Rich and Happy" was cut, as was "Thank You for Coming." I was disappointed, but the cuts made sense; I had been uneasily expecting them.

Then, a week later, Hal took me out of the ending of "Opening Doors."

I was devastated. And embarrassed. I must really be untalented, I thought. My stomach hurt like I'd eaten razors for breakfast.

I understood that the changes were necessary—the audience needed to invest in the lives of the main characters, not in the back-stories of minor ones—but it was impossible not to take it personally.

I tried not to sulk at the rehearsal where Hal restaged the end of "Opening Doors" without me. It went quickly. Sondheim modified some lyrics for Frank and Beth; Larry Fuller gave me an exit and adjusted the other actors' spacing. It was like I'd never been there. Later, I sat in the back of the darkened house, weepy and miserable. Beverley must have seen me.

That evening, as we gathered onstage before the show, she took me aside. I followed her into the dimly lit stage right wing. Stagehands worked quietly around us. Sounds of the orchestra tuning drifted up from below. Beverley, standing at her calling desk, her face and pearls gently illuminated by the glow from the blue running lights, looked at me sympathetically.

"You know," she said, "I'm going to miss you at the end of 'Opening Doors' tonight." Her words were instant balm. "A piece of advice?" she asked.

I nodded.

"Count your blessings, not your wounds." She squeezed my hand, smiling kindly.

I resolved to try.

During that mad preview period, the changes were relentless. We never did the same show twice, sometimes with disastrous results. One night we charged onstage, eager to perform the new Transition we had practiced all afternoon, only to discover that the orchestra was playing the *old* Transition. The music copyists had forgotten to distribute the new orchestra parts. That audience must have thought that Stephen Sondheim wrote very avant-garde music indeed.

The stage crew rarely had time to practice each night's new set moves. Once, an entire party scene arrived facing upstage instead of facing the audience. We adjusted, awkwardly negotiating the backward furniture, but the crew then decided to rotate the stage into its proper alignment, so again we found ourselves with our backs to the audience. On nights like those, I would try to recover from the chaos around me by connecting with the one constant we had: Paul Gemignani, down in the pit.

When you perform in a Broadway musical, you inhabit a bright, vibrant space. The blaze of lights is blinding, rendering the audience invisible. You speak, you sing, and you move inside that space, all for the benefit of a looming black void.

At the bottom edge of that void, you see the face and hands of a conductor guiding you, signaling how fast the music should be, helping you with entrances, clarifying where final consonants should go. You can look at the conductor, or you can look out at the void, monitoring the conductor in your peripheral vision. It feels awkward, at first, glancing down to get a cue for an entrance or a tempo change, but it becomes second nature, part of the actor's technique.

During the second act of *Merrily We Roll Along*, after we performed "Bobby and Jackie and Jack," my character, Ted, stayed onstage, sitting at the piano.

In a reprise of "Not a Day Goes By," Frank sings fervently to Beth. Mary watches, her heart breaking, and she joins him in the song, though he is unaware of her. It's a powerful duet, the kind of heightened moment that can only happen in a musical.

Sitting at my piano, I had a clear view of Paul down in the pit. I watched how he cued the players and how he connected with the singers. I saw how he stretched certain phrases and pressed through others, giving a supple vitality to the ravishing music. I listened to how he built that reprise. Tender and quiet initially, he let it grow and intensify, delaying the climax until the big low chord when the two characters sing together on "Till the days go by." He used his whole body to conduct that chord, and the orchestra responded with a weight and a depth of feeling that resonated through the theater. *I wonder what it feels like to do that*, I thought.

I noticed something else. Paul's brusque personality had changed a few days after we started previews. He began transforming himself into a jolly, clowning master of ceremonies. He brought a little chalkboard into the pit that he used to write us secret messages. He kept it hidden from the audience, placing it so that we had to look right at him in order to read it. He made funny faces, winked at the girls, pretended his baton was a peashooter, or a sword, or a piccolo. His Halloween performance involved three different gorilla masks, strategically timed for maximum comedic effect. It was a hugely entertaining act and quite a departure from his deadpan rehearsal style. During our curtain call, I watched him bouncing with the music. I could see how much he loved his job.

He told me, years later, that his biggest challenge on *Merrily* had been conducting the young actors. We were so inexperienced. We had no idea how to follow a conductor. Our diction was sloppy; we weren't singing together. At his wits' end, he realized that he had to teach us, night by night, how to always be aware of him. If it took blackboards, mime, and animal masks to get our attention, well, that's what it took.

"It was exhausting," he said, "but it worked."

Doddy came to a Wednesday matinee. She was transparently torn by her conflicted feelings: proud of my achievement but bewildered by the show. As we finished our quick between-shows supper, she reached across the table and grabbed my wrist.

"Tell Hal Prince that everyone needs to speak more clearly," she said urgently. I could tell that she had a list of other things she would have liked to say to Hal Prince, but uncharacteristically, she bit her tongue.

Late one night, after one of the final previews, I sat with Liz Callaway and Eddie Strauss in a restaurant on Seventh Avenue, completely spent. We hadn't had a real day off in what seemed like months. Eddie had the latest gossip. He told us, in excruciating detail, how, at a production meeting that afternoon, one of the interns on the show had snapped, unable to keep his opinions to himself for one more moment.

"They came spewing out of him," said Eddie. "He kept saying *this* was awful and *that* was confusing, and they were fixing the wrong things. He said the show was getting worse instead of better. It was like watching someone commit suicide right in front of you. Hal kicked him out of the room and told him to never come back."

Liz and I were silent.

"So, are we getting dessert?" she said, finally.

But the show *was* getting better. I could feel it. We all could.

The most brilliant minds in the business were focused like lasers on improving every detail. The creative team worked until the last possible moment. Watching them struggle, fail, try again, and succeed was a privileged, priceless education in how to fix a troubled show. Word by word, they refined and refocused. We could hear the difference in the audience's reactions. The story made more sense. The jokes were funnier. The performances grew stronger. The orchestra sounded even more fantastic, and the numbers started really landing. Going into the final week of previews, the show was shorter, clearer, and people weren't walking out.

THAT LAST WEEK WAS MAGICAL. HAL PUT HIS LAST CHANGE INTO THE SHOW. Someone had said to him that the black graduation robes we wore at the beginning were depressing. The next night, they were cherry red.

We played to packed houses, enthusiastic cheers for the numbers, and shouting at the curtain call. In six weeks of previews, *Merrily* had been transformed.

As the big night approached, I knew that our hard work had paid off.

We were going to be a hit.

Chapter Twelve

1981

{O}pening night: a cold November evening, family in attendance. Friends from Exeter and Yale sent cards and flowers. Norma Nannini, Van, and Rasheed from *Variety* sent a telegram.

George Furth gave me a framed picture of himself, with an inscription saying that I was his favorite one in the show. He gave the same gift to everyone in the cast.

Performing the show that night was sublime. Backstage, we hugged and held hands, watching and silently cheering each other's scenes and songs. Onstage, the script dazzled and the songs soared. Surrounded by battle-tested comrades, I had never felt such pure, loving support from a company. We were unveiling a new musical to the world. The road to that night may have been bumpy, but together we rejoiced in the show that we had all been a part of creating.

After the performance, which received an instant standing ovation, we changed into our fanciest clothes and bustled over to the Plaza Hotel for a massive party.

Two enormous ballrooms had been combined, yet the party was still oppressively crowded. Hollywood stars and Broadway royalty; fancy food and endless drink. My family left after about twenty minutes. I wandered around. I felt like I had been invited by mistake. My fellow cast members seemed to have been erased. At one point, I ran into Lonny Price. He was holding a few newspapers. He looked dazed and fragile. "Not good," he muttered to me, pointing at the papers. The party suddenly felt unbearable.

I left the Plaza and bought a few newspapers of my own at a chilly corner newsstand. The reviews were harshly dismissive. I had never read anything so poisonous—the words burned like shrapnel. Distraught, I stopped looking at them. I thought about going back to the party, but instead, I walked through the deserted Midtown streets to my sublet. The cold wind stung like knives on my face.

WE KNEW OUR DAYS WERE NUMBERED.

I treasured each performance. I stood just offstage, watching as much of each show as I could—breathing it in. Listening. Savoring. Memorizing details of the other actors' performances, each piece of underscoring, the smell of the makeup, the sound of feet clattering up the spiral staircases from the basement before big ensemble entrances. The way the lights glowed from the wings, the way the air vibrated when the crew pushed big set pieces past me, how the orchestra sounded from the stage.

I packed it all inside me, every morsel, every shred I could grab, layering the precious fragments in a special strongbox, carefully protected.

WE CLOSED TWO WEEKS LATER, ON NOVEMBER 28TH, THE DAY I TURNED TWENTY. I have a card from the whole company that says, "Happy Fucking Birthday."

Chapter Thirteen

1981

{T}he day after our final performance, we recorded the original cast album, starting at 9:00 a.m. and finishing well after midnight. We sang with every bit of strength we had left, doing multiple takes of each number. Thomas Z. Shepard, who produced the album, was not interested in simply recording what we had done in the theater. He was intent on creating an aural experience that worked on its own terms. Notes on diction, intonation, and attitude were administered liberally. The whole orchestra played live on every take. Jonathan Tunick regularly darted out of the control room to give sharp, detailed corrections to the players.

The trumpets blasted out the five-note "Merrily vamp" again and again, until their lips were swollen and split.

While Lonny Price recorded "Franklin Shepard, Inc.," I sat by Eddie in the orchestra area, turning his pages so he could play every single note of his fiendishly difficult part.

We recorded the a cappella chorale "The Hills of Tomorrow," with its brightly optimistic lyric, "As our journey starts, Behold, our hearts are high!" The raw irony made the words catch in my throat.

The day was simultaneously wildly exciting and a shattering reminder of everything I had just lost.

The last song we recorded was "Bobby and Jackie and Jack." This was to save money. The producers could send the orchestra home early because I accompanied the song myself on the piano. The orchestra gathered their instruments and departed. Most of the cast had gone by then as well. The recording studio, which had been so crowded all day, was conspicuously empty and strangely quiet. I sat at the piano, bleary and tired, trying to focus.

A sound technician came by to check my headphones. As he fiddled with the wires, he said to me, "Weird, isn't it? Everyone working so hard on an album nobody's ever going to buy." He chuckled. "I mean—those reviews!" He grinned at me as if he hadn't just stomped on my bleeding heart and ambled away.

We did a take, and Paul emerged from the control room.

"Loud," he said, pointing at me. "Recording booth."

He brought me into the control room to listen to the playback, explaining to Sondheim and Tom Shepard that I had been the music director for the number. I collected their notes and gave them to the actors, along with a few of my own. I was touched beyond words by the generosity of Paul's gesture. But it was emblematic of the entire experience—moments of extraordinary grace in a shitstorm of chaos.

We did two more takes. Everyone was happy, and we were dismissed. As weary as I was, I didn't want to go. Leaving would mean it was really over, the most amazing thing that had ever happened to me.

I slowly gathered my coat and my music. As I reluctantly walked to the door, I looked through the glass window into the control room. Sondheim was sitting by himself, his head in his hands. He looked drained by the long day and the arduous three-month roller coaster of rehearsals and previews and opening and closing. I wanted to go into the booth and hug him and profess my undying admiration and tell him that I knew he would continue to write astounding songs. I wanted to thank him for the life-altering experience and let him know how much it meant to me. I wanted to tell him how I hoped that one day, the score for *Merrily* would be recognized as a masterpiece. I didn't do any of those things, but as I was leaving, he looked up and gave me a nod and a sweet, sleepy half-smile through the glass window. I waved to him and left.

I SPENT DECEMBER IN NEW YORK, NUMB WITH DISAPPOINTMENT, TRYING TO recover. It hit me that Jonathan Tunick, perhaps unwittingly, had captured the essence of *Merrily We Roll Along* when he put that odd tuba solo into the overture. A galumphing elephant of an instrument, trying to play a delicate ballad. Clumsy and heartbreaking, yet somehow noble in its impossibly optimistic struggle.

Dreamgirls opened on Broadway, getting the rave reviews I had imagined *Merrily* would be receiving. The city seemed cold and soulless. I wearily picked up the phone and called Yale to negotiate the terms of my surrender. The university graciously accommodated my much-earlier-than-expected request to re-enroll in January.

I was twenty years old, and my outrageously ambitious lifelong dream had just come true.

Now what?

The serendipitous chain of events that led to my being onstage at the Alvin Theatre did me the favor of illuminating exactly where I belonged in musical theater. Singing and dancing in a Broadway musical had been enormous fun, but I discovered that I wasn't nearly talented enough to have a career as an actor. Looking at my fellow cast members made that clear. Watching Lonny Price and Annie Morrison open their souls each night, watching Jason Alexander and Terry Finn spin their comedic moments into gold, hearing Liz Callaway sing Mary's songs in understudy rehearsals . . . These people had gifts I didn't have and didn't think I could acquire.

I was in Rockefeller Center on a lightly snowy evening, surrounded by strangers, staring up at the giant Christmas tree, when it came to me.

The answer had been, literally, right under my nose—I wanted Paul Gemignani's job. I belonged on the podium. As soon as it hit me, I knew it was right.

I packed up my stuff and vacated my sublet.

The next summer, I decided I would not return to my messenger job. Instead, I would look for work as an assistant music director. I had a Broadway credit on my résumé. Surely, I could find a job at a nice theater somewhere.

In January, safely back in my dorm room at Yale, I grabbed the latest issue of *Variety* and leafed through it.

Chapter Fourteen

1982

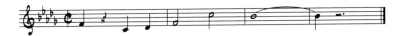

{S}ix months after opening on Broadway in a brand-new Stephen Sondheim musical, I was playing second piano for a third-rate summer stock production of *Little Mary Sunshine*. In the dark.

The theater was on Long Beach Island—a long, thin sliver of sandy land off the New Jersey coast. I was holding a flashlight in my mouth, trying to see the music in front of me because a thunderstorm had rocketed across the island earlier that evening, knocking out the power. The crew had driven a few cars up to the doors and windows of the theater, illuminating the cast's rehearsal with the cars' headlights. Fog swirled, dancing eerily in the bright beams. Certain areas of the stage were pitch black, but the actors lurched bravely around, holding their scripts at odd angles to catch what light they could. Canceling rehearsal was not an option. Pages and pages of dialogue hadn't been rehearsed. Three musical numbers hadn't been staged. The first performance was tomorrow night.

"Once more from the top, sweet boy," the director said to me. He was a tall, thin, bald ex-dancer who liked to dress up as a warlock, with a staff and a cloak, and prowl the dark beaches after midnight, terrifying anyone who caught a glimpse of him. For the forty-fifth time that evening (or was it the hundred and forty-fifth?) I played the introduction to "Look for a Sky of Blue," and the actress playing Little

Mary began her song with the chorus of Forest Rangers. Halfway through, the director clapped his hands smartly.

"No!" he shouted. "Step LEFT on 'When e'er a *cloud* of grey,' step RIGHT on 'Seems to *waft* your way,' and tilt your head up to Jesus on "Look, for a sky of blue." He demonstrated gracefully in the aisle as an apprentice aimed a dying flashlight at his feet. The actors repeated his movements.

One of the actresses from the company plopped herself down on the piano bench next to me. She was wearing a voluminous set of rehearsal petticoats. They flopped onto my lap.

"Let me hold your flashlight, big boy," she said, taking the torch from my mouth.

She pointed the light at her face and quickly introduced herself.

"I'm Arden," she said. "I don't think we've met."

She was playing the maid, Nancy Twinkle.

"I'm David," I said. "You can hold my flashlight any time. It's really uncomfortable holding it in my mouth. But I don't want you to miss an entrance."

She pointed the light at her face again and elaborately rolled her eyes.

"At this rate, we'll be getting to my song around four in the morning. Wally the Warlock here ain't built for speed."

She was gangly and cute, with a Peter Pan haircut.

"You're gay, right?" she said.

She aimed the light at my face.

I nodded.

"Yeah," she said. "You play the piano like you give a shit."

The director finished his corrections.

"You'll get it, darlings," he said. "And remember, boys, you're going to be wearing big butch Forest Ranger hats." He looked at me with a wicked grin, amused with himself.

"Once more from the top, sweet boy."

Arden held the light for me as I played the introduction yet again.

• • •

THE SURFLIGHT THEATRE IN BEACH HAVEN, NEW JERSEY, WAS A DUMP. A defunct auto-repair shop had been reincarnated as a summer theater, cement floor and tin roof intact. Incomprehensibly, the raised stage area was positioned so that the actors could only enter from stage right or down the two aisles. In the corner, where the stage left entrance should have been, was the "orchestra pit," which was not a pit, just a cramped area holding two elderly pianos and a damaged set of drums.

We put on twelve shows in twelve weeks, with no days off. On Sundays, we didn't rehearse, but we performed in the evening. The morning after *Little Mary Sunshine* opened, we began rehearsals for *No, No, Nanette*. A company of twenty actors had been hired for the summer, along with musicians, stage managers, and designers. We lived in a dilapidated former rooming house a few blocks from the theater. Bunk beds, two to a room. As Assistant Music Director, I was paid $105/week, minus $30/week to cover my meals and lodging.

A seedy cabin near the theater was reserved for the directors. They rotated in and out, staying only for the week that their show rehearsed. On Tuesdays, exhausted and frustrated, they would run their last late-afternoon rehearsal, give their final notes, pack their bags, and vacate the cabin, making way for the chipper, unsuspecting schmuck who would start rehearsals with the company the next morning. On opening nights, the outbound director had to watch, helplessly, the fruits of his labors.

Unspeakable things happened those Tuesday nights. Actors missed entrances, essential props never appeared, set changes dragged on and on, while the orchestra repeated the same eight measures of music. Entire songs were skipped because lines got confused and cues never came.

Eleanor Miller, the ferocious little woman who ran the theater, had many ironclad RULES she had developed over the years. The hardest of her RULES for me to follow was that after the opening night performance, the music staff wasn't allowed to fix any mistakes or mishaps. The moment the opening night curtain came down, all creative energy had to be channeled into the *next* show. The disasters usually worked themselves out, and by the weekend, even the most under-rehearsed productions would be running more smoothly—the jokes landing, the singing improved.

But pity the poor twenty-year-old assistant music director who got caught giving an actor a lyric correction in *South Pacific*, or fixing a sloppy chorus cutoff in *Carousel*. I started making detailed wish lists, like, Nineteen Things I Would Fix in *Camelot*, if I were given fifteen minutes of rehearsal time. It was the only way I could bear hearing the same mistakes every night.

Eleanor's deeply tanned face betrayed years of beach town living. She wore form-fitting muumuus in bright colors: pinks, blues, and greens. Most of Eleanor's RULES centered around saving money. If an actor used a paper cup at lunch and casually threw it out, Eleanor, appearing out of thin air, would remind him that each of those cups cost her THREE and a half cents, and would he please retrieve the cup from the trash and drink from it for the rest of the afternoon? Or BETTER, she would continue, use the mug from the Bait 'n Tackle shop down the street, on which she had personally taken the time to magic-marker his name at the beginning of the SUMMER.

She fed the company, grudgingly, three meals a day, repeating the same inexpensive items ad nauseam. I once observed her calmly spooning potato salad from an actor's plate back into the tub from which it had been served.

Another of Eleanor's RULES was that she didn't tell the cast until *after* Tuesday's opening night performance which part they would have in the show that began rehearsals Wednesday morning. She knew how badly the actors wanted the good parts. She dangled upcoming plum roles in front of them, using casting as leverage to keep the company well behaved. This manipulation worked, but it meant that the actors had to learn enormous parts like Dolly Levi or

Harold Hill in six days, with no advance preparation. Panic was the general mode in which we operated.

We conducted music rehearsals in a cement cell called The Bug Room, and dance rehearsals on a six-foot-square wooden platform in the parking lot. The sets, built by overworked apprentices, were minimal. Sometimes just a painted sign announcing the scene's location, like "The Gym," if we were doing *West Side Story*. As for the costumes . . . well . . . plucked from a moldy attic full of kitschy gowns and unstylish suits—donated by Long Beach Island's smart set—the clothes tended to repeat themselves. Audiences grew to accept that a dress worn by Miss Adelaide in *Guys and Dolls* in June might very well reappear on Meg Brockie in *Brigadoon* in July and on Agnes Gooch in *Mame* in August.

One unforgettable week, late in the summer, the director of *Anything Goes* arrived driving a van filled with crisply ironed white sailor suits. He must have bought them at his own expense, or borrowed them, or stolen them. Nothing that splendid, or that clean, had ever been near that stage.

On opening night, when the chorus of sailors marched out in dazzling white uniforms, the astounded gasp from the audience was heart-stopping. If Ethel Merman herself had appeared, belting "I Get a Kick Out of You," she wouldn't have received half the applause those costumes got.

And then there was the tin roof. If it rained, which it often did, we had to stop the performance. The gentlest of showers created a noisy tattoo that easily drowned out the unamplified voices. When a rainstorm struck, Eleanor would strut down the aisle twirling a colorful blue-and-green umbrella over her head. Loudly interrupting whatever drama was unfolding onstage, she would announce an unscheduled intermission. Patrons could buy SOFT DRINKS in the lobby and COOKIES on the patio.

Eleanor was a staunch proponent of the theatrical tradition that the show MUST go on, as well as its corresponding custom: refunds would NEVER be given. During our opening night performance of

Annie Get Your Gun, a stubborn tropical storm kept the audience waiting for nearly two hours between the first and second scenes. Back in the dressing room, we used the time to stage the final reprise of "There's No Business Like Show Business," which we had never reached in rehearsal. The cast finally took their bows after midnight.

The deck was stacked against us at Surflight. I discovered that when terrible things were transpiring onstage, my body would try to disappear into the "pit," involuntarily shrinking down behind my piano, trying to disassociate itself from whatever theatrical atrocity was being committed a few feet away.

But, in the most unlikely moments, magic could happen. The lack of amplification meant that the audience leaned forward to catch every word, creating genuine intimacy. When the right actors landed in the right roles, I could feel the concentration of the audience escalating, supporting the young performers, willing them to grow, to reach, to fly.

The music director that summer was a petite, feisty spitfire with big bouncy hair, who played the piano with lots of dramatic head-tossing. She taught the music to the cast with precision, which I admired. Her husband, dark and brooding, was a talented drummer. He had also been hired for the summer. Making music with them was a pleasure. Unfortunately, as the summer ground on, their marriage crumbled, and our daily "orchestra" rehearsals became more and more volatile. Pointed comments about each other's musicianship escalated into snide digs and personal jabs. It began to feel more like a shark tank than an orchestra pit. I would sit, embarrassed, hearing marital details I never wanted to hear, wondering if we would ever get back to practicing the dance music from *Finian's Rainbow*. Sometimes, we didn't.

After rehearsing with the actors until four, followed by an hour of music and marriage counseling, I had one hour to myself each day before dinner in the cast house.

The ocean saved me that summer. Late in the day, the beach was a perfect remedy. The families had mostly disappeared. The water was bracing, the sunlight danced on the white foam, and the waves grew large. Floating in the ocean, swimming parallel to the shore, I could feel the tensions of the day melting into the salt water. Sometimes my new actress friend, Arden, joined me. We would swim for a bit, then walk hand in hand along the water's edge, barefoot on the wet sand, talking about *anything* other than the musical we were rehearsing.

Seagulls swooped through the air. We gathered unbroken shells and unusual stones and tried not to step on stranded jellyfish or the little crabs that skittered along the shore. Every twenty minutes, a small plane would drone by, trailing a banner advertising cheap beer at the local watering hole, Buckalew's.

Arden was recovering from a bad breakup and was struggling to heal. She needed to talk, and I was happy to listen. Gradually, I realized that I needed to talk as well.

I had been experiencing aching periods of sadness. I was able to talk to Arden about my parents' divorce, a subject I hadn't discussed with anyone, least of all myself. She listened, concerned and attentive.

My father had married, quite suddenly, a much younger woman. Before I knew it, I had a half-brother. I told Arden how uncomfortable I felt going home. My mother was living in an apartment in Lake Placid, dating a series of men I couldn't stand—each year, there seemed to be another one. I did find myself warming to Pat, my father's new wife, a former emergency room nurse. Her salt-of-the-earth practicality seemed like a good match for my father, but her obsessive Catholicism was foreign to me. I didn't know what to do about any of it.

Arden dropped my hand and stopped walking. We looked out at the sea. The limitless sky. The ocean nipped stealthily at our bare toes.

"Here's something I've been thinking," she said. "People who follow their dreams and move to New York have already decided to leave their families behind. It doesn't mean we don't love our families, but we are compelled to sing, or act, or dance, or make music, and we put that longing first in a powerful way. This is not a crime. I think it's good to separate from our families for a while.

Especially now, when we're starting out, trying to figure out who we are, and what we're good at, and just how much we're willing to sacrifice to be in the chorus of *They're Playing Our Song* at a shitty summer theater."

We started walking again. The setting sun warmed our backs; our shadows stretched long and thin in front of us. Dark-green seaweed decorated the sandy beach. She slipped her hand back into mine.

"Your family isn't going anywhere," she continued. "And you've got things to do. Big things. The only people who really get that are other people in the same boat. Show folk. You're stuck with us."

She smiled at me.

A sandpiper trotted by, on a mission all its own.

ON STORMY DAYS, WE CLIMBED THE EMPTY WOODEN LIFEGUARD TOWERS, WATCHing the grey clouds mingle with the mist and the seaweed-flecked waves. Lightning danced under dark thunderclouds over the churning ocean. I told her how the thought of starting life as a gay man in New York City was terrifying to me. News of the spreading "gay plague" was suddenly everywhere. I sometimes woke up in the middle of the night, sweating with fear.

Arden looked perturbed. And deadly serious.

"I need you to swear," she said, "on this clamshell, that you won't sleep with any of the actors in the company."

I took the oath. It seemed a small price to stop the panic attacks.

At six, we tore ourselves away from the sea and braced for reentry to the land-based maelstrom of jealousies, romances, ambitions, and disappointments that bound our summer stock company together.

If it happened to be a week when Arden had a leading role, we would wake up early and walk along the sandy sidewalk to the beach. I would plunge into the ocean and then, shivering, bundle up in a sweatshirt. Sitting back-to-back on the sand, we would run Arden's lines.

At the end of the summer, Eleanor took me aside and asked if I would be interested in returning the following summer as music director. She offered me $50 more a week. I was steadily accumulating a mountain of student-loan debt at Yale. I pleaded for more. She dug in her heels—she was a tough old bird. Finally, she offered to throw in my meals and lodging for free, as long as I didn't tell ANYONE.

Another summer at Surflight would mean another year of poverty. But returning as music director would give me valuable experience. It would also mean learning *another* dozen classic musical theater scores from the inside out: how their vocal arrangements were voiced, how their dance arrangements were constructed, and how they moved from dialogue to song. I accepted the offer.

Arden returned to Surflight the following summer as well. We became lifelong friends.

Over the years, as she cycled through various boyfriends before meeting her husband, none of the men she dated ever seemed quite comfortable with the way Arden and I would instinctively walk hand in hand through the New York streets, as if we could still feel the warm sand on our bare feet and the fresh ocean air on our faces.

ONE PUNISHINGLY HOT WEEKEND IN JULY, MY FATHER; HIS NEW WIFE, PAT; AND their two-year-old son came for a two-night visit. Pat was quite pregnant with their second child. I had booked them a room at a bed-and-breakfast, but it didn't have air-conditioning, and they were miserable. They sat through the Saturday-night performance of *Shenandoah* but decided to cut their trip short. As they hightailed it off the island, I caught a glimpse, through their eyes, of how my decision to spend summers doing non-Equity stock on a tacky New Jersey island must have looked. Was this where my expensive Ivy League education was leading? Weren't my classmates all doing summer internships at blue chip law firms or sailing with Greenpeace?

I walked into the lobby of the theater. The audience had dispersed; the bright red carpeting was stained from years of flooding. The black-and-white headshots of the acting company, with their false smiles and feathered hair, looked back at me from the wall where they had been thumbtacked at the beginning of the season. Some of those actors would never get further than that wall. This summer marked the apex of their showbiz trajectory. Others would keep at it, some even gaining recognition in the business. The sickly sweet smell of stale soda drifted over from the concession stand.

The theater was supposed to be closed, but I could hear voices. I poked my head inside. We had spent the day rehearsing *Pippin*. The two actors playing the leads that week were reviewing their staging with the help of two apprentices who were filling in the other parts. I walked to the orchestra pit and sat down at the piano. Opening my *Pippin* score to the number they were rehearsing, I joined them. "We've got magic to do, just for you." Without missing a beat, they kept going, and together we ran through as much of their material as we could.

Afterward, the actor who was playing Pippin came over to the piano to thank me. He gave me a hug and offered to buy me a beer at Buckalew's some week when he didn't have a big role.

"Anyway," he said, "I thought you were with your family tonight."

I didn't say it out loud, but I remember the startling clarity of my next thought.

I am with my family.

Interlude : 2007

I am an accomplished procrastinator. Seven weeks after my physical therapist handed me the neurologist's card, I am sitting in an uncomfortable folding chair, having finally made an appointment. It's my first visit. I don't know what to expect. The bleakness of the hospital matches my mood.

The receptionist, a greying woman, dressed in grey, parked at a dark grey desk in an unpleasantly public office with grey cement walls, looks up from her computer, which is grey, and says, "The doctor is ready. Please go in."

I walk into the neurologist's office. It is cozy and warm. The doctor looks up at me—he is quite old. White hair, a soft blur of a mustache, a kind face. He reminds me of someone—who is it?

"How long have you had Parkinson's?" he asks.

I don't respond.

"How long have you had Parkinson's disease?" he asks.

The wizard. That's who he reminds me of. He looks like Frank Morgan, the actor who plays the wizard in *The Wizard of Oz*.

"I didn't know I had Parkinson's," I say.

As an expert in bifurcated thinking, I had actually thought I was coming to the neurologist to discuss my shoulder injury.

"What's Parkinson's?" I ask.

He motions for me to sit.

"My first thought, when you walked into the office, was that perhaps you'd had a small stroke or Bell's palsy. Your face is quite irregular. One side is droopy. But when I saw you walk toward me, I knew you had Parkinson's. How long have you had it?"

"What?" I ask.

This is going so fast. Why can't I slow it down?

"Parkinson's disease," he says, "is a neurodegenerative disorder that affects the brain cells in the *substantia nigra*, the brain cells which produce dopamine. Dopamine is a neurotransmitter. It helps communicate messages across different parts of the brain. The loss of dopamine in the brain can lead to movement problems. Symptoms can include tremors, stiffness in your body, and a slowing down of your physical activity. Your face may show little or no expression. One of your arms may not swing naturally when you walk. Your speech may become soft or slurred."

I can hear everything the doctor is saying, but I have left my body, and I am looking down on the scene from high above. The doctor looks quite small, sitting at his desk; the younger man sitting across from him looks small as well.

"There is no cure," he says.

Maybe I'll wake up, I think, from high above. Maybe I'll wake up and feel that surge of relief when I realize it was all a dream and everything's okay.

Please, I say, to a God I don't believe in. *Please, God, let this be an awful dream.*

"But there is a lot we can do," says the doctor. "There is medication which can relieve your symptoms; there are things we can do to limit further deterioration."

Deterioration.

Deterioration of my brain?

$2 \times 2 = 4$, $2 \times 3 = 6 \ldots$

These are too easy.

$12 \times 17 \ldots$ what is 12×17?

"Do you have any questions?" he asks.

Yeah, I have a question. What the fuck is 12 x 17?

204. It's 204. Is that right?

I sit silently.

He sits silently.

It's definitely 204.

My deteriorating brain wants to be far away.

Anywhere but here.

Maybe if I close my eyes, when I open them, I'll be somewhere else.

I close my eyes.

Chapter Fifteen

1984

{I} have never had any fun in a gay bar.

Never.

Okay, once.

In January of 1984, when I moved back to New York after graduating from Yale, I found gay bars unpleasantly smoky, loud, dark, and intimidating. (After New York's passage of the Smoke-Free Air Act, I found gay bars loud, dark, and intimidating.) I would go so far as to say that gay bars are where I have *least* enjoyed being a gay man. But there was one night . . .

ON A BRIGHT SEPTEMBER DAY, I SAT IN A CROWDED PEOPLEXPRESS AIRPLANE on the tarmac at Newark International Airport, waiting to fly to Portland, Maine. I was going to Portland for eight weeks to perform a two-character play-with-music, called *Billy Bishop Goes to War* at the Portland Stage Company. I had arrived early, boarded quickly, and managed to stow my large bag in the now completely stuffed bin. As the plane filled, passengers searched for storage space, calling anxiously to family members about the absence of options. The seat next to mine remained empty. I wondered if it belonged to my castmate, whom I hadn't yet met. The cabin crew began collecting the luggage that couldn't fit and sending it below, charging fifty dollars a bag.

As the cabin doors were closing, a solidly built man with a dashing smile bounded on board, holding a large carry-on suitcase. Quickly grasping the situation, he sweetly convinced the four elderly nuns in the row ahead of me to stow their little suitcases beneath their seats and hide their purses under their habits. In under two minutes, he freed up enough space for his bag in the bin above them. I watched him perform this magic trick in rapt awe. He slid into the seat next to me and introduced himself. Scott Ellis, my castmate, could clearly charm the pasties off a stripper.

The company manager met us at the airport and took us to the Sonesta—a gargantuan, cavernously empty hotel on a hill overlooking downtown Portland. I had a two-room suite on a lower floor with at least forty other suites, all of them unoccupied. The wide wooden hallways, threaded with the ancient remains of what must have once passed for elegant carpeting, were home to giant dust bunnies and roaming gangs of white mice. I unpacked my clothes and wandered the chilly hotel, trying to find the lobby. Both hotel restaurants were closed for renovation. I found a cruddy store and bought a frozen dinner. Heating it up in the toaster oven in my dark, dreary room, I felt forgotten and completely alone.

A WEEK EARLIER, I HAD SPENT THREE DAYS WITH MY MOTHER AT GRANDMOMMY AND Granddaddy's house in Syracuse. The kitchen in that house was the coziest place in the universe. Its walls were painted a buttery yellow. At sunset, warm light came through the windows, giving the room a creamy, saffron glow. The mouthwatering aroma of browning meat and braised vegetables floated in the air—Grandmommy's pot roast.

My mother and I sat at the wooden kitchen table. I had finished chopping vegetables; my mother was darning socks. It was almost cocktail time—Grandmommy had already laid out a tray with cheese crackers and olives.

I had been trying to find the right moment to say something for the last twenty-four hours. Over and over, I had postponed the conversation, and the longer I waited, the more complicated it seemed to be getting. I couldn't put it off one more instant.

"I have something to tell you," I said.

They both looked at me.

I felt like I was stepping off a cliff.

"I'm gay."

My mother took a quick, sharp breath in. She carefully put the curved darning needle she was holding into the bright red pincushion that she kept in the pocket of her sewing apron. Then she burst into tears, hugged me, and said, "I was so worried that you were going to be alone all your life. I hope you find someone wonderful to be with."

Grandmommy hugged me, too. Later that night, she asked me if I knew of any worthwhile gay organizations. She wanted to donate money. I mentioned the Gay Men's Health Crisis. She wrote the name down on the same three-by-five card that held her pot roast recipe.

Within a year, she helped found the Syracuse chapter of PFLAG (Parents and Friends of Lesbians and Gays). Two years later, she was the grand marshal of the Syracuse Gay Pride Annual March.

SCOTT ELLIS AND I WERE THE ENTIRE CAST OF *BILLY BISHOP GOES TO WAR*, A Canadian musical about a World War I fighter pilot. Scott played the title character and eighteen other parts, including the formidable dowager, Lady Saint Helier, without a single costume change. I played the piano, sang a few songs with him, and underscored the scenes with music.

We rehearsed for three weeks in a large, cluttered studio with big dusty windows. A coffee and tea table stood in the corner. I started arriving early so I could help Scott with his lines. I would sip my coffee, and he would guzzle mug after mug of the herbal organic blackberry tea that made his throat feel better.

We worked slowly through the play. The director allowed us great freedom as we rehearsed. Scott worked on differentiating the characters, looking for physical indications—hand gestures, changes in posture—and vocal clues—accents, changes in register—to particularize each one.

I decided that my character, unnamed in the script, would be called Spike. I thought the musical underscoring could help identify Scott's different characters. I associated certain chords and short melodies with specific people. We discovered that with the right combination of a musical flourish and a simple shift in posture, characters could enter and exit, clearly and cleanly, in an instant.

The script for *Billy Bishop Goes to War* contains passages in which Billy, alone in his airplane, recounts aerial battles that he fought. The director explored different ways of staging these, finally arriving at a disarmingly simple solution. Scott used a wooden chair that he straddled, facing the audience over the back of the chair. Rocking back and forth and side to side, he described the action—surprise attacks and midair shootouts with enemy aircraft. Between his lines, he made whirring and clicking noises, like the sounds of an engine. The music I played supported the action: climbing chords as the plane ascended; descending arpeggios as it dove; spare, star-like notes for the moonlit night flights; and Hollywood-style adventure themes for the battles with the German fighter planes. Would any of it work? We had no idea.

We couldn't rehearse for more than four or five hours a day since the entire play was just Scott talking and talking, so we usually stopped midafternoon. I explored Portland, scouring used bookstores for old sheet music and theater books, as well as poking around the picturesque harbor. Scott would glue himself to the pay phone at the theater, wheeling and dealing with agents and producers. He wanted to direct, and he was trying to find a project to launch his new career. We usually met for dinner, alternating between the two tolerable cafés in downtown Portland, then trudging up the hill to the Sonesta.

As rehearsals proceeded, Scott got increasingly tense. He was having trouble sleeping, and his voice was strained. He seemed unnaturally exhausted. When he forgot a line, he panicked. He would compulsively start over from the beginning, struggling past the mental blocks, agonizing about what came next.

In the third week of rehearsal, the theater had scheduled a run-through for the artistic director. We didn't make it past the second scene. The director called a break. Scott was instantly on the pay phone in the hall, muttering angrily. I decided to make him a cup of tea. As I took the teabag out of the box, I noticed that the "herbal" blackberry tea he had been chugging was, in fact, fully caffeinated. Scott had unwittingly been drinking fourteen or fifteen mugs a day of full-strength tea. No wonder he couldn't sleep. Scott went back to the hotel and collapsed.

The next day, we worked through the whole script, and on our last day in the rehearsal hall, we ran the show again for the artistic director without stopping. A stoic flour sack of a woman, she reclined, motionless and emotionless, on a low, leather couch. We sailed through the story, singing our duets, changing characters precisely, gliding and swooping through the daredevil flying sequences, illuminating, we thought, the futility of war. No response. When we finished, she murmured something to the director and left. I was baffled. Scott was outraged.

"She lay there like a beached whale," he said. "Like a fucking beached whale."

AFTER A TENSE WEEKEND OF TECHNICAL REHEARSALS, WE WERE ABOUT TO FACE our first audience.

I stood in the wing, feeling severely under-rehearsed. My heavy military shoes pinched my feet, and the director had decided, at the last minute, that my glasses weren't "period." The theater had hurriedly commissioned a new pair, using my prescription. I was wearing them for the first time. I didn't know if I would be able to see anything onstage. I shifted my weight from side to side, flexing my feet, trying to break in my shoes. Scott stood in the corner, furiously racing through one of his monologues, cursing and banging on the brick wall whenever he stumbled over a word. We looked like the inmates of the world's smallest mental institution.

"Places," said the stage manager. "It's places."

I stood behind Scott in the dark. For the next two hours, it would be just the two of us.

"Go," said the stage manager.

We marched out together. I went to the piano, sat down, and started to play.

The taut silence of the people watching that performance was unlike anything I had ever encountered—it shimmered with concentration, with the collective power of people listening together, imagining together. The audience completely accepted that there were nineteen characters in the play, sometimes three or four onstage together—chatting, reacting, arriving, and departing—though their eyes told them otherwise. When the formidable Lady St. Helier arrived in the second act, it was a relief, even to me, to have a woman onstage, after all those men! The music helped the story spring from scene to scene, painting pictures with sound, intensifying the characters' emotions.

Billy and Spike sang their final duet, and the audience leapt to its feet. As Scott and I marched into the wings, the artistic director, all smiles, opened her arms to embrace us. Scott walked right by her. I did stop to hug her, and Scott turned around and mouthed to me, still outraged, "like a fucking beached whale."

The Portland production got rave reviews. We had only been hired for a five-week run, but we ended up spending the next two years together, traveling around the country, performing *Billy Bishop*. At that time, all the regional theaters were strapped for money. Most of our engagements came from theaters canceling large Shakespearean productions and booking us, instead, at a fraction of the cost. We certainly were inexpensive. All we needed was an upright piano, that wooden chair, and a few props. We each only wore one costume—a khaki green World War I Canadian flying uniform. Neither of us ever missed performances.

Crisscrossing the country together, we had a terrific time.

Scott's mother came to each engagement, no matter how remote, usually driving with an ever-changing gaggle of energetic older women. Most of these women were physically challenged. The ladies would emerge slowly from the car, followed by a clanking barrage of walkers, braces, canes, and, occasionally, a collapsible wheelchair. Nothing on Earth could stop those women from seeing that show. Or from taking us out to dinner after. Scott and his mother had a complicated relationship, but she and I grew quite attached to each other. In Allentown, Pennsylvania, she appeared with presents for the two of us. Scott's was a pair of socks he had accidentally left in her dryer two months before. Mine was a freshly homemade lemon cheesecake with a delicate graham-cracker crust. It had survived the journey unharmed, cradled carefully in the lap of one of her aged posse.

MEN FLUNG THEMSELVES VORACIOUSLY AT SCOTT. THERE WAS ALWAYS SOMEONE waiting shyly at the stage door, or sending him fresh notes backstage, or more worryingly, tracking him down at our hotel. This never happened to me.

I understood why. Scott's innate charisma, combined with the simplicity of the production, made his performance irresistible, like it was happening just for you.

Oh, and he also spent inordinate amounts of time with the costume designer and his dressers, making sure that his ass looked fantastic in the khaki green uniform.

He was a brazen flirt. Once he got comfortable in the role, he discovered a moment early in the show where he could discreetly check out the audience. If he saw something he liked . . . during our next duet, he would put a fancy spin into the choreography, turn smartly upstage toward the piano, and whisper, "Left aisle, fifth row." Certain lines would then be delivered directly to that seat, and he made sure its occupant had a good view of his well-costumed rump. Later, during one of his monologues, when I could feel that the light had dimmed on me, I would subtly try to locate the spot he had mentioned, hoping no one would notice.

It's funny. When you're onstage, you assume everyone is watching you—even when you're sitting still, in the shadows. It is the director's job to firmly guide the audience's eye to what is important. The lighting design for *Billy Bishop* included "shin-busters"—special lights set at floor level focused up on Scott—intensifying the illusion that he was flying, giving him an almost supernatural glow.

I realize now that there was no need for me to be so painstakingly careful about looking at the audience. I could have banged on the piano keys and set my hair on fire—no one would have taken their eyes off Scott.

He believed, with childlike certainty, that the wooden chair was a biplane. He believed that the whirrs and clicks he made were the sounds of that airplane's engine. The audience, watching him on the chair, listening to him describe the action, had no choice but to believe it as well. When the German planes attacked him, the audience cringed with fear. Each enemy aircraft he shot down was a collective victory.

And at the awful moment when Billy realizes that he is out of fuel and will surely crash, well behind enemy lines, the sudden silence of that engine was devastating. The entire theater held its breath, willing the engine to turn over, to spark to life, to whir or buzz or click . . .

The fall of the plane seemed to go on forever, the silence stretching . . .

And stretching . . .

Then one little chugging sound . . . and another . . . then another and another . . . the audience exhaling with grateful relief, as the engine sputtered back to life.

• • •

WHEN I DID GET A CLEAR LOOK AT THE LEFT AISLE, FIFTH ROW, I WOULD inevitably see some dreamy, square-jawed hunk—a dark crew cut bobbing in the sea of white hairdos and pink balding domes. True love for Scott, at last? No. Scott rarely gave his admirers more than a handshake. He had impossibly picky standards, and the slightest oddity disqualified even the most attractive candidate.

Doddy came to see us when we were playing the Forum Theatre, in Chicago. She was enchanted by the show and extended her trip to see it again. She loved that I was both actor and musician.

"Nobody but you could play this part," she crowed, inaccurately.

I knew she was relieved to see me doing a piece of theater that audiences enjoyed. Earlier that year, I had been the music director for a wacky mess of an off-Broadway show called *Paradise!*. Before the first preview, the leading man faked a heart attack to get out of that evening's performance. He never returned. When we opened, the *New York Post* wrote, "The only sensible direction the director could have provided would have been to post a KEEP OUT sign on the door of the theater." With the wounds of *Merrily* still fresh and the frustrations of non-Equity summer stock still gnarling my guts into knots, the failure of *Paradise!* had been yet another kick in the teeth. The audience's affection for *Billy Bishop* was a more-than-welcome change.

DURING A SHORT HIATUS NEAR THE END OF OUR MAKESHIFT TOUR, I VISITED MY father at North Country School. There was something I needed to tell him.

A few weeks before, Pat, my father's second wife, had called me. A friend of my mother's, who still worked at the school, told Pat that she'd heard from my mother that I was gay. She assumed Pat knew. Pat hadn't known, so she was now in an awkward position, keeping a secret from my father. I understood her concern and promised to visit soon, to tell him in person.

That whole weekend, I repeatedly tried to engineer a moment when my father and I could speak privately, failing each time. Pat kept throwing questioning, wide-eyed looks at me. It wasn't until the visit was over, and he was taking me back to the train station, that we finally found ourselves alone together.

He was driving.

Coming out to my friends and colleagues in the theater had been unnecessary. But their loving acceptance, I knew, was the exception, not the rule. North Country School, the land of "be rugged, be resourceful, be resilient," clearly had no place for "be homosexual." The unwritten school policy was, "Let's not speak about this."

My father and I were both looking straight ahead. The comfort of talking without seeing each other made it easier.

"I have something to tell you," I said.

I felt like I was stepping off a cliff.

"I'm gay."

To my relief, he did not drive off the road.

He paused, expressed his surprise, asked a few questions, and changed the subject.

Later, on the train back to New York, I wondered why on earth I had waited so long.

OUR FINAL *BILLY BISHOP* BOOKING WAS A SIX-WEEK RUN AT THE VIRGINIA STAGE Company in Norfolk, Virginia, a naval town. Sailors, everywhere. We had long afternoons with nothing to do. Scott made it his mission to find out where the homosexuals in the navy went at night. They weren't coming to our show. There was no intersection whatsoever between the theater's antiquated subscription audience and the buff young men strutting around town in their blue and white uniforms. Where was the big naval gay bar? Danger lurked around the subject.

At that time, sailors caught at such an establishment were court-martialed and removed from the navy.

The question taunted Scott.

Near the end of the run, a friend of his with a cousin in the service visited. Scott pleaded for the name of a bar, an address, anything. No luck.

"I give up," he said to me, sadly, before the show one night.

A likely story, I thought.

Having long ago seen him do his act on those nuns, I knew he had vast reservoirs of untapped resources.

Scott took his friend out for one more drink. I can't imagine the depths to which he sank, but certain clandestine information was, at last, imparted.

That Saturday night, after the show, we dashed back to our hotel, showered, and took a cab to the address Scott's friend had given us. We got out. The cab sped away, stranding us by a dilapidated gas station in a deserted, rough neighborhood. I looked around, horrified. Clearly, this was to be our last night on Earth. Scott went around to the back of the gas station. He tugged at various doorways in the brown brick wall until he found one that opened. A stairway led down. We gathered our courage and descended several flights of stairs, eventually reaching a window. Scott knocked. An old man appeared. Scott leaned forward to talk to him.

"We're going to the Garage," he said.

No response.

"Delta Echo Foxtrot," he said, putting two twenty-dollar bills on the counter.

The old man pressed a button, and a door on our right clicked open. We walked along a hallway and down more stairs. We could hear club music pounding. Finally, through a big industrial gate, we entered the Garage.

The club was huge—room after room packed with young men and the occasional manly young woman. They weren't in uniform, but their close-cropped hair and stiff bearing confirmed that we had, indeed, found it—the bar that didn't exist. A secret spot so needed that all these people had risked their careers to gather here.

Scott and I fit right in—we both had short World War I military-style haircuts for the show.

The sailors danced to the loud music, some of them shirtless. Lights flashed. Puffs of dry ice swirled through the air. The pulsating bodies glowed with an otherworldly sheen. The crippling shyness I had always felt when I had ventured into gay bars before didn't seem to be appearing. Instead, I relaxed, like I didn't have to pretend to be someone I wasn't.

We found our way to a less crowded area with a bar. Bottled beer seemed to be the favored drink. I looked at the vibrant, electric scene surrounding me. The men were rugged and scrappy-looking. They danced aggressively, occasionally slamming their chests against each other, letting off the steam that had built up inside them as they marched through their military lives.

I sipped my beer.

I noticed a brawny, dark-haired man staring at me.

I looked back at him, but I was too nervous to hold his glance for more than a few seconds.

This went on for a while.

Eventually, he sauntered over to where I was standing. He loomed over me, well over six feet tall. Smiling, he looked me up and down. He waited for a lull in the music, then spoke. His voice was low and rumbly.

"What boat are YOU on?" he said.

I had no idea how to respond; I went with the first thing that came into my mind.

"I'm on the *Show Boat*, sailor!" I said cheerfully.

Scott laughed so hard I thought he was going to hyperventilate.

My sailor didn't seem to think it was a funny answer. He led me out onto the dance floor and put his arms around me, and we danced, my head on his chest, moving as if a slow song had started, even though the music hadn't changed. At one point, he lifted my head and kissed me. It was the sweetest thing that had ever happened to me. We danced for a long time.

Scott found a sailor, too. The four of us ended up in a diner at three thirty in the morning, eating scrambled eggs and hash browns. The sailors had to be back on their ship by 5:00 a.m. The unspoken certainty that we would never see each other again generated an intimacy that seemed to break down walls. We talked and talked, and even though I suspect we never learned their real names, it was a magical night . . . and the only fun I've ever had in a gay bar.

AT THE FOLLOWING AFTERNOON'S PERFORMANCE OF *BILLY BISHOP GOES TO War*, the two actors onstage may have looked a bit tired, but when the actor playing Billy put a fancy spin into his choreography and whispered, "I'm on the *Show Boat*, sailor!" to the actor playing the piano, things seemed to perk up a bit.

Chapter Sixteen

1990

{T}wo years of barnstorming around the nation's theaters can bond people in a lasting way. Scott soon realized his dream of becoming a director. He hired me for my first Broadway show as a music director and four other Broadway shows. But before that, he introduced me to John Kander and Fred Ebb, the celebrated writing team behind *Cabaret*, *Chicago*, and *New York, New York*. The three of them had become pals when Scott appeared on Broadway in their memory musical, *The Rink*, a year before *Billy Bishop Goes to War*. His friendship with them led to an idea: an evening of Kander & Ebb songs, simply done, in which each song functions as a one-act play and reflects interestingly off the song before it and after it. Without knowing whether I was the right person for the job, he decided I would be the music director and arranger.

I had been busy for the three years since our *Billy Bishop* sojourn. In addition to serving as music director for as many projects as I could, I had met a sweet, funny actor. We had moved into a strange, leaky apartment in Hell's Kitchen. We had a dog. When my actor-boyfriend was cast in the First National Tour of *Les Misérables*, I applied to be one of the pianists on the tour and got the job. We ditched the leaky apartment, packed up the dog, put our stuff in storage, and went on the road. After a few months, I was promoted to assistant

conductor, which gave me my first experience of standing up to conduct an orchestra rather than conducting from the piano. But after a
year and a half, playing the keyboard part for *Les Misérables* eight times
a week and conducting one or two performances a month was getting
monotonous. So when Scott offered me the as-yet-unnamed Kander
& Ebb project, I leaped at it. My boyfriend and dog decided to remain
on tour, so I returned home alone, though still attached.

One of the perennial stresses of life in the theater is the constant
starting over.

You do a show. You form a community. It's your world, your
universe.

You make friends, you learn lessons, you grow.

You meet idiots, they annoy you, and you vow, "Never again."

The show closes. You start over.

It's only natural to want to work with people with whom you
have worked successfully before. It means one less unknown on
that revealing first day of rehearsal when you look around the room
and see the princes and the putzes who, like it or not, will soon be
your world, your universe. It might be for a month or two. It could
be for a year, or more. If you're the fortunate one who gets to do the
choosing, choose carefully.

Scott chose carefully.

Susan Stroman, a pert, blonde Broadway dancer turned choreographer, lived in a drab, dark, rarely dusted apartment on West Eighty-
First Street.

"Call me 'Stro,'" she invariably said, when introduced.

In 1990, Scott and I, along with book writer Tommy Thompson,
started spending afternoons in Stro's cramped living room, examining every song John Kander and Fred Ebb had ever written. She
owned a tired spinet, rarely tuned. I parked myself there for hours
as we sang through the stacks of music. There were familiar songs
from their well-known scores, plus songs from *Flora, the Red Menace*;

Zorba; The Happy Time; 70, Girls, 70; The Act; and *The Rink*. There were songs that had been cut from those shows, boxes of "special material" (songs written for specific performers), and songs from shows in progress, shows abandoned, and shows in gestation.

Hundreds of songs. We batted ideas around about each one. The collaboration felt unforced, instinctive, familiar. As if we were around a Harkness table at Exeter, where everyone's ideas were considered equally.

One day, Tommy suggested that we look at the song "Me and My Baby," from *Chicago*. Tinkling on the upper keys of the piano, I toyed with the idea of starting it as a baby's lullaby.

Hearing that, Scott had a vision of the cast pushing prams and swaddling infants.

"And then," said Stro, "they reach into the prams and pull out . . ."

She paused. I thought she was going to say machine guns.

"Banjos!"

"Big modulation and a double-time chorus," I said, starting to play.

"They're dancing around with their banjos!" said Tommy.

"It builds and builds and builds . . ." said Scott.

"Then the whole cast comes down front, faces the audience, and plays their banjos!!" said Stro. "Really well."

We looked at her in disbelief.

"Oh, come on—anybody can learn how to play the banjo," she said, almost convincingly.

It turned out to be true. After a lot of lessons.

We decided to begin the show simply, with a solo, to express our idea that a great song needed nothing but a great singer to send it into orbit. But which song? Our list of "essential" numbers had forty titles on it—many more than we needed. We planned to cut the list down during rehearsals, tailoring it to the specific talents of the cast. We held auditions, searching for five spectacular singing actors.

On the day of the auditions, I arrived at the last minute, rushing into the Midtown studio just as the session was about to start. Scott hurriedly introduced me to the casting director, a former actor named Joe Abaldo. When I heard his name, my heart did a somersault. Joe had been the star of *The Magic Show*, the first Broadway musical I ever saw. He had taken over the role of the magician from Doug Henning and had played it for several years. His name was emblazoned in my brain from reading it over and over in the *Playbill* I had saved.

The specialness of the day swept over me. I couldn't believe that I was sitting with John Kander, Fred Ebb, and Joe Abaldo, auditioning professional actors for a show I was helping to create. Again, I instructed myself to savor the moment.

That afternoon, I worked up my nerve and walked over to the big table in the corner where Joe was setting out the headshots of the actors we were calling back.

"Mr. Abaldo," I said like I was meeting Judy Garland, "I loved you in *The Magic Show*."

I told him how inspiring that night in 1974 had been for me and how influential he had been in my dreams of a career in musical theater. We became pals. If he got tired of my questions about *The Magic Show*, he never let it show. He told me that it had also taken him a while to figure out exactly where he belonged in the business. The thought had come to him onstage, he said, years into his long run, while pulling an endless string of colored scarves out of someone's ear. He liked performing, but what he loved was connecting people. Within a year, he had left the show and opened a casting office. Like Joanna Merlin, who also started casting after a busy acting career, Joe treated actors with kindness, a result of having walked in their well-worn shoes.

I started creating the arrangements. For me, this meant discovering something fresh in each song that allowed an audience to hear it as if for the first time. It also meant unifying a vast and contrasting collection of songs, written for many different projects, into one evening. Scott, Stro, and Tommy encouraged me to go beyond what was on the page, to take as many chances as I could while remaining true to the essence of the material, promising to rein me in if I went too far.

John Kander's music is unerringly tuneful, deceptively simple, and never fails to delight the ear. Fred Ebb's lyrics can be caustic, funny, wise, or rueful, and never what you expect. Their work together is somehow greater than the sum of its parts. A third element, something unknown, is conjured: the "&" in Kander & Ebb.

Each song came with its own challenges. Some songs I presented exactly as written. Others I gave a slight twist—emphasizing a specific element or adjusting the accompaniment to reveal the song in a different way. Reconceiving solo songs as group numbers often meant restructuring them. In the first act, I wove two songs together as a duet for two men. In the second act, I wanted to top that duet with a trio of songs, all of which used a similar underlying chord progression. I modeled it on the way Sondheim had shaped his trio in *A Little Night Music*.

We wanted to try the show out at a theater where Scott and I had played *Billy Bishop*—the Whole Theatre Company, in Montclair, New Jersey. Situated in an old bank, the theater was intimate and unpretentious, like the couple who ran it, actress Olympia Dukakis and her husband, actor Louis Zorich. They lived, cozily, in the house next door to the theater. Olympia invited us to dinner. She served Greek meatballs. We played them some Kander & Ebb songs, and they handed us the keys to the place.

In rehearsal, it became clear which songs best suited the talents of our gifted cast. For our opening number, we chose a slow-to-build scorcher called "The World Goes 'Round," which gave our show a title.

I started teaching my arrangements. I didn't know how the authors would respond to my ideas. Scott let me work with the actors on their material for a full two weeks before bringing John and Fred in to hear the score. By then, the actors had become comfortable with the music, and I had been able to refine my work.

I couldn't sleep at all the night before the presentation, certain that I would be fired and replaced. The songs twisted through my brain as I gyrated in a sweaty panic. I had made so many changes. What would the authors say? At 6:00 a.m., I got up, grabbed my score, and started walking downtown. The sun was just beginning to rise. Rehearsals were in Greenwich Village. I walked the entire way from West Ninety-Sixth Street, stopping at my favorite greasy spoon, the B&H Dairy, for breakfast. I arrived at the rehearsal studio and started practicing obsessively. Actors drifted in, one by one. I could tell that they were feeling the pressure of the presentation as well. Stro arrived, hugged me, and looked me in the eye.

"Don't fuck up," she said.

Scott arrived with Kander & Ebb.

I waited in the corner, drained from the long walk, too nervous for chitchat.

Suddenly it was 10:00 a.m.

The actors sat in a semicircle, at music stands, and I sat at the piano.

We sang through the show.

The result was unexpected and enormously gratifying. John and Fred loved everything about what we were doing. They put themselves entirely at our disposal, never insisting that things had to be "a certain way," simply because they had been that way before. They fussed and helped and worried and kibitzed. They gave the actors insights into what they were thinking when they wrote the songs—personal details that deepened the performances immeasurably.

Stro wanted to create an extended dance sequence that told the story of an entire relationship, using no words, just Fred-and-Ginger-style choreography. Jim Walton, my friend from *Merrily We Roll Along*, was in the cast. Jim was a crackerjack dancer, and we paired him with a dynamite singer-dancer-actress named Karen Ziemba. Stro and I chose many different Kander & Ebb melodies; I started writing the dance arrangement—the music that the orchestra would play while they danced—weaving the melodies together to tell the story. The sequence got longer and longer. We worked on that dance every day for the entire rehearsal period, and when we started tech, it still wasn't finished. Scott began hinting, none-too-subtly, about cuts. Stro kept right on choreographing.

Karen Ziemba could float with gossamer ease through the most challenging choreography—an iron butterfly. There was another Karen in the show—Karen Mason, a deep-voiced cabaret singer who could build a song like nobody else—the queen of the crescendo. I called them KZ and KM, which was how I marked their vocal parts in the show. The KZ stuck; to this day, people who work with Karen Ziemba call her KZ.

The Whole Theatre Company, which generally did plays, not musicals, never hired understudies for their productions. But singing a Kander & Ebb song is like climbing one of the Adirondack 46-ers. You start slowly, on a slope so gentle you barely notice it. As the climb gets steeper, the melody builds, and when you finally reach the top of the mountain, you linger a while, holding out the high notes, taking in the view. Singing an entire evening of songs like that turned out to be an arduous marathon, made even more taxing by Stro's ambitious choreography. The whole company danced with heavy coats and top hats during "Money," roller-skated for "The Rink," and played those banjos in "Me and My Baby." The actors rarely had time to rest between solos. There were multiple group numbers, laced with my challenging vocal arrangements, culminating in an intricate tight-harmony rethink of "Cabaret."

After our third preview, the cast started to lose their voices. We hired understudies and frantically rehearsed them, but we ended up canceling four performances. This was a first for the Whole Theatre. I will never forget the alarming sight of barefoot Olympia Dukakis, her white hair askew, a red knitted shawl wrapped over her pink nightgown, staggering into the theater during our morning rehearsal.

Furious, she brayed at the top of her lungs, "What the FUUUUUCK is going on in my theater??!!"

Actually, something special was going on in her theater. Once the actors got their voices back, the show started connecting in a way that had audiences welling up with emotion in unexpected places, laughing at the clever lyrics as if they'd never heard them before, and cheering, often standing, as the music for the bows started. The long dance sequence stopped the show every night, and the trio in the second act served as the emotional apogee of the evening.

The World Goes 'Round is, essentially, an act of faith—an exploration of the power of simplicity. Put a terrific song on a talented actor, and don't muck it up with anything extra. Trust the audience to use their imaginations. I had already seen, in my young career, how the best theater *requires* an audience to participate mentally in the experience. Giant sets and lavish costumes can never compare with a creative idea, satisfyingly realized.

Peter Neufeld, an experienced general manager and producer of countless Broadway shows, fell in love with our little revue. He proposed moving the show off-Broadway, to the Westside Theatre on Forty-Third Street, which was being renovated. It would be worth the wait, he said confidently. Peter changed the title of the show from *The World Goes 'Round* to *And the World Goes 'Round*.

"Why?" I asked him, mystified.

"I'm glad you asked," he said cheerfully. "Shows that are listed at the beginning of the "ABCs"—the alphabetical theater section of the *New York Times*—run longer."

Among his hit shows were *Annie, Aspects of Love, A Chorus Line, A Christmas Carol,* and *Cats,* so I guess he knew what he was doing.

We had to do some recasting when we brought the show into New York, which meant spending a few more audition days with Joe Abaldo, listening to New York's finest singers serenade us with Kander & Ebb songs. One day at lunch, he confided in me, quite casually, that he was HIV positive. In 1990, this was unusual; there was still so much fear and stigma attached to the disease. Young men were dying every day, but most kept their HIV status secret, at least professionally. We discovered the truth later by carefully scanning obituaries and occasionally reading between the lines even then.

Joe and I sat opposite each other at a small table, eating sandwiches. I told him how touched I was that he had trusted me and how sorry I was for what he was going through. He said that his partner had been heroic and supportive, and he told me how grateful he was to have love like that in his life. His serene acceptance of his fate seemed impossibly brave to me. I went to the bathroom and burst into heaving sobs.

When we went back for the afternoon session, the first actress to audition was Brenda Pressley. She had prepared the title song, and she sang it in a way I had never heard—as an inspirational sermon from someone who had been at the bottom but who had found a way to get through life's hardest challenges. "Sometimes you're happy, and sometimes you're sad, but the world goes 'round." I felt as if she were singing only to me. Her luminous presence matched the powerful empathy of her interpretation. We offered her the job on the spot, and she joined the company.

The only disappointment I had on *And the World Goes 'Round* was that Doddy never got to see it. The holiday season fell during the hiatus between Montclair and our off-Broadway run. Doddy, now ninety, hadn't been able to manage the trip to Montclair but was looking forward to seeing the show in New York. On Christmas Eve, late at night, she called me, alarmed, complaining of stomach cramps. Could I come over? I was worried—she had never asked me for help like this.

Snow had been falling all day. Unable to get a cab, I tromped through deep drifts in Central Park, hoping Doddy would be okay.

My heart sank when I got to her apartment. I could hear shouting; mud and ice had been tracked in everywhere. Two paramedics were pleading with her, trying (and failing) to convince her to get on the stretcher they had wheeled into her small living room. She was yelling, pointing at the stains on her beloved burnt orange carpeting, furious about the mess they had made. When she saw me, she relaxed a little, and I coaxed her onto the stretcher. The paramedics loaded her into their ambulance, and they let me ride with her to Lenox Hill. She was in severe pain during the short trip. I held her hand and she stared at me, terrified. When we arrived at the hospital, they took her straight to the emergency room. In the commotion, I was left holding her fur coat.

The warmth of it felt comforting on my lap.

The label on the coat was faded, and the fur was thin in places. The familiar smell (mothballs, bourbon, Doddy's perfume) reminded me of my childhood theater trips, the two of us gleefully seeing as many plays and musicals as we could in our limited time. The coat also brought back the memory of a bitterly cold afternoon when my family had gathered to pay their final respects to Grandpa, her long-estranged former husband.

Grandpa's funeral was in 1984, at St. Bartholomew's, on the East Side. The weather was sleety, but the church overflowed with people. Various relatives had traveled from all over the country. Grandma was inside, inconsolable. Doddy had staked out a place for herself just inside the heavy outer doors. She hovered awkwardly in the chilly vestibule, unwilling to attend the service but desperate not to miss any of the gathered family. It was February, it was frigid, and the vestibule was damp and drafty, but she would *not* go into that church. It tore my heart, seeing her caught so painfully on the horns of her dilemma. She looked frailer to me than she ever had. She pulled her fur coat tight around her shoulders, crossed her arms against the cold, and stood there stubbornly, shivering.

The precise definition of "family" had never seemed so convoluted.

Doddy died that New Year's Eve, a week after falling ill, without regaining consciousness. She had been my lifeline to the world I dreamed about, and she loved me with an unconditional fervor that gave me confidence in myself. Her occasional brutal honesty bespoke a trust that my standards would, one day, be as high as hers. The thought of living in New York without her was crushing.

But sad as I was to lose her, I was dazzled by the grand style of her exit: three days before her hospitalization, wearing a bright red Chinese-style dress with a Mandarin collar, she had hosted a crowded party for twenty of her closest friends. When I arrived, the apartment was filled with old people—gossiping, drinking, nibbling. Holly and wreaths hung everywhere, candles flickered, and the carpeting gave the room a festive glow. She hugged me tightly and told me how eager she was to see the Kander & Ebb revue. She was spirited, independent, and in firm possession of every one of her original marbles.

Whenever I find myself near East Sixty-Sixth Street, I walk by her apartment building. I can see the two of us, a little boy and a hunched old woman, bustling into a cab or running for a bus, theater tickets in hand. I hope, in the great beyond, there are plays to see. I picture Doddy attending the theater nightly, then settling happily down with a glass of something strong and sharing her opinions, generously, to anyone within earshot.

After a brief re-rehearsal period, *And the World Goes 'Round* opened to good reviews and settled in for a healthy run at the Westside Theatre. Life in New York suddenly had a crisp routine: eight shows a week instead of the unpredictable collage of my freelance existence. I thrived under the structure that having a show running in New York provided. I loved waking up knowing that I had a performance to conduct that evening, or that afternoon and evening.

As I settled into this new rhythm, my perpetually touring actor-boyfriend took another job out of town. We tried to talk on the phone every night, but it was often difficult with our busy schedules and changing time zones. We had promised that we would never let more than two weeks go by without seeing each other, but that proved impossible. Intervals between visits grew longer. I missed him, but my additional commitments—understudy rehearsals, publicity appearances, and the day-to-day maintenance of the show—kept me occupied.

And the World Goes 'Round had an angel of a stage manager, a good-looking southern boy named Michael A. Clarke, who everybody called MAC. He described himself as "a self-educated cracker." He managed to be both a firm authority figure and a sympathetic listener, a combination that can make all the difference in the run of a show, especially one with a crowded backstage.

But the words "crowded backstage" don't even begin to describe the experience of doing a musical as ambitious as *And the World Goes 'Round* at the Westside Theatre. Five actors, three understudies, and six musicians shared two minuscule dressing rooms. Two stage managers and three indentured servants, who served as crew and dressers, occupied a closet the size of a telephone booth. Early on, I claimed a few inches of hanger space in the women's dressing room as my spot, and I changed there every night for the whole run.

The musicians had to climb a tight circular staircase and a long ladder to get to the cramped orchestra loft. Neither of the wings had any space. Banjos and baby carriages and chairs were intricately fit, puzzle-like, on high shelves raised and lowered on pulleys. The roller-skating number, "The Rink," ended the first act. Much more challenging than any of the skating tricks that the actors did onstage was the sharp ninety-degree turn they were required to execute after sailing blithely offstage to avoid slamming face-first into the brick wall that immediately confronted them.

MAC happened to be an expert roller-skater, and he maintained the wheels and brake pads that kept the actors safe. He would skate, shirtless, around the small stage before every show, checking for bumps and slippery spots. We both loved the card game Hearts, and we started a chatty little tournament group. We played between shows on Wednesdays and Saturdays, usually in the carpeted aisles of the Westside Theatre, as there was nowhere backstage that could accommodate a card table. MAC had a vivid vocabulary of colorfully southern swear words, and I learned all about the rectal insertion practices of various animals.

One Wednesday afternoon, playing Hearts, MAC told the story of how he had met his older partner, Ron. When MAC first moved to New York, he had been an actor in the long-running, quasi-pornographic revue *Oh! Calcutta*, in which the actors performed naked. Ron had been the stage manager there for years.

"The actors," MAC said, "all had secrets they used to make their ding-dongs look bigger onstage. Old fluffing tricks and warming sleeves—one guy went around with a bright pink tea cozy, right on his cock-a-doodle-doo!"

"The first night I went on," he continued, "that was the *last* thing on my mind. I had to do a long dance number—just two of us—butt naked. It was cold enough on that stage to freeze the balls off a pool table, and I guess I was kind of shriveled up. When I came off, one of the other actors congratulated me, saying that my wing-wang looked just like a real pecker, only smaller. Ron, the stage manager, was standing next to the guy. Ron had watched my number, and for him it had been love at first sight. He 'accidentally' spilled his ice-cold soda pop all over the jerk's jim-jam, asked me out on a date, and we've been together ever since."

CONDUCTING *AND THE WORLD GOES 'ROUND* FELT LIKE BEING AT THE CENTER of a complicated neural network. The orchestra was behind the cast, concealed by a set of sliding doors, so the whole company—musicians and singers—had to concentrate especially hard to achieve the precision and musicality that the piece required. The success of the show depended entirely on how well we listened to each other.

Despite the challenging conditions, the mood backstage was always positive. We knew how lucky we were. The whole run seemed to be watched over by a particularly good-natured fairy. Which, incidentally, is a pretty good description of Peter Neufeld, though he didn't come out of the closet until three years later, at the ripe age of fifty-five.

Keeping an off-Broadway show running is like trying to keep an emphysema patient alive with a bicycle pump. The profit margin is so tiny that the slightest extra expense (an unexpected rehearsal, a new costume) can change a profitable week into a losing one, and it doesn't take many losing weeks in a row to persuade most producers to throw in the towel. Peter, eternally optimistic, was not in the habit of hurling linens. Tall and chunky, with a wide, ready grin, he kept that show running using every trick he'd learned in his long career. I overheard him once on the phone with the piano tuner, offering a personal backstage tour to the guy's stage-struck daughter if he would lower his weekly tuning price.

When our off-Broadway run did finally come to an end, Peter threw a party for the company. MAC and I sat at a table with John Kander and Fred Ebb. At one point, John turned to me and quietly mentioned that he would like me to be the music director on his next project, whatever it might be. I couldn't believe what I was hearing. Trying not to gush, I thanked him and told him that I was available. I reached over and squeezed MAC's shoulder. It felt thin and bony. For such a hunky guy, I thought, he sure had gotten skinny.

Chapter Seventeen

1991

{T}he following year, Peter Neufeld produced a national tour of *And the World Goes 'Round*, which is not something that usually happens to a mildly successful off-Broadway show. Scott Ellis asked if I would conduct the tour. My actor-boyfriend had accepted another out-of-town job, so nothing was keeping me at home. I accepted the offer.

Our first stop turned out to be the Taft Theatre in downtown Cincinnati, Ohio. I hadn't been back to Cincinnati since the day we had moved away, twenty-four years before. One afternoon, I took a long bus ride out to Madison Road to see the small red house.

It wasn't there. A Lutheran elder-care facility stood in its place, bland and cheerless. The yard where I had played with Fang and Panther was a parking lot, sections of which were overgrown with weeds.

I walked up to the door and looked through the glass panel. I couldn't bring myself to enter. I stood in the doorway, unsure of what to do. There seemed to be no relation whatsoever between the little boy who had lived there and the thirty-one-year-old who had returned.

I felt disconnected, unmoored.

I don't know what I had been expecting, exactly, but it wasn't this.

Coming here was a mistake, I thought.

As I turned to go, glancing down, a trace of color caught my eye. I stopped.

It was a small violet, squeezing its way up through a crack in the asphalt.

Looking down at the tiny flower, I felt my chest filling with emotion. The little boy was suddenly there beside me. Together, we examined the violet, drinking in its exotic color and marveling at how the delicate blossom had found its way through the stone and tar.

After a few minutes, I took a long, last look around the bleak suburban sprawl and walked to the corner, where I boarded the bus to go back downtown.

WE HAD A GLORIOUS CAST ON THAT TOUR, LED BY THE RADIANT MARIN MAZZIE. Marin had a luminous voice, which ranged from sultry growl to operatic soprano, but her voice was never the focus of her performance. She instinctively connected with a lyric in a way that exposed new depths in familiar songs. Deliriously funny, Marin could be Kewpie-doll-cute, Hollywood statuesque, icy Nordic goddess, or friendly girl next door. She opened the second act with "Ring Them Bells," a story about a girl who travels the world searching for love, only to meet and fall for her next-door neighbor. Stro's staging ended with Marin swinging dementedly on a giant rope, gleefully exhorting the whole world to go out and RING THEM BELLS! On tour, the orchestra was down in the pit instead of behind the set. At the first performance, looking up from my podium and seeing Marin careening back and forth, singing with every bit of breath in her body, I suddenly knew what the words "musical comedy" truly meant.

As we were loading into the Majestic Theatre in Dallas, Texas, an early stop on the tour, a local crew member managed to erase every single lighting cue from the system. Showtime was approaching, nobody could figure out how to make the backup program work, and it looked like we might have to cancel our first performance. MAC jerry-rigged an improvised lighting design and somehow got us through the show.

I went to congratulate him afterward, but he wasn't in the stage manager's office. I finally found him in the parking lot, hiding behind a dumpster, sobbing after the ordeal. I calmed him down. His briefcase was lying open on the pavement. When I picked it up, I noticed that it was packed with different bottles of pills. When he could speak, he looked at me for a long moment, not saying what we both knew he didn't want to say.

"It's hard enough being a faggot gay stage manager, dealing with these local crew guys," he said, finally. "If they knew I was a sissy-Mary *crying* faggot gay stage manager, they would eat me for lunch."

I hugged him and told him what an amazing job he'd done. I could tell what it had cost him to get through a grueling evening like that. It was terrible to see him struggling with what, under other circumstances, would have been his dream job.

"You're my brother," he said to me.

I put my arm around his scrawny shoulders, and we walked back into the theater to find out where the company had gone drinking.

As the national tour proceeded, MAC's fragile condition became clear to the whole company. His dramatic weight loss, his elaborate medication schedule, and the occasional sick day that stretched into a sick weekend were telltale signs that AIDS was stealing another exceptional human being from our community. He preferred to keep the details of his illness private, so we all pretended that we didn't know. I was just grateful whenever he'd have a good week or two. We would use the occasion to gather a group and play Hearts between shows. He would grin and swear, and we would discuss the shortcomings of whatever city we were in that week. The other players could never figure out why MAC and I preferred playing in the carpeted aisles of the theater, instead of at a card table.

MARIN MAZZIE LIKED HER WINE.

But her drinking never affected her performances.

Except once.

The tour was scheduled to play Chicago, and one of our under-studies, Jeanne Croft, who lived in Chicago, had family and friends who wanted to see her in the show. She asked if she could go on one night, while we were in Chicago, in one of the parts she understudied. Marin graciously agreed to schedule a night off, and Jeanne invited everyone she knew.

The evening began with MAC's pre-show announcement, "Ladies and gentlemen, the songs usually sung by Marin Mazzie will be sung tonight by Jeanne Croft." After the opening number, another actress, Shelley Dickinson, who Jeanne also covered, got violently ill, throwing up in the bathroom, unable to continue. MAC figured out that Jeanne could keep the show going, playing both parts, for the next twenty-five minutes, and he put his assistant in charge of calling the cues. He ran to the restaurant, four blocks away, where Marin was enjoying her night off, eating dinner with friends.

And when I say eating dinner, what I mean is drinking wine.

She was three glasses in when MAC appeared at her table, apologized to her friends, and led her away, explaining that she had to come back to the theater immediately, as she would be going on in the next group number. Which was "The Rink." On roller skates.

Down in the pit, I had almost figured out what was going on, never quite knowing who would be entering to sing the next song, but nothing prepared me for the sight of Marin, face flushed, shooting out onto the stage on her roller skates, laughing hysterically. She was waving excitedly—I don't know to whom—and she did a few tipsy laps to get her footing, cackling to herself while the rest of the cast was trying to perform the number. Miraculously, nobody got injured, and at intermission, MAC had a pot of coffee brewing back-stage. Then he made the strangest mid-show announcement I've ever heard. "Ladies and gentlemen, as you may have noticed, the songs usually sung by Marin Mazzie are now being sung by Marin Mazzie, and for the remainder of the evening, the songs usually sung by Shelley Dickinson will be sung by Jeanne Croft. I think."

.   .   .

I ENDED UP LEAVING THE TOUR EARLY, MISSING THE LAST FEW CITIES, BECAUSE Scott Ellis requested that I join him back in New York on his upcoming revival of *She Loves Me*. It would be his Broadway debut as a director, and my Broadway debut as a music director. My last week was in Palm Beach, Florida, and the company threw me a goodbye party during what turned out to be a major hurricane. Wind howled through the streets, and palm fronds flew through the air like javelins, but our little troupe gathered in a café that had stubbornly remained open.

When MAC arrived at the party, he looked upset. He took me aside and told me that Joe Abaldo had died that afternoon of AIDS. I was shocked. I had no idea that he was so close to the end. I steadied myself, gripping the back of a chair with both hands. Joe's passing was the first AIDS-related death to occur within my immediate circle of friends. I looked at MAC. He was staring out the doorway at the storm. His eyes looked haunted and distant. One by one, we told the rest of the company. Rain lashed against the windows; we cried and toasted Joe and laughed and told stories. When the power went out, we scavenged as many candles as we could and kept right on with the party.

Chapter Eighteen

1993

{B}ackstage at the Gershwin Theatre, four conductors lined up in a hallway outside the orchestra pit. The 1994 Tony Awards were about to be broadcast live across the nation. The opening number was a cavalcade of excerpts from the four musicals nominated for Best Revival of a Musical. *Grease* was up first. As the conductor of *She Loves Me*, I was standing second in the line. Behind me were the conductors of *Damn Yankees* and *Carousel*. We made nervous small talk. It was my first Tony Awards experience.

Margery, a petite, no-nonsense woman with tortoiseshell glasses, dark hair, a buzz cut, and a clipboard, had been assigned to keep us in our proper order. The producers of the Tony Awards left nothing to chance. Margery had us in our places forty-five minutes before the broadcast began. As we waited, the ridiculousness of the situation became apparent: four men in tuxedos, preparing to *pretend* to conduct a Broadway orchestra, live on national television. Earlier that week, we had each recorded our show's orchestra track. During the broadcast, the actors would sing live to those pre-recorded tracks. The conductors were there to keep the singers synchronized to the recordings, and to create the illusion that the orchestra was actually playing live. Each nominated revival had exactly two-and-a-half minutes of airtime. Each of the excerpts would be introduced by Victor Garber, who was playing the devil in *Damn Yankees*.

Elliot Lawrence, a distinguished Broadway music director who had conducted every Tony Awards broadcast since they were first televised in 1965, bustled past us with a phalanx of CBS flunkies. They escorted him into the pit. Margery nodded curtly to us, and we followed Elliot Lawrence in, watching as the elderly maestro slowly climbed the staircase up to the podium. We remained, obediently, in our line. The live broadcast began.

Elliot Lawrence conducted the opening bit with Victor Garber. Then, as the company of *Grease* ran onstage with their hula-hoops and poodle skirts, he turned, smiling as he graciously offered his baton to the conductor of *Grease*, who had climbed halfway up the stairway to discreetly wait his turn. The baton having been passed, Elliot Lawrence sat down on a green wooden chair and the younger man stepped into the spotlight, raising his arms to cue the music for "We Go Together," seamlessly making the transition between numbers. Of course, the music would have played perfectly if a baboon had been standing on the podium scratching himself since it had all been pre-recorded. This, however, was the peculiar game we were playing that night: a disorienting exercise in show-biz phoniness, desperate hopes, and dashed dreams.

To make this bizarre musical relay race even more surreal, there actually *was* a live orchestra in the pit, staring up at us, not playing. The orchestra was there to play the appropriate "Winner's Theme" when each Tony winner was announced, and to play the annoying music that interrupted the winner's speech, should that speech run long.

She Loves Me had everything riding on those two minutes and thirty seconds of national airtime. Box office receipts had plummeted, and our producers had made it clear: a strong performance on the Tony broadcast combined with a win for Best Revival of a Musical was the only way *She Loves Me* could stay open. The pressure weighed acutely on my shoulders. We were an extraordinarily happy company. The thought of closing was deeply depressing.

When the cast of *Grease* had sung their last "RAMA LAMA LAMA KA DINGITY DING DE DONG," Elliot Lawrence returned to his place at the podium. The *Grease* conductor, having returned Elliot's baton, squeezed by me as he descended the narrow stairway. He was done for the evening. He looked relieved. Elliot Lawrence cued Victor Garber to sing, and soon it was my turn. With the same gracious smile, the maestro turned to me, offering his baton.

One of the musicals in my parents' cabinet of Broadway LPs was *Fiorello!*—Jerry Bock and Sheldon Harnick's warm, witty portrait of Fiorello H. LaGuardia, the first Italian American mayor of New York City. That score made me happy whenever I heard it. The jaunty melodies, brimming with hope, are combined with a satirical look at the corruption in New York politics, producing a musical that is both fun and adult, simultaneously innocent and knowing. A more obscure Bock and Harnick show, *She Loves Me*, appeared on Broadway in 1963, but it only managed a brief Broadway run. Bock and Harnick went on to write *Fiddler on the Roof* (a smash) and *The Apple Tree* (a modest hit). Then, in 1970, on a show called *The Rothschilds*, they argued bitterly and split, never to collaborate on a new show again.

Scott Ellis convinced the Roundabout Theatre Company to revive *She Loves Me* at their large off-Broadway theater in Times Square. Our new collaboration as director and music director felt as natural as our relationship had been as fellow actors. Rehearsals were highly enjoyable. Our star was the Tony Award–winning actor Boyd Gaines, leading a company whose work was subtle and free of artifice. The inventive choreography was by Rob Marshall (before he decamped to Hollywood).

Jerry Bock (the composer) and Sheldon Harnick (the lyricist) were frequently in attendance, always cordial and respectful of each other but very clearly . . . divorced.

As an expert on the subject, I recognized all the signs. Rarely speaking, never sitting together but always subtly monitoring the

behavior of the other, they spent noticeable amounts of energy trying to seem unconcerned by each other's presence. Joe Masteroff,
the librettist, attended rehearsals as well. Quiet and gentle, he would
sit unobtrusively in the corner, occasionally getting up to whisper
something into Jerry's ear or, on a separate trip, exchanging a few
soft words with Sheldon. He navigated sadly, carefully between
them. I knew that dance well—every step of it. I knew the toll it took.
But clearly, being in the rehearsal room was important enough to
each of them that it was worth going through the awkward gavotte.

The three of them gave the tiniest notes—subtle tempo adjust-
ments, slight changes of emphasis or pronunciation for the actors,
phrasing details for the players, delicate dynamics for the chorus.
Their suggestions were exquisite, and the effect on the work was
striking. Like jewelers fixing up a fancy watch, they carefully polished
and cleaned, coaxing the intricate mechanism to run more smoothly,
sparkle more brightly.

Set primarily in an elegant Hungarian *parfumerie*, the score for
She Loves Me is a music box stuffed with sugared confections. There
are sprightly patter songs, rapturous ballads, waltzes, marches, a
tango, a bolero, a vaudeville two-step, a Hungarian czárdás, and a
mock aria that ends with a soprano-flute duet, finishing on an ecstatic
high B natural. All executed with a lighthearted Broadway pizzazz. A
virtually perfect score.

But Rob Marshall, the choreographer, thought one of the numbers could be better.

"Twelve Days to Christmas," which comes late in the second act,
was written for the chorus to sing, giving the leads a break before
the end. It's a mildly funny ensemble piece, set on the street outside
the shop, but it doesn't advance the story or develop the characters,
aside from counting down the days until Christmas Eve. Rob wanted
to set it *inside* the shop, involving all the store clerks, the people the
audience cared about. We came up with the idea that each of the four
verses would have an increased tempo and that the staging would
repeat itself four times, starting calmly but getting more and more

desperate as the tempo got faster and faster. I added phrases from the Christmas carol "The Twelve Days of Christmas," to pressurize the countdown, and we cut one section of each verse. Rob's new staging was hair-raisingly precise and deftly comedic. The final "button" was especially perfect: the clerks collapsing in an exhausted pile as they slammed the door behind the last frenzied shopper.

The three authors loved the changes. I'm sure the *She Loves Me* purists were scandalized, but the reconception of that song stopped the show every night, giving a helium boost to the second act. And as an unintended bonus, because the revised staging was so strenuous, the final scene had a touching, breathless quality. "Twelve Days to Christmas," which now included all the leading characters, provided the show with a true climax, instead of a charming interlude.

Rob's sister, Kathleen, was his assistant. They were a fascinating pair, communicating telepathically, unfailingly gracious, always in agreement. Rob was infinitely creative; Kathleen, a genius of the details.

She Loves Me is a prop-driven show. The action is largely dependent on the bottles of perfume, bars of soap, lipsticks, and lotions sold in the store. Horrible things could happen if one tube of face cream was out of place.

When we began doing run-throughs, the stage managers checked every prop twice. But invariably, as Scott would cue me to start the overture, Kathleen would shout, "WAIT!" Apologetically, she would say, "Shouldn't there be two more eyebrow pencils in the small canister on the makeup counter, and I'm so sorry, but didn't we decide yesterday that in order for the Christmas wrapping hand-off to work, we need *four* music boxes in the stage left pile, not three?" She was never wrong. The stage managers, mere mortals, would scurry, frantically updating their lists. After getting a definitive nod from Kathleen, Scott would cue me again, and only then could I finally begin the overture.

• • •

As we approached the first orchestra rehearsal, everything about the production was looking promising: the acting and singing were delectable, the set spun cleverly from scene to scene, the clothes were stylish. Jerry Bock had chosen a California-based orchestrator to reduce the original orchestration, which required twenty-four players, down to a size that the Roundabout Theatre Company could afford: a chamber group of eight players. Orchestral reductions like this are difficult to pull off, requiring much time and creativity. This orchestrator, an experienced computer copyist, had also offered to do all of the music copying, for much less than the usual rates. The Roundabout, keen for a bargain, eagerly agreed. During rehearsals, I checked in with him regularly by phone. I couldn't wait to hear the new orchestrations.

Four days before the first preview, at 9:00 a.m., the orchestra gathered in the lobby, instruments tuned, ready to play. There was no music on the music stands and no orchestrator in sight. No answer in his hotel room, either. I waited, red-faced and embarrassed. Orchestra rehearsal time is a precious commodity. There's never enough of it, and it's costly.

Forty-five minutes late, the orchestrator sidled in, nervous and jittery. He muttered an inaudible apology to the waiting group but offered me no explanation. He had brought three numbers for us to rehearse. One of them was "Arpad's Exit," a sixteen-measure piece of scene change music. He promised more, soon, but the details were fuzzy. He looked terrible (pale, greasy skin, red eyes), and he smelled worse. He had clearly been up all night. After a short rehearsal, I sent the musicians home. Grabbing my assistant, Todd Ellison, for support, I cornered the guy.

"What the hell is going on?" I asked him.

Trembling, he confessed. He was massively behind. The copying was taking forever. His computer kept erasing his work. He had been scared to tell me because he didn't want to let me down . . . he was sure he could catch up . . .

There was another problem. The pieces he had managed to finish sounded lousy—disappointingly thin, with exposed solos on the unpleasant electronic keyboards he had insisted we use.

I was mortified. Every other element of the production was proceeding perfectly; the music department was a disaster. Instead of insisting that we use an experienced Broadway orchestrator, I had blindly taken Jerry's recommendation, entrusting a vital, difficult job to an unknown, letting the show down with a rookie mistake. Lesson learned: you MUST know the people with whom you get in bed.

I held an emergency meeting with the Roundabout producers, and I started calling in favors. I located a competent copyist. I begged the orchestrator for *And the World Goes 'Round* to redo the music that had been orchestrated poorly, and I found two other orchestrators to start work on the rest of the score. I tracked down a better synthesizer programmer. And I convinced the Roundabout to hire an additional musician to fill in the tinny, hollow sound.

Todd and I worked nonstop for four days, writing out music by hand, pasting it into the players' parts. The programmer refined the keyboard sounds. I canceled the *sitzprobe* and rehearsed the orchestra during tech, as the finished numbers appeared, one by one. By the first preview, we had an orchestration ready, but it was a thing of shreds and patches.

Jerry Bock seemed singularly unconcerned with the whole fiasco, apparently secure in his trust that we would make it better, eventually. We did, but it took every preview. The musicians patiently tolerated the fussing, contributing many improvements themselves. It never got great—that would have required a complete rethinking from scratch—but by the time we opened, it was acceptable.

If the actors were alarmed, they never showed it, and I discovered the power of a company leader. For some reason, Boyd Gaines, our leading man, had faith in me. He had set the tone at every rehearsal, arriving early and staying late, working harder than I had ever seen an actor work. Moreover, he treated everyone in the company with affable respect. Self-deprecating and cheerful, his behavior lifted the other actors into a place of contentment and ardent dedication. Boyd trusted that I would solve the orchestration catastrophe, and the cast followed his patient lead, avoiding what could have disintegrated into a demoralizing crisis.

WE WERE A HIT, AND AFTER THREE MONTHS, THE ROUNDABOUT MOVED US TO THE Brooks Atkinson Theatre. The Broadway run was a delight to conduct, from start to finish, despite a strange string of unexplained events that plagued us there. As our run proceeded, I became convinced that there was a cranky theater ghost at the Atkinson. With a vendetta.

Props would disappear for weeks at a time, reappearing, finally, in the most unlikely places.

Strange howling noises would occasionally come echoing down from the flies.

I shared a crowded dressing room in the basement with four understudies and the man who maintained the shoes. Mysteriously, the door to that room occasionally would not open—the old iron lock seemed to freeze in place—once resulting in a calamitous series of missed entrances involving the elderly understudy for Mr. Maraczek, the owner of the *parfumerie*. The worried stage doorman eventually rescued him, finally locating the plaintive calls of "Help!" echoing spookily through the basement steam pipes.

Tony Walton's whirling set for *She Loves Me* was a two-story confection with a central spiral staircase. The orchestra was on the second floor, visible to the audience. I sat at a keyboard, playing and conducting the orchestra, with my back to the stage. Two small TV screens—one for the onstage scenes, the other with an infrared view—showed me everything that happened, even during the blackouts. I caught visual cues throughout the evening, coordinating the music with the movement of the actors and the scenery.

Forty-five minutes into our Broadway opening night performance, one of the dressers decided to heat up a pierogi in the basement microwave. The microwave exploded—blowing several fuses—knocking out the backstage running lights, the power to the orchestra, and my video system. The stage lights kept working, and the rotating set was powered by stagehands, not electricity, so the show proceeded, but it was a blood-chilling experience. With the running lights out, it was pitch-black backstage. I could hear crashes and muffled swearing. Many of the props were glass—perfume bottles and jars of face cream. Since the stagehands couldn't see, the set started lurching, sending heavy silver combs and brushes flying, shattering bottles. I could hear glass crunching under the actors' feet. The orchestra's music stand lights weren't working, so the players were squinting at their parts in the semi-gloom, and both electronic keyboards were without power. Diane Fratantoni, playing Amalia, sang "Will He Like Me?" accompanied by a single cello and a glockenspiel. The electricians finally restored the power after eleven minutes. It had felt like eleven years.

These unsettling episodes continued, bedeviling us throughout the run.

In the last moments of the play, Amalia and Georg finally realize that they are in love with each other. It's Christmas Eve. They each hold elegantly wrapped presents, snow is falling, and the music swells romantically. They drop the packages and kiss. Blackout. The scene was beautifully staged. Scott had invented the unconscious release of the packages as a physical gesture that demonstrated the powerful emotion of the moment, as they shed their doubts and fears. But it created a technical problem: the presents had to be removed from the stage before the lights could come up for the curtain calls.

The solution was decidedly low-tech: in the final blackout, Amalia and Georg had to kneel quickly on the stage, grope around in the dark, gather the packages they had dropped, then scoot off into the wings. I watched this every night on the infrared camera. As soon as both actors were heading offstage, I could begin the music for the bows.

The actors in *She Loves Me* rarely missed performances. When Diane Fratantoni took her weeklong vacation, her understudy, Teri Bibb, performed Amalia for the first time. Teri was amazing, making it through the entire performance perfectly. In the final blackout, however, she could not find those boxes. On my screen, I saw Teri crawling blindly around the stage, waving her arms, just missing them each time she got near. Suddenly, she disappeared. She had crawled off the edge of the stage, slipping on the paper "snow" that had fallen during the scene, launching herself out into the audience.

She landed on top of a woman in the front row, who, unfortunately, had a broken arm. A noisy woman, it turned out, who, understandably, screamed and kept on screaming through the bows. Teri had broken two ribs in the accident, but unaware, she ran up the aisle, exited the theater onto Forty-Seventh Street, and reentered through the stage door, making it into the wings just in time for her bow. As she came out to accept her hard-earned applause, the woman in the front row screamed even louder, apparently convinced that she was going to be assaulted again. Teri, valiantly, played the rest of the week with taped-up ribs.

The Brooks Atkinson Theatre ghost had struck again.

WHEN MAC RETURNED FROM THE TOUR OF *AND THE WORLD GOES 'ROUND*, he dropped by the theater to say hello. It took me a moment to recognize him. The final months of the tour had been especially hard. His skin drooped from his fragile frame, and he had visible lesions on his neck. We caught up over chicken soup at the Edison Café. I was very worried about him. Miraculously, his strength slowly returned, and when he was well enough, Scott Ellis hired him at *She Loves Me* as an extra stage manager. I would see him backstage at the Brooks Atkinson, sitting on the steps in one of the stairwells, catching his breath. Never complaining, he would grin cheerfully and mutter something filthy as I passed.

Eventually, he ended up in the hospital. I hiked through an apocalyptic Valentine's Day blizzard to visit him at New York-Presbyterian. His partner, Ron, sat by his bed, holding MAC's skeleton-like hand. MAC couldn't see very well at that point. I told him who I was, and we chatted a bit. Talking was difficult for him, but he wanted to know everything that was going on at the theater. I caught him up. He told me that Marin had visited him the previous day and how touched he was by that.

"I don't think I have very long," he said.

"You're my brother from a southern mother," I said.

He smiled. His lips were dry and cracked.

"You know what you do?" he asked me.

I didn't know what he meant.

"You make music matter," he said.

Then he got tired and faded away.

The snow melted.

MAC was gone.

THE VOID THAT MAC'S PASSING LEFT HAS NEVER BEEN FILLED. DESTROYED, I threw myself into putting together the music for his memorial, which we held at the Westside Theatre. I called my actor-boyfriend after the ceremony, needing comfort. We had been together for eight years. We had moved to a nice apartment on the Upper West Side. He was currently in Toronto, with the dog, in the middle of a yearlong contract. He was sympathetic, of course, but he hardly knew MAC, having met him only once. I considered taking a week off from *She Loves Me*, maybe even going up to Toronto, but ultimately decided not to. The unrelenting hamster wheel of eight-shows-a-week seemed as good a place to numb the pain as anywhere else.

• • •

S*HE* L*OVES* M*E*'S BOX OFFICE BUSINESS HAD BEEN STRONG FOR THE FIRST SIX months of our run, but by the end of May, the show was struggling to make its weekly costs. The Tony Awards were our last hope.

And lo and behold, one radiant spring morning, I woke to the welcome news that *She Loves Me* had been nominated for eight Tony Awards!

The mood at the theater that night was euphoric. The producers all appeared, bearing cake and champagne.

They were humbled, honored, hopeful.

We ate the cake and sipped the champagne. During the bubbly celebration, one question was on everyone's lips: Which number would we perform on the Tonys?

O*VER THE COMING DAYS, MEETINGS WERE HELD.*

"Nominations need to be advertised if they're going to do us any good, right?"

"Of course it's costly, but how else are people going to know?"

"All the other shows are advertising."

"We should do a big number on the Tony Awards, show off the whole company, right?"

"Well, that's quite pricey," said the general manager quietly.

I noticed fear in the producers' eyes.

"The producers of the nominated shows have to pay each actor who performs at the Tony Awards," the general manager continued. "The producers have to pay for a set to be built and for a new orchestration for that medley that everybody wants; they have to pay the stage managers and the dressers who work on the Tony broadcast; they have to pay the pianists and the conductor and the stagehands for the extra rehearsals . . . and did you see the balcony last night? Sparse, to put it kindly."

Fingers drummed nervously on tables. Looks were exchanged.

It sounded so . . . expensive.

•   •   •

I took the baton from Elliot Lawrence, and I gave my cue to the unheeding recording. The three other revivals had arrived with full companies, painted drops, and sturdy scenery. We brought three actors, two chairs, a bicycle, and a table.

Our chosen-by-committee medley began. Stagehands whisked the table and chairs into place, and Diane Fratantoni and Sally Mayes, our two leading ladies, appeared in front of me. The actresses sang their duet beautifully, perfectly synchronized to the recording, so I had done my job. I said a silent prayer as the music transitioned to the next excerpt. Backstage, Boyd Gaines had been tense, trembling with nerves, but onstage, he was charming. He sang his solo, the title song, flawlessly.

As we finished, Elliot Lawrence stood up from his green wooden chair. I passed his baton back to him and ducked down the stairs, squeezing past the waiting *Damn Yankees* conductor. My duties were complete for the evening. I felt relieved. Margery briskly checked me off her list. The *Carousel* conductor, an old friend, waited at the bottom of the stairs. I was afraid that *Carousel* would win the award for Best Revival that evening. I gave him a hug and wound my way through the musicians toward the door at the back of the pit.

A trumpet player waved to me—a former band member from *And the World Goes 'Round*. I stopped at his stand and silently mouthed a greeting. The music that lay open on his music stand was titled "Winner's Music—Best Revival." Surprised, I looked more closely. Did the orchestra know, ahead of time, who would win? It made sense. How else could they so quickly be playing the appropriate music the instant the winner was announced? If I could figure out, by looking at the second trumpet part, which excerpt they were about to play, would I know who tonight's winner would be?

Closer inspection revealed the truth. There were four brief selections printed on the page, one for each of the nominated shows.

When the winner was announced, Elliott Lawrence would simply hold up the appropriate number of fingers—one, two, three, or four—and the band would launch into the winning tune. Relieved, I made my way out of the pit.

The backstage corridors of the Gershwin were unfamiliar. I had trouble finding the stage door. When I finally located it, the doorman was watching the program on a small TV. I looked over his shoulder. The opening sequence had finished, and Gwen Verdon was about to announce the Best Revival of a Musical. Gwen Verdon stood next to George Abbott. Mr. Abbott was about to be a hundred and seven, she said. He didn't look a day over a hundred and one.

"The winner is," she said in her trademarked quavering voice, "*Carousel!*"

The orchestra struck up a majestic "If I Loved You," and the screams of the winning company ricocheted over the swelling music. Those orchestral excerpts of "Heart," "Summer Nights," and "She Loves Me" would remain unplayed, at least for the moment. I stepped out into the warm evening air on West Fifty-Second Street. I didn't know what to do or where to go. I felt empty and numb. The disappointment of the evening swept over me like a massive wave, crushing the air out of my chest, leaving me weak and unsteady.

I found a diner on Eighth Avenue and ordered a piece of lemon meringue pie. The sharp taste of the sour filling cut through the frothy sweetness of the topping. I ate carefully, trying not to get any goo on my tuxedo. Eventually, I meandered over to the television viewing party that the Roundabout Theatre was throwing for the rest of the cast in their lobby. I watched Boyd Gaines win Best Actor in a Musical. He gave a gracious speech, thanking me by name, a thoughtful gesture that moved me to tears. But that was the only Tony *She Loves Me* won. One week later, we played our final performance, our 354th. As I led the company through that beautiful score for the last time, every note seemed tinged with sadness but also with gratitude for the shared experience.

• • •

SHELDON HARNICK, THE LYRICIST, TOLD ME YEARS LATER THAT HIS FAVORITE performance of *She Loves Me*, out of the many productions he had seen, had been during our 1993 revival. The original Broadway run in 1963 hadn't had a performance on Christmas Eve, but our producers had scheduled one. It was a snowy December twenty-fourth. Business was still good, and, by chance, all three authors stood separately at the back of the sold-out Brooks Atkinson Theatre, observing the first Christmas Eve performance of *She Loves Me* on Broadway.

They stood watching the show and watching the audience watch the show, as the story built inevitably to that snowy Christmas Eve outside the lovely Budapest *parfumerie*.

I remember that night as well. After spending the day doing their own last-minute New York Christmas Eve shopping, the audience thoroughly enjoyed the chaos of "Twelve Days to Christmas," which led to the emotional final scene. The collective realization of the synchronous timing of that evening seemed to bind the show, the audience, and the actors into one radiant, jubilant entity.

As the presents fell and the music soared and the snow swirled, long-held feuds and disagreements were suddenly forgotten. The authors found that they were holding one another, gripping each other's hands tightly, bound together again as well, at least for the moment.

Chapter Nineteen

1994

{I}f *She Loves Me* hadn't closed when it did, I might never have met the love of my life.

When I moved back to New York City in 1984, after graduating from Yale, I attended a concert of new songs by "young composers" (composers who had never had any of their work produced). Near the end of the program, two songs stood out like emeralds in a handful of coal. The music was tuneful and interesting, the lyrics succinct and surprising. Both songs were the work of Stephen Hoffman and Mark Campbell. I tracked down a phone number for Stephen, the composer of the team, and I left him a message offering to be the music director, rehearsal pianist, or coffee boy on any upcoming projects.

Two days later, I journeyed from the Upper West Side to a distant downtown neighborhood. A pair of tall, not-so-young men welcomed me into Stephen's ill-lit, one-room apartment, which held a tall, not-so-young piano, manuscript paper, piles of books, and some somber Germanic paintings.

Stephen supported his composing habit by waking at 3:00 a.m. to bake baguettes and pastries at a nearby restaurant. Mark maintained a dreary day job in a soulless advertising factory. They had designed their lives to be in service to their collaboration.

Stephen offered me a glass of tea. Mark asked if I would like to hear their current project. Stephen played the piano while Mark sang quietly, without expression.

Sitting on a futon, the smell of mint rising from my glass, I listened to breathtaking song after breathtaking song. The show—*The Tenants of 3R*—looked at one New York apartment and all the people who had lived there over the last hundred years. Every song told a complete story, starting with a Jewish immigrant couple marrying off their daughter, then a German man struggling to learn English, three bootlegging flappers, a naked man sitting at a piano, and more. There was even a clever tap dance, performed by the cockroaches that had taken over the kitchen during a long vacancy between tenants. Cumulatively, the stories wove an intimate history of the city.

"Collaborating on projects like this," I told them, "is the reason I'm in New York."

Over the next ten years, between jobs, I helped Stephen and Mark develop four shows, each as interesting and original as the others. We did readings relentlessly. Private readings, to let the writers hear their material; public readings with invited audiences, to attract producers. We collected an informal repertory company of talented actors who were always willing to donate a week or two of time. But in the late 1980s, Broadway was headed elsewhere. The enormous poperettas—*Les Misérables, The Phantom of the Opera, Miss Saigon*—were gushing money. Producers weren't searching for quirky little gems. We had negligible success. Then, in 1994, as *She Loves Me* was sputtering toward its demise, an intrepid regional theater called with an offer.

The Sweet Revenge of Louisa May, based on several of what Louisa May Alcott called her "blood and thunder" stories, was a lightning-lit exploration of melodrama and madness, with a romantic, Brahms-like score.

If *She Loves Me* had run one more week, I wouldn't have been able to travel down to the Olney Theatre, in a Maryland suburb of Washington, D.C., to start rehearsals with the company. Miraculously,

Stephen and Mark had nervously waited for me, secretly hoping, I guess, that my Broadway show would expire.

So, the day after *She Loves Me* closed, ten years after cold-calling the composer, I began teaching the music for an actual production of a Hoffman/Campbell musical.

For *The Sweet Revenge of Louisa May*, the Olney Theatre cast four actors from New York and three D.C. locals. To portray Manuel, the fiery romantic lead, they hired Pedro Porro, a local actor who had recently won a Helen Hayes Award playing Anthony in *Sweeney Todd*. Stephen Hoffman, who had seen Pedro's audition, said, "You're going to love him. It's the most beautiful tenor voice I've ever heard. And he's very cute."

Music rehearsals were held on a spacious porch that encircled the large house where the New Yorkers were staying. I was sitting at the piano on a balmy June day. An adorably handsome man appeared. He had a wide, ready smile, light brown hair, slightly tousled, and truly, a tenor voice like spun gold. A joyful light seemed to shine out of him. I was smitten.

I made subtle inquiries. He was living with his boyfriend of four years. Well, that's that, I thought.

Then I discovered that he had been making similar inquiries. We began a tantalizingly slow flirtation, lasting through rehearsals, tech, previews, and opening night. Then, finally, we went out to dinner.

Ignoring the messy truth of our current relationships, Pedro kissed me, long and hard, after that dinner. Suddenly, he was all I could think about.

As the run of *Louisa May* continued, I started racing backstage after the first act, hoping to sit next to Pedro on the ratty couch in the green room, where the cast gathered every intermission. I couldn't get enough of him. We spent afternoons together, taking walks through the countryside, enjoying the picturesque horse farms and meadows around Olney. We often wound up at a bustling little restaurant on a river near the theater, eating fried catfish sandwiches and talking and talking. It was an exceptionally beautiful fall. The leaves blazed

in rich colors, and every day seemed to be both sunny and cool. I
wanted it to go on forever.

DURING THAT RUN, A NEW YORK CASTING DIRECTOR CALLED ME WITH AN
opportunity to audition for the role of Manny Weinstock in a new
play by Terrence McNally.

"They're looking for a pianist who can play operatic arias and say
a few lines," he said.

"I'm interested," I replied.

The script arrived the next day. I read it in one gulp, sitting at the
communal kitchen table that the *Louisa May* company shared, laughing out loud and wiping away tears at the end. The play, called *Master
Class*, was about Maria Callas, the Greek American opera singer. It
focused on a day near the end of her stormy, operatic life when she
taught a master class for opera students. Essentially a monologue for
the character of Callas, there were also parts for three aspiring singers, who each had a scene with the diva, in which they attempted to
work on the aria they had prepared. Manny, the pianist for the class,
was onstage for the entire play.

I wanted that part. The play was outstanding—a biting, funny
look at *La Divina*, as Callas was known to her fans, and a devastating
exploration of the emotional costs of living an artist's life. I didn't
know the arias, but Pedro, a passionate opera student, coached me
through "Recondita armonia" from *Tosca*. When he sang it, I got
goose bumps. I hunted down recordings of Callas singing, and I
prepared the other two arias. On our next day off, I took the train to
New York for my audition.

TERRENCE MCNALLY HAD WRITTEN *MASTER CLASS* WITH THE GREAT THEATER
actress Zoe Caldwell in mind. To his delight, she agreed to play the
part. Chic and svelte at sixty-one, the three-time Tony Award winner
had originated roles by Tennessee Williams and Arthur Miller. Her

husband, legendary theater impresario Robert Whitehead, was producing the play. Debonair at seventy-nine, with a pencil-thin Errol Flynn–style mustache, he had presented over seventy-five plays on Broadway.

I was now accustomed to being behind the table at auditions and quite unused to auditioning. Ten years had passed since I had auditioned for *Billy Bishop Goes to War*. Ironically, I had spent a great deal of time over those ten years coaching actors for *their* auditions, dispensing calm wisdom as if I were some sort of expert on how to transform paralyzing fear into focused performance energy.

Sitting in the hallway, waiting to audition, stricken by a deadly combination of dry mouth, shaky knees, and trembling fingers, I tried giving myself the advice I gave my students.

"Remember, they have a problem, and you are the solution."

Meaningless gobbledygook.

"Remember, you love performing, and this is a chance to perform."

False. I hated performing. Why would anybody want to perform?

"Focus on what your character wants and how to get it."

Blah blah blah.

I should leave, I thought.

Too late. The casting director had opened the door and called my name. Reluctantly, I walked into the studio. Terrence McNally, Zoe Caldwell, and Robert Whitehead, all dressed in black, were lined up behind a table, along with the director, Leonard Foglia.

My heart was pounding. I couldn't hear anything they said. They wanted me to read the scene first, then play the piano? I nodded, pretending that I understood. Zoe Caldwell got up from the table and walked toward me. She was tiny. She looked up at me with her cat-like eyes. Smudged gently with charcoal makeup, they crinkled with support. Putting her back to the table where the auditors were sitting, she discreetly indicated the spot where I should stand so the focus would be on me.

She said her first line.

• • •

Mr. Marriott, my theater teacher at Exeter, had died while directing a play in Calcutta, India. Septic shock, his obituary said. With a sharp pang, I remembered doing his theater games, learning to trust and follow. From somewhere, I heard his voice: "Theater is only interesting if it is a matter of life and death."

Suspended in that moment, I examined the scene. What did I want?

I wanted to please Maria Callas.

A matter of life and death, said Mr. Marriott.

I wanted to please her so that she would ask me to play more master classes.

Life and death.

Deeply in debt from spending all my money on piano lessons, I needed to impress Maria Callas or be evicted from my apartment. In the dead of winter.

Better. Now, what is the obstacle that is preventing you from getting what you want?

I hesitated. Then it came to me.

She is. Her behavior is the antithesis of what I expected. She is capricious, self-centered, and cruel to the students. Everything she says is a complete surprise.

As I focused on what I wanted, how much I needed it, and the obstacle that she presented to my achieving it, I found I could swallow again. My knees stopped shaking.

I listened to the great actress say her line.

Surprised and confused, I said my line to her. Everybody in the room laughed. I silently thanked Mr. Marriott and continued through the short scene, focusing on what I wanted and my frustration at not getting it.

When we finished, Zoe looked at me appraisingly.

"Nice suit," she said mysteriously.

I had worn a plain black suit, trying to bring out my inner music nerd. Like it took a suit to bring out my inner music nerd.

Nobody said anything.

I sat down at the piano and played excerpts from the three arias while the creative team stared at me, whispering to each other.

I finished.

Complete silence.

I thanked them for the opportunity and left the room with no idea what they were thinking.

I arrived back in Maryland to find a message from the casting director saying that it was down to two of us for the role of Manny. For our callbacks, they wanted us to separately accompany one day of auditions for the prospective singers. A week later, I put my black suit back on, took the train to New York, and played the three arias all day long for a parade of young hopefuls. *That* night, when I returned to Olney, I was greeted by a message offering me the role. They also requested that I play for the final day of auditions.

I was thrilled. I loved music directing, but part of me missed being an actor. And I needed something to focus on besides my increasingly tangled romantic life.

When the run of *Louisa May* came to an end, Pedro and I didn't know what to do. How could we return to our real lives? He drove me to the train station and kissed me goodbye. I tore myself away and climbed onto the train, confused about what our next step should be. In New York, the apartment felt bleak and strange. I lay awake, unsure of what I was feeling.

In *Master Class*, Sophie, the first student to sing for Callas, only sings one note before *La Divina* stops her. She never finishes the phrase. For this role, the casting director brought in New York's finest young comediennes. Zoe Caldwell and Robert Whitehead didn't like any of them.

Eight months earlier, Zoe had done a reading of the play at an author's workshop in Montana, using Seattle-based actors to read the smaller parts. Karen Kay Cody had played Sophie, and they couldn't get her out of their minds. For the final day of auditions, Robert Whitehead flew Karen in from Seattle, hoping that she would measure up to their memories. She read the scene, and I instantly saw what they meant. Adorable, with tightly curled blonde hair and bee-stung lips, she had a hilarious, puzzled innocence and an ability to blush slowly in shame and confusion, her pale pink cheeks blooming with an ever-deepening ruby glow.

For the role of Tony, the good-looking tenor who infuriates but then charms Callas, five singers were called back. Accompanying them, I didn't get goose bumps once. At the end of the session, Robert Whitehead asked the casting director to keep searching. I recommended Pedro and gave them his information. Not knowing what the future might hold for us, I didn't share any details about our budding relationship.

The role that I had assumed would be the most challenging to cast—Sharon, a young soprano who sings Lady Macbeth's insanely difficult "letter" aria and plays a confrontational scene with Callas—turned out to be a no-brainer. I played for some talented sopranos that day, but once the creative team saw Audra McDonald, fresh from winning her first Tony Award (for *Carousel*), she was the only contender. Playing the piano for Audra felt like having an intimate conversation with someone while flying through the air. She listened to what I was doing and instinctively responded with her own musical ideas. As I accompanied her, I could feel my technique stretching and growing to meet hers. None of the other singers called back that day could compete with Audra's effortless command of her glorious voice, or her vulnerable, fiery reading of the scene.

A week later, they saw more tenors, including Pedro, who traveled from Washington for his first New York audition. I was at the piano, sending support his way. He sang well, and at the end of the day, it was down to two singers: Pedro, and Jay Hunter Morris, a jovial, strapping blond Texan with an enormous voice.

That night, Pedro and I had a romantic dinner in Greenwich Village. It was one of the only real dates we managed to enjoy in those hectic, unsettled weeks. I had been unsure of how I felt, but looking at him across the candles and the crystal, I realized I could spend the rest of my life with this man. He smiled at me, and the world lit up. When the food arrived, he pronounced it "the best steak I've eaten in my entire life." His passion for the present moment was an inspiring reminder: the universe may deal us challenges and disappointments, but there are always things to be cherished and celebrated. He was smart, funny, creative . . . I felt myself letting my guard down . . . falling . . .

In the morning, we got the news. The role had gone to Jay Hunter Morris. Pedro was disappointed, not having yet developed the impenetrable leather skin required for the actor's life. I could only hold his hand and sympathize. He got on the train back to Washington, a little bruised. I worried that our complicated situation was only getting more complicated.

But the cast of *Master Class* was complete. Rehearsals would start in New York soon, and we would be going to the Plays and Players Theatre, in Philadelphia, for our out-of-town tryout. Robert Whitehead wanted to give Zoe Caldwell ample time to craft her performance.

And I knew, now, that I had to be with Pedro. Preparing myself for the worst, I got on a plane to Toronto holding a round-trip ticket with a flexible return. After a dramatic twenty-four hours, filled with enough anger and sorrow for several seasons of some sad gay soap opera, I returned to New York a single man. Which felt right. Except that I was now living in an apartment I shared with my very-angry-ex, surrounded by my very-angry-ex's belongings.

It was an awful time. He got the dog; I got the apartment. I put his things into boxes. A friend of his came and took them away. Meanwhile, Pedro was playing out the D.C. version of the same story, ending his relationship and temporarily moving in with his parents in Bethesda.

But now what? *Master Class* was rehearsing in New York, so I couldn't even visit him. Pedro wanted to move to New York, eventually, but he had no money saved. He had earned a degree in architecture before becoming an actor, accumulating a large student loan debt. We wanted to be together, but the truth was . . . we barely knew each other. We certainly weren't ready to live together.

Finally, on a frigid February morning, Pedro did the sensible thing. He rented a U-Haul, threw his stuff in the back, and drove to New York to move in with me.

Risking everything and leaving behind his friends, family, and career, he arrived, shivering in the arctic air. I was overjoyed. He looked exhausted and fragile and in need of warmth. We unloaded his belongings and postponed the conversation about where to put things by crawling into bed and staying there for the rest of the day. Eventually, he stopped shivering.

His courage and commitment dazzled me, though there was the occasional hiccup. Within forty-eight hours of moving in, he had rearranged the furniture, put a bunch of my clothes into storage, and reorganized the kitchen. I came home to a suddenly spacious apartment and thought, *My God, what a catch! But where are the forks? And my pants?*

There was no time to sort out what we were doing. The very next day, I had to leave for Philadelphia to start tech rehearsals. It killed me to walk out that door. Would I always be putting my career above my personal life?

I kissed Pedro goodbye. "I'll see you in seven weeks," I said, leaving him alone in the apartment into which he had just moved all his possessions.

I couldn't read the look on his face as I turned back to wave goodbye. Was it, "I'm so sad to see you go," or, "Dear God, what have I done?"

Chapter Twenty

1995

{Z}oe Caldwell had never missed a performance in her entire career. She belonged to a generation of actors who regularly pooh-poohed doctors' orders, entering stage doors without regard for life or limb. But the first thing I heard, when I walked from the brightly lit lobby into the darkened theater in Philadelphia, was Zoe Caldwell pleading with Robert Whitehead to cancel the production.

"Shut it down," she was saying. "Shut the damn thing down."

I stopped walking and stood still, listening. My eyes hadn't yet adjusted to the darkness of the tech rehearsal, but I could hear Zoe's theatrical baritone.

"I cannot do it," she continued. "What was I thinking? It's too much. I implore you, Robert—find a way out. I'm miserable. We don't need the money. We have far too much money. I *cannot* do it."

I couldn't believe what I was hearing. Was the play really going to be canceled?

Robert Whitehead's voice was surprisingly calm.

"You can do it, and you are doing it," he told his wife. "And what you're doing is marvelous."

I could see them now in the gloom, standing in the aisle. Zoe looked up at Robert, deeply skeptical.

"Do you really think so, darling? I'm *beyond* miserable . . ."

She sighed and moved away from him.

He stood there quietly.

It occurred to me that they might have played this scene before.

"Where's the nice girl who makes my tea?" Zoe called into the darkness.

One of the apprentices at the theater had been assigned to her as an assistant. The nice girl, blonde, maybe sixteen, materialized.

"Would you like a cup of tea, Miss Caldwell?"

"No, dear," said Zoe. "What I would like is to get out of this fucking play." She glared back at her husband. "But what I'm going to do is run my lines with you. Again, and again. It's going to be most unpleasant."

She stalked down the aisle. The girl scampered nervously after her.

Robert Whitehead turned his attention back to the lighting rehearsal. "Lenny," he called to the director, "it's a little dark, don't you think?"

I understood why Zoe was scared. In a few days, she would be onstage for over two hours, talking the entire time. Yes, the rest of us had lines here and there, but she carried the show, and nobody else ever changed the subject. There were also several long monologues, moving backward and forward in time, where she played other figures in Callas's life—her voice teacher, her husband, and her lover, Aristotle Onassis. In rehearsal, Zoe had loved playing the men, especially the foul-mouthed Onassis. Her whole body changed. Unrecognizable, she would saunter across the room, saying, "Do you have any idea just how much money I have? I breathe money, I sweat money, I shit money."

But her memorization of the monologues wasn't going well. And when she blanked, unable to remember what came next, there was no one to help her.

Zoe was also struggling with the musical elements of the show. Recordings of Callas singing underscored the monologues, and Zoe had to time her speeches to the music, waiting for certain phrases to finish before continuing. Strictures like these were antithetical to her charged, in-the-moment style. As the first preview approached, the inflexibility of the recorded cues was driving her mad. No amount of rehearsal helped.

We were all on edge. The housing was crummy, the theater cramped. The director was spending precious rehearsal time endlessly tweaking one technical effect, which involved a complicated series of projectors. Most of the play took place, realistically, on the stage of a recital hall. But, as Callas got lost in her memories, the white walls of the recital hall transformed into the crimson ones of *La Scala*, the Italian opera house. It was the view from the stage—the view Callas had when she performed there, her voice filling the luxurious red and gold auditorium. The transformation happened imperceptibly. And as the walls changed color and texture, the play itself changed, bursting the tight boundaries that had been set at the beginning, shifting perspective and scale. Suddenly, anything was possible.

THE DRESSING ROOMS WERE JAMMED TOGETHER IN THE BASEMENT, BUILT LIKE office cubicles, with walls that didn't reach the ceiling. I could hear everything. Zoe's nerves grew worse and worse, and I felt like I experienced each new crisis with her. The fascinating characterization that she had been developing in the rehearsal room had vanished. Watching the great actress dissolve into a jumble of insecurity and fear had been dispiriting and unexpected.

After a rocky dress rehearsal, pocked with pauses and mangled words, the producers decided to have a prompter for the first preview the following night.

The nice girl who made Zoe's tea was promoted to a position off left, with a music stand and a script. If Zoe got lost, she would say, in her smoky contralto, "Yes?"

The nice girl, who had a high-pitched, breathy voice, would cue her with the next line. Zoe would repeat it, continuing with the play.

That was the plan.

It was midnight when I stumbled back to my dingy apartment in the damp March air. The streetlights cast cold circles of light.

The next evening, Karen Kay Cody and I stood in the stage right wing, wondering when the first preview would begin. The genteel buzz of excitement from the audience had faded to awkward silence. Zoe had been sulky and catatonic at the afternoon rehearsal, vanishing well before we broke for dinner. We hadn't seen her since. The potential for a mortifying evening was sky-high. I felt nothing but dread and a strong desire to be anywhere else. Karen and I looked at each other solemnly, not speaking. I wondered if Zoe would even attempt the performance.

Then, accompanied by the sharp click-click-click of high heels strutting confidently on wood, a figure appeared out of the shadows. Glistening in her elegant, black Chanel pantsuit, a Hermès scarf at her neck, and a wig that transformed the actress into . . . not Callas exactly, but a woman who contained both Callas and Caldwell, ready to explore what it meant for an artist to say farewell to a career. Gleaming with vitality in the soft light of the wings, Zoe put her hand on Karen's shoulder and whispered something private in her ear. She darted over to me and took my hands in hers, gripping them tightly, glowing with excitement. Callas's favorite perfume, *Detchema* by Revillon, wafted delectably off her wrists.

"On the greensward," she said, her eyes lifted up to mine. I wasn't entirely sure what she meant, but I could feel her energy flowing into me, connecting us for our upcoming maiden voyage through the play.

"On the greensward," I repeated back to her, guessing that we were reenacting some Shakespearean tradition. Her eyes were fiery and determined. Dropping my hands, she click-click-clicked away to prepare for her entrance.

Suddenly, I was excited. I picked up my props, a stack of opera scores, and stood by the stage right door. Linda, the stage manager, tapped me on the shoulder. I opened the door and entered the recital hall. I arranged the opera scores into a neat pile on the piano, sat on the piano bench, adjusted it to its proper height, and then looked directly out into the audience, searching for a friendly face. Seeing one, I waved. The audience tittered. I settled back onto the piano bench and waited.

A minute passed.

The center door flew open, and Maria Callas entered, sternly admonishing the audience, "No applause." A tumultuous ovation washed over us. When it subsided, she went on with the play. "We are here to work."

Her performance was phenomenal. The panicked creature haunting our theater for the last few days had vanished, and in its place was a practiced technician, expertly gauging laughs, timing pauses, and making mental notes about what could be better the following night. The prompting situation seemed to be working. Terrence McNally's portrait of Callas, especially at the beginning of the play, is so eccentric that the audience didn't question the occasional deeply voiced "Yes?" and the high-pitched muffled prompts. It was thrilling, watching her from the piano bench. The first act ended, and Zoe strode offstage.

Act Two was even more compelling, with the appearance of Audra McDonald, who seemed to me to be challenging the diva more aggressively than she ever had in rehearsal. Audra tossed off her difficult aria like it was "The Itsy-Bitsy Spider."

As Zoe launched into her climactic monologue, the theater felt electrically charged, suffused with anticipation. The slow scenic transformation to *La Scala* began. Zoe stalked the stage, growling out her lines with force and precision. She seemed unstoppable.

But then, switching characters, she got confused—unable to remember what came next. Silence. Audra and I, sitting next to each other in the dark, held hands tightly, willing her to remember the words.

More silence.

"Yes?" Zoe said, finally. Her voice was low and guttural.

No response.

"Yes?" she said again, more firmly.

The nice girl, her voice audibly blushing with mortification, quietly gave her the next line.

"Um . . . you like it when I fuck you . . ." she whispered, trailing off unhappily.

"What?" said Zoe.

"Um . . . YOU LIKE IT WHEN I FUCK YOU WITH MY BIG GREEK DICK!"

The girl's high-pitched voice had grown surprisingly loud and shrill. She was completely audible throughout the theater. I have no idea what the audience thought was happening, but Zoe paused, became Onassis, and continued.

"You like it when I fuck you with my big Greek dick . . ."

She sailed confidently through the last section of the play. Which was a good thing since the nice girl, traumatized, had left her post and fled the building, never to return.

DURING OUR THREE WEEKS OF PREVIEWS, ZOE METHODICALLY REFINED EVERY moment of her performance. Her timing became more precise. She solved pronunciation issues. Clumsy bits of business would either suddenly make sense or be eliminated.

She arrived at the theater two hours before each performance, stretching, vocalizing, studying her script, occasionally sipping a spoonful of broth. She encouraged us to drop by her dressing room when we arrived backstage. She would greet me eagerly, hungry for news of how I had spent my day. I got in the habit of stopping onstage before heading to my dressing room to warm up my fingers with some scales on the grand piano before the house opened. Routine quickly became ritual, and Zoe considered any deviation unlucky. Once, running late, I arrived at the theater as the house was about to open. Zoe appeared in her wig cap and dressing gown, insisting that the audience be held in the lobby.

"It'll all go to hell if he doesn't play those scales," I heard her muttering darkly to the house manager.

I invited Grandma and Pedro to opening night. I allowed myself to be cautiously optimistic. The well-dressed Philadelphia audience lapped up the play and Zoe's performance like kittens around a bowl of cream. Robert Whitehead's impossibly generous gift to the company was to move us out of the dreary actor housing and into lovely, clean apartments in a sparkly high-rise. At the opening night party, he announced his plan: another out-of-town engagement before heading to Broadway. The Mark Taper Forum in Los Angeles was interested, he said. I couldn't help wondering, wistfully, how *Merrily We Roll Along* might have fared if Robert had co-produced with Hal, carefully shepherding the production through a string of out-of-town tryouts . . .

THREE WEEKS AFTER WE OPENED, ON A WEDNESDAY AFTERNOON, JAY HUNTER MORRIS played his second act scene, received his customary round of affectionate applause from the matinée ladies, exited, and collapsed, writhing in pain. The company manager drove him to the hospital, where the diagnosis was concise: acute appendicitis; operate immediately. The theater had not hired understudies for our six-week run. An urgent call to the casting director from the producers yielded a consensus of one tenor's name: Pedro Porro, the runner-up for the role, who lived in . . . Washington, D.C.?

Walking past the stage manager's office around 5:00 p.m., on my way to dinner, I overheard Linda trying to reach Pedro, unsuccessfully, at his old D.C. phone number. I sheepishly suggested that she try my New York number instead, which then required an explanation of how Mr. Porro had come to be in residence there.

That cat having sprung from its bag, Linda called Pedro in New York and explained the urgent situation. I listened helplessly, trying to imagine what he was thinking.

"Can you drop everything and take the next train to Philadelphia?" Linda asked. "Your fax machine is beeping because I'm faxing you the current version of the tenor's scene with Callas, which has changed since your audition. Can you memorize it on the train? And could you wear clothes you'd wear to a master class with Maria Callas? Please hang up the phone and hurry to Penn Station. Oh, wait—can you stay three weeks?"

Pedro, being the capable, responsible sort, got himself on a train leaving Penn Station at 6:05, clutching a sheaf of freshly faxed pages, dressed like a tenor.

He arrived in Philadelphia at 7:33. The artistic director of the theater was waiting, the engine of her car running. She sped Pedro to the theater, where the house manager was holding the audience in the lobby. Zoe Caldwell, in full costume and makeup, waited onstage. She greeted Pedro with a no-nonsense handshake and thanked him for uprooting his life. Linda quickly gave him his blocking, and we rehearsed his scene and his aria. Rehearsal ended at 7:55, and we finally had a moment to say hello.

I marveled at how calm he was. He whispered in my ear that he couldn't wait to be alone with me. The wardrobe mistress dragged him away to try on some shoes. At 7:58, the house manager opened the house, explained the situation, and at 8:10, the play started, a mere three minutes later than usual.

While Zoe, Karen, and I performed the first act, Pedro went to the dressing rooms and introduced himself to Audra McDonald, who put herself at his disposal. For the next hour, Audra played Maria Callas, rehearsing Pedro's scene over and over. Audra was only twenty-four at the time, but Pedro reports that she was a brilliant Callas. He remains the only person on the planet to have witnessed her interpretation, which, during their hour together, apparently grew to include a flawless Greek accent.

As the first act ended, Zoe came offstage doing a little jig of jubilation. She had remembered, during her first monologue, to wait for some music to finish before starting her next line. One more bump smoothed out as she meticulously polished her performance. "It really is better when I do the things that everybody tells me I must," she announced to the world, her voice full of wonder.

Audra had to prepare for Act Two. Karen took over, making sure Pedro had tea and lozenges. When I checked on him, he was staring at himself in the mirror in Jay's dressing room, pale and frozen. The reality of what was about to transpire was just dawning on him. He was inside the horrific nightmare from which every actor, at some point, gratefully wakes. Walking onto an unknown stage, in a role you've never rehearsed, with people you don't know.

"Ladies and gentlemen, this is your five-minute call. Act Two will begin in five minutes." Linda, like all stage managers, said everything twice, phrasing it differently the second time. I hugged Pedro and reluctantly left him, still staring at himself, promising that I would definitely be in love with him in the morning, no matter what happened.

Even in a short run, any variation in the daily routine is a source of enormous interest—especially if it has the potential to become a great disaster. A combination of anxious dread and giddy excitement flooded the theater, and the contradictory emotions were churning up my insides. I tried to focus on my second act performance but I kept thinking about what Pedro was about to undergo.

Linda tapped me on the shoulder. Relieved to have something specific to accomplish, I opened the door and entered the recital hall. No fussing with the scores. No cute wave. Maria Callas was behaving strangely. The master class wasn't going very well. Tense, I sat on the bench, waiting.

The night was a triumph for Pedro, who breezed through his scene and poured his honeyed tenor into Cavaradossi's aria like caramel over flan. By that point in the run, I was comfortable enough in my part that I was able to take a moment, while accompanying him, to acknowledge and enjoy what was happening. I thanked the crazy vagaries of show business for leading me to this beautiful person who was shaking up my life. My life had needed shaking. And I marveled at the luck that had somehow placed us here, together, on a small stage in Philadelphia, trying out this challenging, remarkable play.

Another miracle that occurred that night was Zoe Caldwell's response to the arrival of a new actor into the play. She navigated the scene completely differently, listening to what Pedro said and how he said it, then answering with what she felt, using Terrence McNally's words to do it. It sounds simple, but I have never seen anyone else achieve it. The dialogue was unchanged; each moment was new. How could it not be?

But really, every night was new. There was always a detail, an insight, belonging to that performance only. At a moment where she was usually harsh, she would try a gentler approach and then trace where that led her, investigating what had shifted as she wound through the familiar material. Or she would pause, speechless, after one of the students' lines, wondering if she had heard correctly. When she continued, the tension she had created made everything different. Watching her, night after night, from my piano bench was another kind of master class. She brought her entire wealth of experience to the stage—a lifetime of lessons and embarrassments, triumphs and failures.

Pedro continued in the role for a week while Jay recuperated, and then stayed on another two weeks, performing the matinées, to lighten Jay's load. It was the first extended time we were able to spend together. We explored Philadelphia, walking hand in hand through Rittenhouse Square and the Rodin Museum. Being with Pedro felt easy. Natural and romantic. Each day seemed to affirm that we had made the right choice, that it might be worth all the upheaval, and the pain we had caused.

SPENDING TIME WITH ZOE AND ROBERT FELT LIKE BEING PART OF A LONG THEATRICAL tradition, stretching back to the Greeks.

Zoe had played *Medea* on Broadway, originated the title role in *The Prime of Miss Jean Brodie*, and she had directed or acted in every

Shakespeare play in the canon. She told me that the secret to acting Shakespeare (or any great playwright) was simply to honor his punctuation.

"If Shakespeare writes a comma . . ." she said, lingering . . . "I pause."

"And if he writes a period?"

She waited. A long time.

"Full stop."

On one of our nights off, to thank Pedro for saving the show, Robert Whitehead took the two of us out for an elegant dinner. Utterly charming, he regaled us with star-studded stories from his eminent career. Robert said that when he had watched Pedro enter that first night, he felt he was witnessing "an act of unparalleled bravery." His eyes filled with tears as he said it.

Zoe and Robert, from the start, made each of us in the cast feel that we were essential to the success of the play and that we were irreplaceably precious to them.

THAT SUMMER, WE PERFORMED *MASTER CLASS* IN LOS ANGELES AT THE MARK Taper Forum. Pedro got a job in Walnut Creek, a suburb of San Francisco, doing *Forever Plaid*. To see each other, we commuted up and down California on the inexpensive Southwest Airlines shuttle. One weekend, Pedro rented a bright blue convertible, and we drove along the coast, eating at restaurants overlooking the Pacific.

During our Los Angeles run, a certain subset of Hollywood stars with ties to the New York theater came backstage to see Zoe after the show. One evening, it was Carol Burnett, another Julie Andrews. On opening night, as I was changing out of Manny's black suit, I heard a brisk knock. Thinking it was one of the stage managers, I opened my dressing room door wearing only a pair of white briefs. There stood Angela Lansbury, in a glittery black dress and a fur wrap. She kissed me on the cheek, told me how much she loved the show, and moved on to the next dressing room.

• • •

BEING IN LOS ANGELES ALLOWED ME TO RECONNECT WITH MY MOTHER. QUITE unexpectedly, she had married a much younger man—a cheerful, down-to-earth scientist named John—and they had moved to Switzerland. They shared a passion for folk dancing. During the eight years they lived abroad, they attended every dirndl-clad festival they could find. Happy as they were, however, my mother missed her parents and children. John had recently taken a job in Pasadena, outside Los Angeles, so my mother could at least be in the same country as her family. I visited their Victorian fixer-upper on our first day off. They seemed meant for each other.

The night they came to see *Master Class*, I brought them backstage afterward. My mother, terminally shy, could only manage a whispered "Hello." Zoe gathered my mother's hands in hers, saying, "You must know, my dear, that as mean and rotten as I am to your son onstage, back here I love him dearly. Thank you for giving birth to our Manny."

LATE THAT FALL, WE OPENED AT THE GOLDEN THEATRE ON BROADWAY. ZOE WON a Tony for Best Actress, Audra won Best Featured Actress, and Terrence McNally won Best Play, 1996. The theater was sold out for the entire nine months that Zoe played the role. Since the event of the evening was Zoe Caldwell–as–Maria Callas, the producers didn't even hire an understudy.

I relished my sabbatical from music directing. I loved that I was only responsible for myself and my performance instead of having to worry about the orchestra, the chorus, the diction, the cutoffs, and the dance tempos. Karen, Audra, Jay, and I had become a simpatico quartet. On two-show days, while Zoe would disappear off to Sardi's, the four of us usually ate dinner together someplace less expensive, dissecting our personal lives in great detail.

Whenever I was doing a Broadway show, Grandmommy baked cookies. She had several reliable recipes. My childhood favorite had been a buttery German confection, dusted with powdered sugar. She would bake a few batches and pack them into a cardboard box, dividing them into servings of two small cookies each, wrapping them, loosely, in a slightly crumpled piece of waxed paper. They unfailingly arrived unbroken, smelling as if they had been baked that morning. I would stroll through the dressing rooms at whatever show I was doing, distributing the cookies, still wrapped in wax paper, to the cast and crew. It made me popular for the day, so I was always happy when a box arrived in the mail from Syracuse.

Zoe couldn't get enough of them. When Cookie Day rolled around, every six weeks or so, she would shyly ask for more than her allotted pair, vaguely implying that she wanted to take a few to Robert and the boys. She loved the flaky, buttery taste, and the generous dusting of confectioners' sugar on each cookie. Most of all, I think, she was fascinated by the care Grandmommy took with the wax paper.

A few months after we opened, when Grandmommy and Granddaddy came to New York to see the play, Zoe stopped the applause during the curtain call to announce, grandly, "The best cookie maker on Broadway is in the house." She paused. The playwright must have written a comma. "David Loud's grandmother!"

Grandmommy was appropriately astonished.

ABOUT THOSE COMMAS—LATER IN THE BROADWAY RUN OF *MASTER CLASS*, AFTER Zoe left, I played Manny for three months opposite Patti LuPone. Without changing or cutting a single word, the show was twenty-five minutes shorter. It made for a zippier evening, but a surprising amount of Zoe's singular potency occurred in those punctuated moments.

Four years later, I played Manny at a glamorous one-night-only benefit in which five different stars—Jessica Lange, Kathy Bates, Edie Falco, Dixie Carter, and Leslie Uggams—shared the role of Callas. Each of those amazing actresses brought unique insights to the role, but one thing became blindingly clear to me that night: nobody else on Earth could wield a full stop like Zoe Caldwell.

One two-show day, about ten minutes into the first act of the evening performance, *La Divina* started wobbling. I watched her from the piano bench, alarmed. Zoe was pausing in strange places and skipping passages of dialogue. At one point, she stopped completely, hanging on to the back of her chair. Forlornly, she turned to me, asking, "Did I say something wrong?" which is not a line from the play. I stared back at her, worried. She looked green under her makeup. She moved center stage, trying to continue, but instead, ever-so-gracefully, her knees slowly buckled, and her head drooped.

She collapsed so theatrically that without quite knowing what I was doing, I was able to reach her as she fell, catching her head in my hands before it hit the floor. I scooped up her tiny body and carried her into the wings. The inky darkness enveloped us as I held her in my arms.

Dressers and stagehands ran toward us. Suddenly, Zoe vomited violently, a great deal of it hitting poor Linda, who was leading the charge. Zoe's dresser rolled up a coat to use as a pillow. A stagehand took the great actress from my arms and laid her gently on the floor. She continued to wretch, moaning and shaking. It was ghastly.

The company manager, a timid man with a quiet voice, went out onstage to inquire if there was a doctor in the house. Nobody could hear him, and people started shouting. Then booing. A lot of the audience thought it was part of the play. When he finally convinced them that a real emergency was, in fact, transpiring, we had our pick of doctors. The first to arrive backstage was a stylish redheaded woman with sunglasses and a Romanian accent. Even backstage, it seemed like it was part of the play.

We were gathered around the fallen diva. The Romanian doctor knelt down on the floor beside her, poking and prodding. Suddenly, the doctor raised her head, saying loudly, "Selfish! Selfish!"

Bewildered, we all backed up, feeling guilty for . . . what? Breathing too much air? What did the doctor mean?

It was Robert Whitehead who figured it out. Quite distraught, he was leaning against the wall, dapper as ever in his three-piece suit.

"It was the oysters," he said. "She had a dozen. Against my advice. What was she thinking? *Shellfish* at Sardi's on a two-show day?"

The EMTs arrived, strapped her to a stretcher, and headed for the stage door. In her soiled black Chanel pantsuit, her wig askew, and her makeup melting, she looked more like a deranged drag queen than the toast of Broadway. They took her to St. Clare's Hospital and pumped her stomach. Getting the disgruntled audience out of the theater took ages. They seemed startled by the revelation that sometimes, truly, the show can't go on.

Three days later, Zoe returned to work. That night, in the wings, instead of her usual "On the greensward!" she raised her right hand and ruefully promised me, "No shellfish."

It took a few bad oysters to do it, but Zoe Caldwell's perfect attendance record had been shattered.

Interlude : 2007

I open my eyes.

To my disappointment, I am still in the neurologist's office.

"What do you mean when you say my face is droopy?" I ask, finally.

"You haven't seen it?" the neurologist says, surprised. "The left side of your face has sagged. It's quite noticeable. Do you have a girlfriend? Hasn't she noticed?"

"Boyfriend," I say. "No. He's never said anything."

"You're kidding—he's never mentioned it?" The doctor chuckles to himself.

I don't know what to say.

"What do you do for a living?" he asks.

"I'm a conductor," I say. "I conduct Broadway musicals."

"Really?" He is genuinely excited. "What have you conducted? We see everything!"

I mention a few credits.

"*Ragtime!*" he says, his eyes twinkling. "You conducted that? Excellent. A little long, if you ask me, but what a cast! Audra McArdle!!"

"And *Curtains*! With Dr. Niles Crane! So funny. We saw it a few weeks ago. Wonderful. What's his name? The actor?"

"David—"

"—Hyde Pierce!" He finishes the name triumphantly. "I loved his dancing. So funny."

I offer up my most interesting credit—the truffle on the dessert menu.

"I was in the original cast of *Merrily We Roll Along.*"

He gets that holy look on his face. I recognize it instantly. A small portion of the human race worships *Merrily* unnaturally.

"Really?!" he says, visibly moved.

He looks me in the eye.

I wait for him to say, "As God is my witness, I am going to cure you."

Instead, he says reverently, "I met Stephen Sondheim once."

Why is this what we're discussing?

"His secretary—nice lady—was a patient of mine."

Wait a minute. I know Steve's secretary. An alarm bell goes off in the back of my head, but it is drowned out by the other nineteen thoughts roaring through my deteriorating brain.

"What do I do?" I ask.

He looks at me, perplexed.

"About the Parkinson's," I say.

"Oh." He seems disappointed. "Back to business?"

I nod.

"The first thing," he says, "is we get an MRI to make sure a brain tumor isn't causing your symptoms. There's also a test I could arrange that involves injecting dye into your brain, but frankly, it's expensive, and I'm pretty sure you have Parkinson's. So, I don't think we'll do that one, right?"

He looks at me as if I've had time to make an informed decision.

I nod, dazed.

"I have all of the symptoms that you mention," I say. "I have a slight tremor in my left hand. The left side of my body is stiff. I move more slowly. My left arm does not swing when I walk. And I have noticed my voice getting softer."

He jots a few notes on his notepad.

Clearing his throat a little, he raises his eyes up to mine.

He looks like he's going to say something important.

"You know," he says, "I have a grandniece who wants to be an actress. Very talented. Sings like an angel. Maybe she could audition for you sometime?"

Jesus Christ.

As appalled as I am, I confess I'm also thinking, *Sure, send the girl in to audition for me. Do I get better medical treatment? Put her in the chorus—I don't care.*

I am overwhelmed and not thinking rationally.

I gather my things.

I have to call Pedro. I have shopping to do. We have forty people coming over for dinner. Today is Pedro's forty-fifth birthday.

The doctor smiles cheerfully as we say our goodbyes.

I stumble out of his office.

The grey secretary looks up at me.

I am tempted to walk right by her, but because it's what I'm supposed to do, I make a follow-up appointment and schedule an MRI. Then I go outside to call Pedro.

I sit on a bench in the Park Avenue median. He answers the phone.

"The neurologist says I have Parkinson's," I say.

Chapter Twenty-One

1997

{ "David, I need a score from you the day before yesterday. We start rehearsals in less than a week. This delay is unacceptable. I'm concerned. Call me immediately."

The scratchy, raucous voice on my answering machine was unmistakable. Beverley Randolph was on the warpath. I couldn't help smiling. Sixteen years had passed since I had been one of the "kids" in *Merrily We Roll Along*.

Beverley was the first professional stage manager I ever met and the best I'll ever know. *Merrily* was only her third Broadway show, but she seemed vastly experienced. Hal Prince trusted her completely. She was always disconcertingly happy and frighteningly busy. During *Merrily*'s chaotic previews, when sets were spinning on for scenes that had been cut that afternoon, and actors were saying new lines of dialogue in clothes they'd never worn, Beverley's skillful competence and startling laugh kept us going. We were so green. There were twenty-seven of us. How she managed to wrangle us, discipline us, mother us, educate us, AND stage-manage a big flop musical, I will never know.

She was instinctively musical. Her lighting cues invariably landed on the right beat. Scenery under her guidance danced into place. I occasionally saw her lie down on the floor and peek under the curtain to make sure that her cues were coordinated with Paul Gemignani's swells and cutoffs.

IN 1997, JOHN KANDER FULFILLED HIS PROMISE TO MAKE ME THE MUSIC DIRECTOR of his next project, and I began rehearsals for a workshop production of *Steel Pier*, a new Kander & Ebb musical with a script by Tommy Thompson. Scott Ellis hired Beverley to be the stage manager. Her greeting to me the first day of the workshop was so violently joyful that she put my back out. If it ever seemed odd to her that one of her "kids" was now in charge of the music department—running music rehearsals and writing vocal arrangements—she never showed it. She supported me with the friendly fervor of a former teacher, bestowing on me the kind of respect that inspired me to live up to her high expectations.

Invited audiences at the *Steel Pier* workshop were enthusiastic, especially about Susan Stroman's inventive choreography, and our producers, believing the show had promise, booked us into the Richard Rodgers Theatre on Forty-Sixth Street. For our Broadway rehearsals, the producers found a cavernous, windowless rehearsal space on the western fringe of Hell's Kitchen.

Beverley needed time to photocopy and bind the score for the cast, but the score was incomplete. Fred Ebb's health, always a crapshoot, was now in perpetual decline. Rewrites that the songwriting team had promised kept not appearing. I had my hands full, trying to finish the vocal arrangements. I didn't want to give her a version of the score that would be out-of-date when rehearsals started.

Steeling my nerves, I called Beverley, promising to hand her the music twenty-four hours before the cast arrived. Her frustration burned through the phone like steam. She snarled something about an intern shortage. Beverley had a reputation for going through assistants like Kleenex. Then she laughed and said she had thought of me on my birthday. I knew what she meant. For a select few, my birthday would always be the anniversary of *Merrily*'s closing. I smiled. We were both quiet for a moment. Then she brusquely hung up the phone.

STEEL PIER WAS A ROMANTIC GHOST STORY SET IN THE DANCE MARATHONS HELD on the New Jersey shore during the Great Depression. The score boasted a cornucopia of vintage treats, and Stro's choreography ran the gamut of 1930s dance styles, performed by a handpicked chorus of the best hoofers in town. Karen Ziemba was period-perfect as Rita Racine, and she had genuine chemistry with her Hollywood-handsome costar, Daniel McDonald, who played a stunt pilot. Add great supporting performances by Debra Monk, Gregory Harrison, and, in her Broadway debut, Kristin Chenoweth, and it sounds like it should still be running, right?

REHEARSALS WERE NOT FUN, DESPITE THE DYNAMITE CAST. EVERY WALL IN THAT enormous rehearsal studio was painted black, and the double-height ceilings seemed to suck the sound out of the air and the joy out of the process. The lack of windows became gloomily depressing. The cast danced continuously in each other's arms, fox-trotting, tangoing, and sweating on their partners from ten in the morning to six at night. Viruses circulated viciously through the company. New York City was being punished with particularly bleak weather that January. At the end of each day, when rehearsal finally ended, and we stumbled, spent, out of the grim building, it would invariably be snowing or sleeting and already growing dark.

The show was complicated technically, requiring constant modifications, and the only time the creative team could meet with the designers was on our lunch break. We got in the habit of having our lunches delivered, eating while meeting in the gloomy, windowless conference room next to the gloomy, windowless rehearsal studio.

Beverley was well aware of the intensity of the rehearsal process, and of the happiness that food can bring. Her assistant would carefully set out our lunches, exactly as we had ordered them. I started looking forward to that lovely moment when we all sat down at our places—a lone bright spot in the dour proceedings.

One drab day, in the third week, which felt like the third month, Beverley hired a new young woman for the coveted job of lowly production assistant. The new young woman's first assignment was to handle the lunch order. We'd spent a difficult morning working on a section of the show where time went backward, the action rewinding as the music played in reverse. It hadn't gone well. As I sat down at the table, Scott Ellis, quite uncharacteristically, had a temper tantrum.

"Goddammit," he said, looking at his lunch. "I ordered a peach yogurt. This is strawberry. I HATE strawberry yogurt." He was genuinely angry.

"GodDAMmit!" He crankily pushed the offending yogurt away.

Beverley calmly stood up, smiled at the young woman, and walked into the hallway. The young woman obediently trotted after her but neglected to close the door completely. We could hear everything.

"You're fired," said Beverley. "Get out, and don't come back."

The young woman, astonished, at first assumed that Beverley was joking, but she soon realized that her chance to work on a Broadway musical had, in fact, just evaporated. I heard a choked sob, then silence. Beverley returned to the conference room and resumed reviewing her notes. We sat in uneasy silence for a few minutes, then went on with our meeting.

Later, privately, Beverley said to me, "Really, how hard is it? The director says, 'Get a peach yogurt'—you get a peach yogurt. What if I had asked her to put down a spike mark?"

The horror of this overwhelmed her. Looking a little pale, she said, "Can you imagine?"

We do have a tendency, in the theater, to treat our work as if it were heart surgery.

It was a brutal episode. But I admit, I saw Beverley's point.

• • •

When we finally got out of that Alcatraz of a rehearsal space, things started looking up. Conducting *Steel Pier* was exciting. Michael Gibson's orchestration was a Big Band marvel, throbbing with period flavor, spiked with copper-hued brass chords and wailing saxophone seediness. The orchestra was stellar, bringing an intoxicating period style to every note. William Ivey Long's costumes were eye-catching wonders, designed to peel away in layers, as the contestants grew more and more exhausted, exposing increasing amounts of skin as the competition wore on. My view from the pit was especially colorful. All the shoes were two-toned, carefully crafted, and specially dyed—in Italy, at great expense—to draw attention to the fancy footwork.

Facing the music at *Steel Pier* came with a unique perk. The dancers in the chorus were putting on a powerful performance of their own. Much more interesting than the show the audience was watching was the background drama improvised each night between the competing dance teams. I would get deliriously lost in the incriminating glances and flirtatious smiles, the whispered arguments, and ongoing rivalries. The subtle detail that the *Steel Pier* ensemble poured into that dance marathon each night was breathtaking, but this "other" *Steel Pier* was only visible from my podium.

IMAGES OF THOSE PERFORMERS BLAZE LIKE FIREWORKS IN MY MEMORY, BURSTING bright, then fading to darkness.

The ensemble's first appearance: as if summoned out of the ocean spray, a line of dancers glides sinuously down to the front of the stage. Reaching into their pockets, they pull out small handfuls of sand. Mysteriously, they let the sand fall through their fingers. The sand represents time passing, or the dust of the Great Depression, or perhaps the ashes of a fallen pilot. It also forms the beach upon which Rita Racine will soon walk barefoot, savoring her last moment of freedom before the marathon. The dancers turn and drift smoothly upstage, vanishing back into the morning haze.

Debra Monk, as Shelby, a good-time gal: on a bench, looking out at the ocean at night, she sings "Somebody Older," a gut-wrenchingly simple Kander & Ebb ballad. The movement of the water reflects up on her face. Lanky Jim Newman, as Happy, listens silently.

Joel Blum and Valerie Wright, as an aging brother-and-sister vaudeville team: they dance harder and brighter than the other couples, half their ages. Anguished, the sister watches her brother disintegrate mentally, trying in vain to find honor in defeat.

JoAnn Hunter and Gregory Mitchell, the fiery, exotic couple: they move faster than the other dance teams, their hips never stopping, their eyes locked in a smoldering gaze.

Tall Jack Hayes and gorgeous Elizabeth Mills, the all-American dream team come true: darting out from the shadows for their perfectly timed Lindy specialty, their smiles gleam with hope. Afterward, slinking off, they are exhausted and angry.

Young Andy Blankenbuehler and Dana Mauro, tip-tapping through a silly routine about balancing eggs on spoons as if it were the most important thing in the world: for a minute or two each night, it is.

The ensemble's final appearance: against a stormy backdrop, silhouetted couples whirl in ever-expanding circles. Executing spot-turn after dizzying spot-turn, they conjure a dark tornado of dancers.

Conducting the dreamlike second act opener, "Leave the World Behind," which depicted a nostalgic ride on an old-fashioned biplane, was like living inside an MGM movie-musical, complete with a chorus of wing-walking girls in sassy leather caps. It featured a satanically complex vocal arrangement of mine that Susan Stroman paired with equally challenging choreography. It ended with the girls lying flat on their backs on the airplane's wings, legs up in the air in perfect V formation, right on the high note. KZ danced fearlessly back and forth along the narrow wings of the plane, seemingly miles above the stage, while the plane tilted dangerously one way, then the other.

Clever theater wizardry helped make this happen. The secret to the success of the vocal arrangement was having two women sit still on the lower wing while the rest of the chorus danced for their lives on the upper wing. One of those stationary girls was Kristen Chenoweth. Her miraculous soprano filled the theater, making ten women sound like twenty. The trick to the plane's tilting involved the painted cloud backdrop, which slanted slightly one way and then the other, while the women on the wings leaned in the opposite direction. I've never divined the mystery behind KZ's ability to dance cheerfully along the wings of a biplane. Some theater magic is best left unexplained.

Vast quantities of dry ice "clouds" were used to help create the flying illusion. By the end of the number, the orchestra pit would be completely filled with dense white fog, rendering my conducting invisible and therefore useless. The fact that the musicians and the actors could still stay in sync was both remarkable and, frankly, disturbing. Nothing deflates a conductor's all-important King-of-the-World confidence like a nightly demonstration of his redundancy. Luckily, the fog generally dissipated pretty quickly, restoring the natural order of the universe.

It wasn't just fog that ended up in the pit. That first appearance of the ensemble, dropping sand onto the stage? A gorgeous image, but it created unending problems for the orchestra. The sand got everywhere: into the delicate fingering mechanisms of the woodwinds, inside the valves and mouthpieces of the brass instruments, between the piano keys, and into the hair, eyes, and mouths of the players. The original orchestra parts for *Steel Pier*'s "Prelude" are filled with scrawled warnings about what is about to happen: "Don't breathe—sand coming." "Cover your instrument and close your eyes!" "Pull cloth over keyboard." That sand became a part of our lives: crusted in the bindings of our scores and under our fingernails.

Tony Walton's set featured a drop covered with light bulbs, which, when lit, spelled out a garish "STEEL PIER." It was stored in the crowded fly space, high above the stage. During a final preview, five minutes before KZ's second act solo (which she performed barefoot), that drop collided with another set piece, shattering the bulbs, raining shards of glass onto the stage. I sped through the underscoring and picked up the phone to tell Beverley that we had to stop the show. Immediately.

"Calm down, Princess," she said. "Not without a fight. Cue 254 . . . go. You just tell me when the deck is safe." I looked up. Two men from the chorus, Casey Nicholaw and Brad Bradley, were entering with push brooms. Impressively, they were wearing janitorial costumes. Using the big brooms, they discreetly swept up the glass while the scene continued. Then they got down on their knees, using damp cloths to wipe up the finest fragments. They were so natural, the scene looked like it had always been staged that way.

As the dialogue ended, the red light on my podium flashed. I picked up the phone. "Is it safe?" Beverley asked me. "I will stop the show if we need to." The stage looked spotless.

I gave her the all-clear. The evening proceeded without carnage.

WE WORKED HARD DURING PREVIEWS, BUT WE WERE RUNNING THAT IMPOSSIBLE race: performing a flawed show cold in New York, with no out-of-town tryout. I felt trapped in a recurring nightmare. Most of our work was devoted to solving the problem of when to let the audience know that Daniel McDonald's character was actually dead. The story was originally written with this revelation happening just before the final song. This, apparently, confused audience members, or at least those with access to our producer's ear. Clues to the character's spectral state started appearing earlier and earlier in the script. Finally, one night, the show *began* with the sound of an airplane crash and Daniel appearing behind a scrim, smoke rising from his body as he tried his best to look . . . transparent? The audience never understood the supernatural aspect of the story, no matter when it was revealed. And the more we explained it, the clunkier it seemed.

Across Forty-Sixth Street, at the Lunt-Fontanne Theatre, another show was in a similar boat. *Titanic* had a gorgeous score by Maury Yeston that was drowning in a chilly production. Technically, it was a wreck, with previews often capsizing mid-performance when the complicated set broke. The tabloids were circling, smelling blood in the icy water.

Pedro and I saw a preview of *Titanic*. It was a night to remember. Halfway through the first act, after a gruesome ripping-of-canvas sound, the amplified voice of the stage manager asked the actors to "Please carefully exit the stage." Stagehands removed the damaged drop and the metal railing that had torn it. Twenty minutes later, the show set sail again. One number, which must have been new, was un-orchestrated. The pit pianist provided the song's only accompaniment. Also, that night, for one performance only, the authors tried a different ending. This involved an interminable wait while stagehands lugged scenery into place. An underwater diorama filled the stage. To lugubrious music, a miniature RMS *Titanic* twisted down from the surface, breaking in half before landing on the stage floor, which was decorated with rocks and seaweed, all seen from the perspective of a passing fish.

Clearly, the two productions had radically different preview philosophies. At *Steel Pier*, we never put anything new into the show until it was rehearsed, lit, costumed, and orchestrated to perfection. No preview audience could ever have detected that songs were debuting, that a new scene was being tried out, or that our leading lady was singing freshly rewritten lyrics.

It was a slow process. If one of us had a great idea on Monday, we were lucky if it materialized onstage Thursday night or even Friday. At *Titanic*, where they bravely appeared in public with their underwear down around their ankles, ideas they had each morning were quickly staged that afternoon and tested that evening. It must have been a nerve-wracking process, but it had its advantages: *Titanic* accomplished a substantial amount of rewriting in the same time that *Steel Pier* managed a few tasteful revisions.

A few days before *Steel Pier* opened, I came upstairs from conducting a matinée to find a handsome man with paint in his hair and a hammer in his hand.

"Surprise!" said Pedro.

As an early opening night gift, he had completely redecorated my dressing room. He sponge-painted the walls Tuscan yellow, hung embroidered curtains in the window, and mounted framed historical prints of the Steel Pier on the walls, transforming the drab cell into a cozy haven. Having such a serene refuge from the backstage commotion made the run quite enjoyable.

Steel Pier received eleven Tony nominations. I was excited! The producers appeared with cake and champagne. They were humbled, honored, hopeful.

That year, the Tony Awards were held at the enormous Radio City Music Hall. We brought a truckload of scenery, and our full company performed the rousing opening number, "Everybody Dance!" Margery, deadly serious in her tortoiseshell glasses, brandishing her clipboard and spiked hair, was once again in charge of the conductors. She surprised me by remembering my name and, once, smiling. She guided me through the serpentine tunnels that wound through the backstage of Radio City Music Hall, and she made certain, when I finished pretending to conduct, that I found the pass door out into the huge auditorium.

So that night, standing in the back of the hall, I got to watch live as *Titanic* won all five of their Tony nominations, including Best Musical. They ran for two years. *Steel Pier* lost all eleven of its nominations. Each loss felt like a punch to my gut. We ran for eight weeks. I was starting to think of awards shows as an unnecessary evil. Why on earth should works of art be forced into competition with each other?

WHEN THE CLOSING NOTICE WENT UP, PEDRO WONDERED IF HE HAD PERSONALLY jinxed the production by decorating my dressing room so confidently.

He vowed that for my next show, if there were one (I had nothing on the horizon), he wouldn't hang so much as a Post-it Note.

The demise of any show hurts, but *Steel Pier*'s failure was a dagger in my heart. I had put everything I had learned over the years into the vocal arrangements, refining and polishing them throughout the process. All that work, vaporized, like dew in the morning sunlight. If only the audience could have seen the show that *I* saw every night, if we'd had more time, if we hadn't been so careful . . .

Pedro and I settled uncomfortably into the end of a hot New York summer, not knowing what the future would bring. I knew I should be trying to enjoy my time off, but the city seemed brutal and uncaring. Music directors don't generally have opportunities to audition for their next job. We sit at home, hoping that the phone will ring.

Two weeks after *Steel Pier* closed, I got a bill in the mail for $312.00. I was expected to cover the cost of repainting the walls of my dressing room back to their original institutional beige.

WHENEVER I OPEN UP MY *STEEL PIER* SCORE, GRAINS OF SAND FALL ONTO THE piano. Musicals are ephemeral by nature, especially the failures. They don't usually leave behind concrete evidence of their existence. But *Steel Pier* lingers on. The feeling of grains of sand on my fingers instantly transports me back to the pit at the Richard Rodgers, looking up at those dancers, watching their tattered dreams vanish into the salty mist.

Chapter Twenty-Two

1998

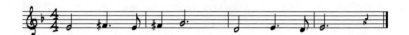

{**P**edro and I come from radically dissimilar backgrounds. I am not referring to his Cuban heritage. My family emphatically embraced the outdoors. His family viewed even their suburban backyard with grave suspicion, convinced that the more time children spent outside, the more likely they were to get deathly ill.

One July, we visited my father in Lake Placid. At dinner, our first night there, my father announced that the three of us would be hiking up Cascade Mountain the next day. For me, this was business as usual. Pedro, not wanting to disappoint my father, agreed. The next morning, four hours earlier than Pedro usually rises, he got out of bed, shivering, and silently dressed himself in every article of clothing he had packed. My father and I had talked up the sumptuous view that awaited us on the top of Cascade Mountain. Pedro grabbed his camera and a bottle of water. We were off.

Most of the Adirondack high peaks require a hike of several miles from the parking lot to the base of the mountain. This part of the expedition, along burbling streams in shadowed forests or across bright alpine meadows, is invigorating. Your body warms up before the hard climbing begins. The trail up Cascade Mountain is different. After parking your car, you are immediately confronted with a steep ascent that continues mercilessly to the top. Pedro's jaw dropped at the nearly vertical trail and the complete absence of water fountains and gift shops.

Cascade Mountain is a popular day trip because it's only a two-and-a-half-mile climb to the summit. Due to its popularity, the trail takes a good deal of abuse, resulting in a muddy, slippery path with challenging rocks to scale. And did I mention the children? Nothing is more annoying, when one is dragging one's aging adult body up a mountain, than being passed by young people, barely out of breath. This happens frequently on Cascade Mountain—a cruel reminder of the ravages of time.

It had been years since I had climbed one of the forty-six high peaks, but the sounds and smells of the forest felt intimately familiar. The sun dappling through the rustling leaves. The faint rushing of a distant stream. The sweet mingling scents of balsam and birch, ferns and sour grass and moss. The fresh, cold air was stimulating. Images from childhood trips floated in and out of my mind. Surprised at how potent my memories were, I hardly noticed the steepness of the trail.

Pedro was not enjoying himself. His shoes were caked with mud, and his legs were aching. At each turn, as the trail rose up again before us, he grew more miserable.

My father, in hiking mode, does not enjoy the question, "How much further is it?"

It makes him crazy.

As a boy, I quickly learned never to ask it, lest I be ridiculed mercilessly.

The path leveled out for a few hundred feet and then curved sharply to the left. As we walked around the corner, yet another steep, muddy climb loomed into view. I could feel the forbidden question coming. Should I tackle Pedro and throw him to the ground to prevent the dreaded words from escaping his mouth?

"How much further is it?" Pedro asked my father.

I cringed, knowing that the sarcastic, emasculating retort would be swift and deadly.

My father took a moment, glancing around to get his bearings.

"We've got about three-quarters of a mile to go," he said, cheerfully. Then he added, kindly, "You're through the worst of it."

I wondered, briefly, if I were dehydrated and hallucinating.

AS WE ASCENDED, THE TREES GOT SMALLER. MAJESTIC OAKS AND MAPLES GAVE way to scrubby pine trees just a few feet high, then dwindled to nothing. The final half mile was above the tree line. Bathed in sunlight, we followed yellow arrows painted on the exposed rock, and cairns—piles of stacked stones.

When we reached the top, Pedro got on his hands and knees and gratefully kissed the small metal disk that marked the summit. Eventually, he wearily tried to enjoy the spectacular view that my father and I kept admiring. We reminded him that this was something he could never have seen if he hadn't undergone the ordeal of climbing the mountain. He snapped a few pictures.

It had turned into a knockout of a day, sunny and windy, not a single cloud littering the bright blue sky. My father can name every high peak within sight, and he proceeded to do so. When he pointed out Whiteface Mountain, I told Pedro that Whiteface was unique among the Adirondack Mountains.

"Not only was it the site of the 1980 Olympic downhill ski races," I said, "but it also has a road winding all the way up to the top and an observatory."

Pedro was still covered with sweat from the climb. His hair was a wild mess.

He looked at me, confused.

It took him a minute due to his depleted state, but his gradual comprehension of what I had just said was a frightening thing to witness. This supposedly unattainable-except-by-hard-labor "view" we were going on about was, on another mountain, conveniently accessible by automobile and easily enjoyed from a cute summit lodge with a cafeteria?

This is bad, I thought. *What have I done?*

Maybe this whole relationship is impossible.

But he didn't strangle me, or leave me, or yell at my father. Eventually, he laughed, enjoying the tragic lunacy of it. I fell more in love with him than ever on top of that mountain.

LATER, I OVERHEARD PEDRO ON THE PHONE WITH HIS MOTHER, DESCRIBING, IN lightning-fast Spanish, the events of the weekend. One phrase, clearly intelligible, kept ringing out: *"Gringos locos."*

Chapter Twenty-Three

1998

{G}arth Drabinsky pounded on the back of a theater seat, raging, his face purple with apoplexy. His suspiciously brown hair, styled to suggest the floppy mop of a teenage Canadian hockey player, remained immobile, despite the banging of his fist. Waving pages of crumpled notes, he looked like a giant schoolboy having a temper tantrum. Over and over his clenched hand slammed down.

"He is definitely going to break that seat," I murmured under my breath to Steve Flaherty, the composer, who sat next to me.

Steve, obviously exhausted, his customary cheerful glow dimmed to a nervous pallor, thought about that, then whispered back to me, "Well, he built it."

It was true. Canadian producer Garth Drabinsky had merged the decrepit ruins of two dilapidated, unused Broadway theaters, the Lyric and the Apollo, salvaging elements from each of the old playhouses to construct his new one. The resulting theater, grandly designed, with a spacious backstage and a swanky three-tiered lobby, was a godsend for the New York theater industry. But he soon squandered the goodwill he had earned in the creation of his showplace. Instead of christening it the Jerome Kern Theatre, or perhaps the Irving Berlin Theatre, he sold the naming rights to the Ford Motor Company, resulting in the baldly commercial Ford Center for the

Performing Arts. *Ragtime*, the epic musical we were previewing at
Garth's new theater, was tainted, in the eyes of some people, before
it even opened.

After each of those previews, the entire creative team of *Ragtime*
was required to sit patiently in Garth's brand-new theater seats, in his
brand-new auditorium, listening to him scream and pound and rage.
No detail was too small to escape his fury. The sullen attitude of the
sales boy in the gift shop was as infuriating a problem as the trou-
blesome scene change into the Morgan Library, which was slowing
down the end of the show. Garth yelled at the costume designer about
the hats. He shouted at the sound designer about the microphones.
He berated the authors and complained about the staging and fumed
over the choreography. He may have been the first person in the
history of Broadway to bellow directly into the face of the burly head
stagehand about the laziness of his crew.

To me, he snarled venomously either, "All your tempos were too
slow," or, "All your tempos were too fast," depending on the day. His
rage was hard to take.

Impressively, he delivered his blistering fusillades of criticism
without consulting the sweaty notes he clutched so tightly. Eventually,
his tirades would subside, and as his handpicked team discussed the
various crises, his face would slowly return to a recognizably human
color. He would become warm and almost friendly, eager to help find
solutions to the problems, quick with an idea, and, occasionally, even
a compliment. It was treacherous terrain to navigate, but I have never
worked for a producer who cared as deeply about his show.

Ragtime was his beloved child. He had overseen every aspect of
its creation: auditioning various teams of songwriters, attending
each rehearsal of each developmental reading, micromanaging every
design decision.

He had spent ten million dollars getting it to Broadway.

BASED ON THE HISTORICAL NOVEL BY E.L. DOCTOROW, *RAGTIME*, WITH A SOARING score by Steve Flaherty and Lynn Ahrens and a miracle of a script by Terrence McNally, was sumptuously overproduced. The weekly running costs of the show were impossibly high, based on projected earnings that assumed every seat would be filled for years to come. Fatally optimistic, Garth simply couldn't imagine a future in which every performance of *Ragtime* wasn't sold out.

On opening night, January 18th, 1998, I had fifty-four singers onstage and twenty-eight musicians in the pit—the largest company I ever conducted on Broadway. A sumptuous party at the Waldorf Astoria followed, filling several floors, featuring a large jazz orchestra, lavish buffets, and American flags of all sizes. The next morning, the reviews were favorable, except from the *New York Times*. Over the next few months, convinced that something fishy was going on at LIVENT (Garth Drabinsky's Canadian theater-producing company), the *Times* published a series of articles detailing LIVENT's questionable accounting practices. Where, exactly, they wondered, was the money for this lavish production coming from?

I conducted *Ragtime* seven times a week. Once a week, I sat out in the house, taking notes to maintain the production's musical quality, while my assistant conducted. Stuffed to the brim with songs, *Ragtime* ran three hours. Conducting it was a strenuous workout. The original cast, a never-to-be-equaled combination of Brian Stokes Mitchell, Peter Friedman, and my friends Marin Mazzie and Audra McDonald, also included an eleven-year-old dark-eyed beauty, Lea Michele, soon to be the star of *Glee*.

The two years I conducted *Ragtime* on Broadway are the most time I ever spent with one show. If it had run longer, I would have gladly stayed.

Frank Galati's direction and Graciela Daniele's choreography were a nightly graduate-level course in both complex and simple staging techniques. My classroom seat was my podium, a beautifully constructed affair with shelves specially designed to hold my massive copies of Bill Brohn's handwritten orchestral score.

Using skewed perspectives and dotted with surreal details, the inspired stagecraft gave the characters a larger-than-life historical resonance. *Ragtime* opened with an intricately woven full-company number that concisely introduced the show's many characters, building to a chaotic celebration of the American melting pot and a surprise triple-confrontation between the races. At its high point, the entire cast marched downstage, directly toward my podium, singing straight at me in glorious six-part harmony. Chills every night.

A nightmarish circus represented Evelyn Nesbit's "Crime of the Century." As her swing careened out over my head, I couldn't help but see that her bloomers were as meticulously designed as the rest of her costume.

An entire factory of Henry Ford's automobile assembly-line workers appeared, choreographed like automatons under moving pistons and blasts of steam that shook the theater.

These spectacular tableaus contrasted with the stark intimacy of "Your Daddy's Son"—Audra McDonald kneeling on an empty stage, just a few feet from me, begging forgiveness from her infant child—and the refreshing clarity of "Back to Before"—Marin Mazzie, barefoot on the beach, a simple silhouette of a lighthouse behind her, illuminating the constrictive history of her marriage and bravely imagining a brighter, more humane future.

An hour-and-a-half into the long first act, there was a moment of relief for which I was always grateful. Dripping with sweat by that point, having conducted sixteen substantial numbers, I rarely had time to catch my breath or sip some water. Each night, as I started the music for "Gliding," a big set piece swept by, turning as it moved, transforming into the caboose of a departing train. A big puff of dry ice "steam" accompanied the effect, and the "steam," cold and restorative, was aimed directly at my head. I lived for that big blast of super-chilled air! It gave me the strength I needed for the four numbers remaining before intermission, during which I could change out of my drenched first act tux shirt and slip into a fresh, dry one for the slightly easier second act, which contained only fifteen musical numbers.

The view from that pit was awe-inspiring. The new theater gleamed with promise. Brohn's ambitious orchestration included a harp, plenty of strings, and a large brass choir to create the genteel New Rochelle world that the white people in *Ragtime* inhabited; a honky-tonk piano, a banjo, and a tuba to evoke Harlem and the African American characters; and two Klezmer specialists, one on the violin and another on the Eb clarinet, plus a mandolin player, to give voice to the Jewish immigrants who entered America through the gates of Ellis Island. When we recorded the original Broadway cast album, a grueling two-day marathon, Garth agreed to double the string section, giving me twelve violins, four violas, and four cellos. The symphonic sound matched the epic aspirations of the musical, lifting it even higher.

Ragtime debuted on Broadway the same year as Disney's *The Lion King*. At the Tony Awards that year, *Ragtime* brought its entire company. The cast, wearing full costumes and makeup, traveled the nine blocks between the Ford Center and Radio City Music Hall in a caravan of buses, as there wasn't enough dressing room space at Radio City to accommodate our enormous regiment. The authors had prepared a carefully condensed version of *Ragtime*'s opening number that ran exactly four minutes and ten seconds, each second having been painstakingly negotiated in meetings between Garth, Disney, and the Tony producers. I enjoyed coming back to the Music Hall. I explored the deluxe art deco lobby for the first time, and, in another first, our massive company actually filled the cavernous stage. Margery greeted me like a long-lost friend, her salt-and-pepper hair as spiky as ever. We gossiped and chatted through the endless waiting required on any project involving cameras and lighting.

Of our twelve nominations, *Ragtime* won four Tony Awards: Best Featured Actress in a Musical (Audra McDonald), Best Original Score, Best Book, and Best Orchestrations. We ran for two years. *The Lion King* won Best Musical and five other Tonys. It's still running, more than twenty years later.

The disappointment I felt was strangely familiar.

The show itself was a privilege to work on, but the Broadway run of *Ragtime* was discomfiting. After an extensive investigation by the Royal Canadian Mounted Police into questionable producing practices, it was revealed, in a plot twist reminiscent of a John Grisham thriller, that Garth Drabinsky was keeping two sets of books: a public set that documented how well LIVENT's shows were doing financially, and another, secret set that exposed how much money those shows were actually losing. He was hoodwinking his investors and defaulting on payments, and he was forced to step down.

I, along with the rest of the company, read about these events in the newspapers. Backstage, whispered rumors abounded. LIVENT's company of *Show Boat* discovered that for the past year, LIVENT had been deducting their weekly Social Security payments without ever sending the money to the U.S. Government.

LIVENT then changed ownership several times, as various plans to save the floundering company were tried. During the second year of our run, every few months, the entire *Ragtime* cast and crew would be summoned to a meeting. The new owners would introduce themselves and express their undying support for the show. Three months later, they would be gone. We would assemble again, and a new set of suits would proclaim *their* unwavering devotion.

I couldn't tell who or what to believe. Publicly traded companies, profit-skimming schemes, and white-collar chicanery are not my field of expertise. I do know that *Ragtime* deserved better producing. Running costs could have been trimmed, advertising could have focused attention on our extraordinary cast, and the whole experience could have been made to feel more Broadway, less corporate.

Eventually, without the one man responsible for its creation, and without his blind, tenacious passion, business fell off. The number crunchers who inherited Garth's behemoth of a show, citing its "unwieldy operating costs," decided to close it. We had played 27 previews and 834 performances.

In 1999, the Ontario Superior Court found Garth Drabinsky guilty of fraud and forgery, sentencing him to seven years in prison for misstating LIVENT's finances between 1993 and 1998. He served five years in jail and was granted full parole in 2014.

I've sometimes wondered if crafty Garth, anticipating the crumbling of his empire, might have stashed bundles of cash in the walls of the Ford Center. If I find myself there for a rehearsal or a meeting, I occasionally knock discreetly on likely looking spots, hoping for the appearance of a secret door. So far, I haven't found a Canadian penny.

IN A BIZARRE POSTSCRIPT TO MY GARTH DRABINSKY EXPERIENCE, YEARS AFTER *Ragtime* closed, I found myself heading to the Newark airport in a comfortable limousine. It was a misty spring morning. The phone had rung two days before. "Please hold for Garth Drabinsky," a woman's voice said.

Intriguing. Frightening.

I could imagine two possibilities: someone was playing an elaborate joke, or the Canadian prison system had surprisingly lenient policies regarding inmates' use of secretarial support staff. It turned out to be neither. Garth was out of jail and wanted to put on a show.

I had no desire to talk to him, but before I knew it, Garth was on the line, pitching an idea to me like I was his oldest friend and most trusted collaborator.

Ten minutes later, in a daze, I wandered into the living room and told Pedro that I needed to go to Toronto for a day. He looked at me, not understanding. My explanation did nothing to dispel his conclusion that I had lost my mind.

AS MY LIMOUSINE ARRIVED AT THE TERMINAL, TWO MORE LIMOUSINES PULLED UP behind me. One held John Kander, the other Terrence McNally. The three of us had been summoned to Toronto for the day to meet with Garth. Garth's powers of persuasion, diminished neither by time nor incarceration, remained so potent that the three of us actually made the trip. We had to meet him in Canada because of the arrest warrants that were still outstanding in the United States.

We flew in first-class comfort, and Garth himself met us at the Toronto airport. His driver whooshed us to a downtown rehearsal studio while the ebullient impresario revealed the details of his big idea—a revival of *Kiss of the Spiderwoman*, the Tony-winning musical he had produced in 1993. *Kiss of the Spiderwoman* is a top-notch show, with a sizzling Latin score by Kander & Ebb and a powerful script by Terrence McNally. Its setting is a prison in an unnamed South American country. This revival, Garth explained to us, would employ an all-black cast, and would be set in an unnamed African country. He had gathered us in Toronto to discuss the necessary changes to the script and score. We would also be auditioning Angela Bassett, the Oscar-nominated actress, for the part of Aurora, the Spiderwoman. He had flown Angela Bassett in from Los Angeles the night before. While Garth met with John and Terrence, I was to work with her on two songs from the show. She would then sing for the authors.

The role of Aurora has no lines and requires an accomplished singer-dancer. Angela Bassett is a powerful dramatic actress who has never done a musical. *Nothing about this makes sense*, I thought.

Miss Bassett and I met in a private studio equipped with a concert Steinway and an opulent spread of fruit and pastries. Stunningly pretty, with eyes that made you want to never look away, she greeted me warmly, as if we were going to be best friends. I think she had decided that I was her only hope of surviving this audition. I played while she sang the two numbers she had prepared. She was nervous and uncomfortable singing but eager for help. I worked with her on her breathing and phrasing, and we discussed ways that she could bring the songs to life as dramatic portraits rather than dance-driven show tunes.

After an hour, we took a break. Garth was showing John and Terrence drawings of a theater complex he wanted to build in Toronto. I told them we were ready. An assistant brought Angela in.

She had changed outfits and looked sensational. She sang the two songs.

I felt bad for her. Classy to the core, she gave it her all. She didn't shy away from the high notes she couldn't quite reach or the rhythms she hadn't yet mastered. John and Terrence were charming and complimentary. Garth explained his plan to try out this new version in Toronto, then bring it to Broadway. No one mentioned the various legal obstacles.

Angela left, thanking me as if I had birthed her child.

Garth, grinning, crowed, "Was I right or was I right? She's our star!"

John Kander laughed.

"She can't sing the role, Garth," he said.

Terrence nodded in agreement.

"She's our star," Garth said. "She's a big star."

It hit me that maybe he didn't know that in the movie *What's Love Got to Do with It*, when Angela played Tina Turner, she had lip-synced to Tina Turner's voice.

I mentioned how well she had lip-synced in the movie.

Garth had a faraway look in his eyes.

He continued to explain his vision. He detailed, scene by scene, how powerfully the story would resonate in this new context. He had thought it through carefully. He instructed us to adjust the entire score, measure by measure, eliminating the Latin flavor and replacing it with an "African sound." To demonstrate what he meant, he produced a boom box and a Starbucks compilation CD called *African Blend*. He played the first track. John Kander reached over to the boom box and firmly pressed the STOP button.

"Thank you, Garth," he said. "You've given us a lot to think about. I think it's time for the three of us to head back to New York."

Garth smiled broadly, told us how great it was to see his "friends from New York," summoned his driver, and escorted us back to the airport.

WHEN WE WERE ALONE, THE THREE OF US BURST INTO A FIVE-MINUTE GIGGLE FIT. The discomfort of the day had been intense, yet we all agreed that there had been moments when Garth held forth about his plans that our interest, and our hopes, had been genuinely piqued. Passion is an aphrodisiac, and in the theater, we're suckers for it. Garth's robust enthusiasm held the power to make rational people abandon common sense and jump on the Crazy Train with him. We *need* mad dreamers. Nobody sane would risk his fortune chasing something as quixotically elusive as a moneymaking musical.

Enjoying the first-class flight back to Newark, the irony of Garth's hopes struck me. His big idea, hatched while enduring five years in prison, was to produce a show about being in prison. The characters in *Kiss of the Spiderwoman* create fantasies that allow them to escape, mentally, from the nightmare of incarceration. Garth had done the same.

Three limos were waiting when we landed. I never heard a word about that project ever again.

Chapter Twenty-Four

2000

{G}randmommy reached into the plastic bag she was holding and pulled out a big handful of Granddaddy's ashes. She looked at the dark beige powder for a moment, then tossed the dusty remains of her husband of sixty-two years onto a rhododendron bush.

"So long, Ralph," she said.

It was a cold, windy day, late April. *Ragtime* had closed a few months earlier. My sister and I, and my mother and her brother— my uncle Johnny—had gathered with Grandmommy in the back-yard of the house in Syracuse. Granddaddy had died over two months before, and his body had been "donated to science." This meant that the local medical school had received the fresh cadaver of a small ninety-three-year-old man. Earlier that day, we had attended a ceremony, at the medical school, where the students had formally thanked Grandmommy for the nine-week loan of her husband's body.

She had responded cheerfully, "You'll be getting mine, too, you know. Soon, I would imagine!"

The dean of the school presented her with a plain cardboard box, which held the plastic bag containing Granddaddy's ashes. We returned to the house for lunch, which Grandmommy served in her cozy kitchen. Then she bundled us outside for the event of the day.

• • •

SHE HANDED THE BAG TO MY MOTHER, WHO GIGGLED NERVOUSLY BUT COULDN'T bring herself, just yet, to sprinkle her father over the lilacs, or the forsythia, or the Japanese maple. Uncle Johnny had no such qualms. He took the bag from her and reached in, making a face that made us laugh when he felt the curious texture of Granddaddy's remains.

"Are those bits of his bones?" he asked, looking at the pebbled, grainy substance in his hand.

"Well, I hope they're his!" said Grandmommy.

A big gust of wind blew, and Uncle Johnny tossed his handful of his father high in the air. It spread out over the lawn.

He handed the bag to my sister.

She grimaced, gathered her courage, and reached in, cautiously scooping up a small portion of the ashes.

I had barely seen her since her wedding, eleven years earlier.

The wedding ceremony had been at North Country School, in a meadow with a view of Cascade Mountain. She had been so anxious that day. Lovely, in the creamy wedding dress my mother had made for her, but endlessly worried over all that might, at any moment, go wrong. Our parents, each remarried, were not speaking. The unacknowledged tension affected everything. When the party finally ended, without incident, I was exhausted. I couldn't wait to get back to New York.

My sister and her husband settled in Colorado on a farm filled with horses, house dogs, and barn cats. They rarely came back East.

She gave me a small smile, then carefully sprinkled some of her grandfather over the forsythia.

It was my turn. I put my hand into the bag.

GRANDDADDY HAD LOVED, ABOVE ALL ELSE, THE MARX BROTHERS.

Just saying their names made him laugh.

"Groucho. Chico. Harpo. And sometimes Zeppo."

Their combination of anarchic mayhem and musical mischief spoke to his soul. They saw the world as he did, through the eyes of first-generation Americans. The stateroom scene from *A Night at the Opera* was, to him, Hollywood's greatest achievement, if not mankind's. Granddaddy had even written a screenplay for the Marx Brothers, long ago, called *A Night at Grand Central*, which he was sure, if only he could have gotten it into the right people's hands, would have been a smasheroo.

The book he'd been writing for the last forty years, however, wasn't nearly as fun: a layman's guide to quantum physics called *The Einstein Legacy*. I found it an unendurable bore. Near the end of Granddaddy's life, Uncle Johnny managed to get a few copies of the book professionally bound and printed, so that his father could, at last, hold a hardcover volume in his hands. As the final version was going to the printer, Granddaddy noticed a mistake in the last chapter.

"Stop the presses!" he shouted.

"Oh, Ralph," said my grandmother, "*nobody* has ever made it that far."

To his credit, he laughed so hard he had to sit down.

When Granddaddy was a teenager, he had worked in the lobby of the old Metropolitan Opera House on Broadway at West Thirty-Ninth Street, hawking librettos—translations of the text that operagoers bought before performances.

He spent his evenings standing at the back of the theater, riveted by the performers. He knew all the legendary anecdotes about the eccentric opera singers. He told me about Leo Slezak, the Wagnerian heldentenor, who was supposed to sing an aria and then exit the stage on a boat pulled by a swan. One night, as he finished his aria, the boat left without him. Flummoxed, he turned to the audience and asked, in his Austrian accent, "Vat time is the next Schwan?"

Granddaddy always did the accent perfectly.

· · ·

I PULLED OUT A HANDFUL OF HIS ASHES. THE TEXTURE WAS PECULIAR. SOFT AND powdery, with hard little chunks of . . . better not to think about it. I thought instead about our early morning swimming trips, and how sometimes we would sit together in his car, long after we had arrived back at the house, our bare feet sandy from the beach, waiting to find out who had written the symphony or the string quartet we had been listening to on the radio.

I let the dust run through my fingers, spreading his ashes at the foot of the Japanese maple.

Then we trooped inside to wash our hands.

Chapter Twenty-Five

2007

{ "WHY . . . ?" asks William Ivey Long.

He speaks in a tone so dire that I am afraid the rest of the question is going to be, " . . . has the sun gone out?"

His dramatic pause having stretched to the proportions of Greek tragedy, he continues, " . . . doesn't the hem on his left sleeve match the hem on his right sleeve?"

Acolytes scurry. Measurements are taken. Brows are furrowed.

I am standing in the middle of a brightly lit fitting room. There are mirrors everywhere. Time has graciously agreed to stand still for a few moments while the master costumer works on my second act suit for *Curtains*.

To be the focus of a William Ivey Long costume fitting is to exist at the center of the universe. Every iota of attention is aimed at you. At making you look thinner or taller. At bringing out your cheekbones, or flattering your hips, or compensating discreetly for that slight irregularity involving your left leg. He sculpts the fabric, the buttons, the zippers, the shoulder pads, tailoring the garment to make you look powerful, or innocent, or dangerous—whichever is required by the story he is telling.

William is wearing what he always wears: a blue blazer, a white shirt, and khakis. That is the only outfit I've ever seen him in, by careful design. He doesn't distract. This magician of velvet, poplin, and lace dresses himself only to disappear.

We are in our first week of rehearsals for the Broadway production of *Curtains*.

Three assistants, their eyes trained on me as if connected by wires, dart like hummingbirds, making chalk marks on fabric, ripping seams, inserting pins, widening plackets.

And there are *his* eyes, seeing into the future, imagining the garment under lights, against the set, from the balcony, from the front row, and from H-101, the seat on the aisle where the critic from the *New York Times* will be sitting.

William's eyes see every detail, every flaw.

"That hem is crooked. The zipper shows. David, darling, raise your arms. So tight in the back. WHY must the fabric bunch like that? Seamstress!"

Underlings scamper. A wiry old seamstress appears. The lining is rethought. Scissors are employed. Needles threaded. Elastic stays installed.

Near the end of the second act of *Curtains*, as I conduct the overture to the show-within-the-show, the podium will rise up, revealing me, as Sasha, in an ivory-colored western-style tuxedo, glittering with black rhinestones. The rhinestones form music notes on a staff, scrolling fancifully across the back of my tuxedo jacket. In razzle-dazzling detail, William has designed the notes to precisely match the melody that the orchestra will be playing as Sasha levitates into place.

The flurry of activity down by the pit will happen in eight measures of music—mere seconds—just enough time to cover a scene change, but William is treating the ivory tux as if it is the suit in which the next King of England is going to be crowned. This is my third fitting, and it won't be my last.

My tuxedo is one of over 250 costumes he has designed for *Curtains*. There are twelve major characters, each with several changes. The full company appears in pajamas in one scene, rehearsal clothes in another, and opening night formal wear in yet another. The men and women in the chorus play cowboys, floozies, stagehands, riverboat passengers, and dream dancers.

But God DAMN it, those hems on Sasha's sleeves had better match, or something evil will happen to somebody! William hasn't earned the discreetly whispered sobriquet "Poison Ivey" for nothing. I raise my arms again, as if I were conducting. He examines the back of the jacket, peering closely at my sleeves.

The world waits.

"Much better," he says, finally. "And the color is fantastic."

Relief floods the room.

"Who's next?" he calls.

A hireling guides me away. As I leave, William is already on his hands and knees, glasses perched on the tip of his nose, intently scrutinizing Debra Monk's costumed derrière, reworking the draping of one of her glamorous businesswoman outfits. She looks terrific.

"Disaster!" I hear him saying.

I change into my street clothes and hurry across town, back to rehearsals.

CURTAINS WAS REHEARSING IN TWO BRAND-NEW STUDIOS ON FORTY-SECOND Street. Floor-to-ceiling windows framed distracting views of the theater district and its gaudy signage. John Kander had brought in a new song, called "I Miss the Music." It was written for the character of the composer to sing about his ex-wife, a lyricist. Both the marriage and the collaboration have collapsed. Jason Danieley was playing the composer; Karen Ziemba, the ex-wife. We were gathered, along with Scott Ellis, to hear the new song for the first time. Kander sat down at the piano. At the venerable age of seventy-nine, he still got noticeably nervous when presenting a new song. I found this amusing and comforting. His hand trembled as he took a typed lyric sheet out of his shirt pocket, placing it in front of him.

There was a ghost haunting the room—Fred Ebb, Kander's collaborator of forty-two years, who had died three years earlier, leaving three of their shows unfinished: *Curtains*, *The Scottsboro Boys*, and *The Visit*. The lyric that Kander had put on the piano was not by Fred Ebb. It was by John Kander. And the song he sang for us that day was a composer's lament for the lyricist who had left him.

Tears ran down my face as he finished. It was exactly the right song for the scene, and it would sound great on Jason's vibrant tenor. Scott Ellis told Kander it was a home run.

"I'm glad you like it," the composer said, looking relieved.

He turned to Jason.

"Now, don't take this the wrong way," he said.

He turned back to us.

"I was having trouble writing it. So, in order to get into the character of Aaron and how he would feel if Georgia left him, I kept thinking about how Jason would feel if Marin left him."

Nobody said anything.

"Anyway," he said, "that's how I wrote it."

Silence.

"John," I said, finally, "don't you think this is a song about Fred and how much you miss him?"

Kander looked confused.

"No," he said, "that's not how I wrote it."

He stopped and thought for a moment.

"Oh," he said, blushing slightly. "Maybe you're right."

LATER THAT DAY, I SAT AT THE PIANO, WORKING OUT THE VOCAL ARRANGEMENT for another song from the *Curtains* score, "In the Same Boat." My left hand kept making little mistakes, over and over. This was not normal for me. I shook it off. *I must get back to practicing every day*, I thought. My technique was clearly declining. Focusing, I attempted

the passage again, certain that I could play it accurately if I concentrated. My left hand stumbled in the same place it had the previous
twelve times.

Baffled, I packed up my music and headed home.

Chapter Twenty-Six

2008

{W}hat on earth was I doing playing the piano on a brightly lit stage at Baylor University, a Baptist Christian college in Waco, Texas? The ferociously talented Marin Mazzie was center stage, singing "Ring Them Bells" at the top of her lungs, while her equally talented husband, Jason Danieley, stood near me, ringing a small pair of handbells every time his wife shook her ample breasts. Which she did, vigorously yet somehow tastefully, every time she sang the title phrase. Which was quite often. Jason looked at me and grinned.

"It's a living," he whispered.

It had all started, years earlier, at the Kaplan Penthouse, a splendid concert venue in Manhattan. Marin and Jason had booked themselves there in October of 2002, promising an evening of duets. The couple had no such evening prepared. They called me, hoping that I could create some arrangements for the two of them. We had exactly three weeks to put together an act.

They came over to our apartment every afternoon. Pedro would have tea, honey, lozenges, and lemons ready. Huddled in my little music room, we sang through every duet we knew, plus all the songs we thought could be made into duets, and lots of songs that we now know should never be made into duets.

I spent mornings working out an opening number: a long, silly cavalcade of all the duets they might be *expected* to sing so that the act could consist of duets they *wanted* to sing. We discovered that Irving Berlin's three contrapuntal duets could be interwoven into one virtuosic medley; I sewed together a suite of sultry Harold Arlen tunes; and we assembled a fifteen-minute, self-contained drama using five Sondheim songs that flowed smoothly into one another. I made them sing every lyric that Cole Porter ever wrote for "Let's Do It," and they found a rare, funny song called "Nellie, the Nudist Queen," to honor the rare, funny coincidence that they had both appeared naked on Broadway (Marin in *Passion*, Jason in *The Full Monty*). For an encore, I slowed the tempo of "Aba Daba Honeymoon," one of my mother's favorite songs, giving it a serious, art-song accompaniment. The golden couple stared rapturously at each other, singing in delicate harmony, intoning the nonsense syllables as if they were Shakespearean couplets.

Before we knew it, we were onstage in the Kaplan Penthouse, and we spent the next seven years together, performing that show wherever we could get a booking. We all had other projects during that time, and sometimes months would go by until the three of us were available, but then, all of a sudden, we'd be performing together in Kalamazoo, Michigan or Skokie, Illinois.

Marin and Jason were heaven to be with, onstage and off. The best part of each engagement was gathering, dressed in our pajamas, in one of our hotel rooms after the show. Surrounded by snacks and wine, we would laugh about the things that had gone wrong, revel in the things that had gone well, catch up on each other's lives, and marvel at how lucky we were—that this delightful collaboration was actually our profession.

We performed the show on huge stages, in tiny cabaret rooms, vulgar New Jersey McMansions, and tasteful East Hampton salons. We did it for Bette Midler at the Cinegrill in Hollywood, for Whoopi Goldberg at Joe's Pub in New York, and for Martha Stewart, a few days after she got out of jail, at the Wave Hill Gardens in Riverdale.

Wherever we were, as we drew near the end of the show and I started playing the vamp for "Happiness," which was the beginning of the extended Sondheim section, Marin would slink by me, trace her finger gently along the back of my neck, and discreetly whisper, "See you in fifteen minutes, my darling."

BUT AFTER MY PARKINSON'S DIAGNOSIS, EVERYTHING CHANGED. PETRIFIED AT THE thought of people knowing about my illness, I worried constantly about my playing and my stamina and my strength. If directors, writers, and producers knew that I was damaged goods, I would never work again. I had long known how easily replaceable we all were. Suddenly, I was keeping a secret. It felt odd—why would I ever feel that I had to keep a secret from Marin and Jason?

I was keeping a secret from everyone I knew, except Pedro and my parents.

After my surprise diagnosis, sitting on that bench in the Park Avenue median, I repeated to Pedro everything the neurologist had said. Pedro remained exceptionally calm. He said he would take care of canceling the birthday party we were hosting that evening. I said no. I didn't want to cancel the party. Pedro told me years later that after he hung up the phone with me that day, he had thrown up right on the street.

It was a strange evening, to say the least. It helped to have something to think about other than I-have-Parkinson's, I-have-Parkinson's, I-have-Parkinson's. But not talking about my diagnosis, which was to become a way of life for me for the next few years, was frustrating and uncomfortable. Pedro kept the party going, but I knew he felt the strain as well. And now every birthday of his would also be the anniversary of my diagnosis. When the last guests left, he held me in his arms while I sobbed.

I called my mother and told her, and then my father. After that, I kept my mouth shut about Parkinson's. If I could keep my condition a secret, maybe I could keep working.

I knew that my piano playing was deteriorating, but I felt that I could still play Marin and Jason's show, and I did for a few years. One summer, we had an engagement at Feinstein's, a swank club on the East Side. A composer I had worked with and her husband, a music director, sent me a note backstage, saying how much they were looking forward to seeing the show that night. This tripped a panic button that I couldn't control. My left hand started to shake uncontrollably.

I didn't know what to do. I had never felt such a violent tremor.

Maybe I could meditate, I thought.

I've always been a terrible meditator.

I tried to clear my mind. I took deep breaths. Nothing helped. I considered pulling the fire alarm and making a mad run for it. And then we were onstage, and the show was happening. My left hand was still shaking violently, so I tried tucking it under my leg. Could I play the entire show with only my right hand? The opening medley was a mess. I needed to still my brain.

I tried to think of a time in my life when I had felt truly calm.

Nothing.

Twenty-five minutes into the show, I remembered . . .

In my mind, I leaned my forehead against the belly of a big brown cow.

The scent of hay drifted gently over me, mingling with the sharper smell of manure. I could hear the pleading meows of the barn cats. I felt the cow's udders in my ten-year-old hands.

I found the rhythm and entered into it, spiraling down.

Squeeze. Squeeze. Squeeze. Squeeze.

My brain, triggered by the memory of that peacefully focused state, did what it was supposed to do. The panic subsided. My hand stopped shaking. Relief flooded through me.

I could play.

It felt like an enormous victory. But even then, I knew it was only a short-term solution.

I scraped through the rest of the performance, mortified, but relieved that it hadn't been worse. I left quickly, dodging my perplexed friends.

Miraculously, I had fooled 'em all, one more time.

But secrets are hard to keep. Like debutantes and chorus boys, they have a way of coming out.

Chapter Twenty-Seven

2010

{T}he record album from my family's collection of Broadway musicals that got the most airtime in our living room was definitely *The Music Man*. I was mad for it, in love with the rapid-fire jargon, the rousing brass orchestrations, and the gorgeous melodies. In *The Music Man*, music is everywhere. In the wheels of a train, the hypnotic patter of a con man, the incessant gossiping of the local women, and the serendipitous rhyme of a lady's name with her profession. I listened to it unceasingly. Barbara Cook's performance as Marian is etched into my DNA. There's a moment in "Goodnight My Someone" that destroys me. She starts it simply, floating the melody over the arpeggiated exercise her student is playing, but then, just before the piano fades and the lush strings of the orchestra discreetly take over, her singing becomes more emotional, more expressive, as if the transformation of the accompaniment is something that she creates, through the power of her imagination.

Each subsequent encounter with Barbara's other cast albums is marked in my memory: At Exeter, when the album of *Candide* arrived, hearing her formidable soprano fireworks in "Glitter and be Gay." At Yale, listening to *She Loves Me* and discovering her definitive "Vanilla Ice Cream." Preparing to music direct *Plain and Fancy* at Surflight, I studied her singing of "This Is All Very New to Me" and "I'll Show

Him," marveling at the seamless "soprano belt" she seemed to have invented. How would we find a girl to sing like that? We couldn't, of course.

In 2010, when James Lapine and I were assembling *Sondheim on Sondheim*, a new revue of Sondheim songs, more than fifty years had passed since Barbara had opened in *The Music Man*, and almost forty since she had played a role on Broadway. In the meantime, she had doubled her weight, battled alcoholism and depression, and reincarnated herself as a legend of the cabaret world, able to pierce the heart of any song she tackled. She agreed to star in *Sondheim on Sondheim*.

Barbara and I met privately before rehearsals officially began. I knew how important her return to Broadway was, and I had created some arrangements that I thought might help her find something new in the material. I arranged an impressionistic, Debussy-inspired "I Remember," and I put a different spin on "The Ladies Who Lunch," a song that Elaine Stritch had sung in *Company*, that I thought would match Barbara's still-optimistic-in-spite-of-it-all persona.

I arrived at her cheerfully decorated apartment on Riverside Drive. An assistant, apologizing, asked me to wait. I sat in her living room for twenty minutes, looking out at the Hudson, watching the barges pass sluggishly by. There were pictures of her singing for presidents, telegrams from Nobel Peace Prize winners, post-performance poses with movie stars. I could hear muffled shouting coming from what I guessed was her bedroom. It sounded like she was having trouble getting paid for one of her cabaret performances. Even at the top of the showbiz food chain, I marveled, sometimes you're just the garbage on the bottom of someone else's shoe.

When Barbara emerged from her bedroom, she was all business. I sat at her grand piano and played the two arrangements I'd brought.

She rejected them firmly, without mincing words.

"This is crap," she said after I played the first for her.

When I played her the second, she stopped me after four bars, announcing that under no circumstances would she sing "Elaine's song."

"Tell James Lapine he should know better than to ask me to do *that*," she said. "Jesus Christ."

Working on "I Read," a difficult song from Sondheim's *Passion*, she was rattled by the constantly changing time signatures and irregular intervals. "Why is this so goddamn complicated?" she said. "I would have to work every day for a month to learn this shit." My assistant cleared his schedule and went to her apartment every afternoon for four weeks. Sometimes they would work on a single musical phrase for an hour. Eventually, the challenging material started to sink in.

She explained to me, at one meeting, that she wasn't interested in clever arrangements or "fresh takes" on the material.

"In order for me to inhabit a song," she said, "to illuminate it from within, I need to investigate it using my own experience—my fears, my frustrations, my heartbreaks. It can be a painful process, but for me, it's the only way. All that other stuff"—she looked at me, pointedly—"really doesn't matter."

She was right, of course. It was a powerful lesson. The best moments in the show were her definitive explorations of "Loving You" and "Send in the Clowns," each presented with minimal arranging.

BY THE TIME REHEARSALS STARTED, SHE WAS WELL PREPARED, BUT I COULD TELL how anxious she was. This manifested itself in her disconcerting habit of delivering harshly accurate performance notes directly to the other actors. They called it "Getting Cooked."

"You're always flat flat flat on that phrase," I heard her say once, quite cheerfully, to one of her colleagues. "You should fix that!"

"Why do you make that funny face when you try to hit the high note?" she asked another one. "Believe me, it doesn't help your sound."

There was no discernible chemistry between her and the other "star"—Tom Wopat—though that was hardly her fault. His surly morning demeanor was insufferable, improving only slightly in the afternoons. Vanessa Williams was fun to be around, but she, too, seemed preoccupied, worrying about her voice and whether she was a good match for the material. We were well on our way to becoming the most dysfunctional company ever.

Sondheim on Sondheim was a Roundabout production, so nobody was making much money. I started bringing my lunch from home, eating communally with the frugal actors, including Barbara Cook, at a big table in the rehearsal studio. Over those lunches, I watched Barbara's prickly shell and judgmental demeanor gradually melt away.

She was just out of the habit of being in a company. She started telling stories about her life and career. We loved hearing them. Slowly, before our eyes, she transformed into a warmly supportive, loving cast member, convinced that everyone around her was marvelously talented. I was fascinated, watching her rediscover the camaraderie, the feeling of collective accomplishment a show can provide.

The effect on the company was noticeable. Nothing can sink a show faster than a crabby leading lady. As Barbara relaxed, everybody's work got better. And the day she actually complimented my arrangement, late in the rehearsal process, of "Losing My Mind" and "Not a Day Goes By" was one of the most satisfying moments of my life.

Sondheim on Sondheim was built around a set of filmed interviews, in which Sondheim talked with great detail and surprising candor about his writing process and his personal life. In one devastating clip, he recounted how his mother had written him a letter saying that her biggest regret in life was giving birth to him.

I happened to be watching Barbara Cook the first time she saw that piece of footage. She gasped quietly, astonished, and a look came over her face of such sadness that I thought she was going to cry. She didn't, though. There was a hardness to her.

Instead, she looked over at James Lapine and nodded slightly, as if to say, "Good for you. You found the key."

• • •

I DON'T KNOW HOW I DID IT, BUT WHILE I WAS REHEARSING *SONDHEIM ON Sondheim*, I was also supervising the first production of *The Scottsboro Boys* at the Vineyard Theatre. *The Scottsboro Boys* opened off-Broadway on March 10th, 2010; *Sondheim on Sondheim* opened on Broadway six weeks later, on April 22nd.

This kind of production piggybacking was murder on my relationship with Pedro. He was grappling with a difficult decision: whether or not to leave show business. Tired of the endless auditioning and bruising struggles, he wanted to open his own architecture practice. I was buried in my shows, unavailable to him and distracted.

Unwisely, we set this problem aside and focused instead on spending all our money. Pedro was pining for a house so that we could occasionally get out of the city. We looked at fixer-uppers all over the Hudson Valley. Nothing seemed right. In the end, we decided to build a new house in the Catskills, which Pedro designed. I took my life's savings, gleaned from twenty-six years of tiny fees I'd received for music directing hundreds of readings and workshops, most of which were never heard of again, and gave a big check to the Actors' Federal Credit Union, in exchange for a mortgage.

Having lived in small New York apartments for all those years, I had never owned a grand piano. I couldn't wait. The first piece of furniture that arrived at our new, empty home was a Sohmer Grand I had found at an estate sale. Sohmers were known as the "poor man's Steinway" because, in the 1930s, the Sohmer factory was down the street from the legendary Steinway factory in Queens, and the Steinway technicians supplemented their incomes by moonlighting at Sohmer. For two weeks, the piano was the only piece of furniture we possessed, besides a mattress and a church pew we had found in Milford, Pennsylvania. I couldn't tear myself away from that piano. My view was of deer and wild turkeys on the snowy lawn instead of the tenement fire escape across the alley.

I wrote the vocal arrangements for *The Scottsboro Boys* sitting there. This was a challenging assignment, as the show used an all-male cast, even though some of the characters were women. I had to figure out how to give the score variety and depth while respecting Kander & Ebb's provocative concept: using the form of a Minstrel Show to tell the story of nine young African American men wrongly convicted of raping two white women in Alabama in 1931. Tommy Thompson's script was pointedly irreverent. Susan Stroman staged it using eleven chairs and a few boards. Those chairs and boards became a train, a jail, a courtroom, and anything else she needed. The result was starkly simple and boundlessly imaginative.

The Minstrel Show concept put enormous pressure on the actors, who had to sing superbly, dance ferociously, and change characters (and sexes) instantaneously. As the grueling first week of rehearsal ended, the actors were realizing how physically demanding the show would be to perform. We were asking the impossible. The singing was challenging, the dancing was exhausting, and doing them simultaneously was inconceivable. Upset and tired, they held a cast meeting after rehearsal. The creative team was not invited.

We had a meeting of our own, disappointed that we might have to simplify the choreography and vocal arrangements. I paged through the score, looking for passages I could adjust.

The next morning, the actors asked to have a word with the creative team. Colman Domingo, who played several roles in the show, stood to speak for the cast.

Here it comes, I thought.

Colman told us that the actors had decided, as a group, that the answer to the seemingly impossible demands being placed upon them was, "Yes, we can." The only accommodation they asked for was our patience. They hurled themselves into the work, supporting each other through the challenges, determined to realize the vision we had for the show. It was an honor to watch that company succeed, achieving things they hadn't thought possible. My favorite production photo is of the cast in midair, suspended over the stage, literally flying. Their mouths are all wide open; they're singing at the top of their lungs.

At the end of the show, utilizing a grotesque historical tradition from the Minstrel Shows, the whole company (with the exception of John Cullum, the only Caucasian member of the cast) put on blackface to perform the final number. I was backstage at the Vineyard Theatre the first time they put on the pitch-black makeup. Several members of the cast were sobbing; the mood was anguished. I wondered whether it was all worth it.

Onstage, the effect was chilling. By that point in the show, the audience knew each of the "boys" quite well. They had each played at least one character, some of them two. When they appeared onstage in blackface, they were instantly reduced to antiquated stereotypes, indistinguishable from one another, their humanity erased. As a cautionary metaphor for how easy it is to see people as a group rather than as individuals, it was shocking.

After the Vineyard production, *The Scottsboro Boys* had a successful run at the Guthrie Theater in Minneapolis, then opened on Broadway in October. It only played six weeks. A bitterly disappointing end to what had been a highly fulfilling artistic journey.

At the Tony Awards, six months later, we were nominated for Best Musical, which meant that we were invited to perform on the broadcast. We needed to reassemble the company and reconstruct what we had created, but the actors had dispersed to other jobs. Luckily, you don't often get the chance to lose a Tony Award six months after closing a show, so they all made themselves available. The ceremony that year was held in the Beacon Theatre, on the Upper West Side. The Beacon seats less than half as many people as Radio City Music Hall. I said to Margery that it felt like people just weren't interested anymore.

She snorted derisively and said, without looking up from her clipboard, "You're serving caviar to hyenas."

We lost all twelve of our Tony nominations that night, setting a new record for the most nominations without a win. The previous record holder, at eleven nominations without a win, had been *Steel Pier*.

Chapter Twenty-Eight

2011

{S}peaking as someone who knows how the chicken gets on the plate, let me assure you that the plucking and gutting involved in poultry farming pales in comparison to the pluck and guts required to survive the long road that some shows take to Broadway.

It was back in 1999, during the Broadway run of *Ragtime*, that I first served as music director for *The Visit*—Kander & Ebb's musical take on Friedrich Dürrenmatt's darkly satiric play, with a stark script by Terrence McNally. That first reading, with Angela Lansbury and Philip Bosco, took place at 890 Broadway, in the same studio where *Merrily We Roll Along* had rehearsed. We only did one performance—on a chilly October afternoon—but the heat generated by the two stars, as directed by Frank Galati, seemed to warm the whole building.

Angela Lansbury, who radiated calm and an endearing charm, found a steely sadness in the role of Claire Zachanassian, the richest woman in the world, bent on revenge. Philip Bosco, as her former lover, had a dazed quality that contrasted with her chilly determination.

Our producer confidently announced his plan: a Boston tryout in December 2000 and a Broadway opening in March 2001. It sounded like a dream come true. Ann Reinking signed on as choreographer; top-notch designers were announced; I conducted "demo" recordings of three of the songs with Angela and a twenty-four-piece orchestra.

That production never happened. *The Visit* did make it to Broadway, eventually, in 2015, fourteen years later than originally scheduled, with different stars, a different cast, and a different producer, director, choreographer, and orchestrator. In fact, with the exception of the writing team, I was the only one from that first reading who survived all three out-of-town productions and crawled over the finish line.

The Visit was part of my life for so long that I associate the various productions with major personal milestones.

SEPTEMBER 11, 2001, THE DAY OF THE ATTACKS ON THE WORLD TRADE CENTER in New York City, was the day of our first tech rehearsal for *The Visit* at the Goodman Theatre in Chicago. The rehearsal was quickly canceled. Pedro happened to be visiting, and we walked hand in hand up Michigan Avenue on a spectacularly crisp, sunny afternoon, wondering what had gone wrong with the world.

Chita Rivera and John McMartin were the stars at the Goodman, an odd pairing of Latina tigress and patrician restraint. Chita was fascinating—earthy yet elegant—singing the role in her feline baritone. Since her character, Claire, had an artificial leg, Ann Reinking and I devised a tango with a limp, in 5/4 time, that Claire performed with her bizarre entourage of bodyguards and eunuchs. Chita made it a nightly showstopper.

Fred Ebb, debilitatingly ill at that point, had flown to Chicago six days before the attacks. He had missed weeks of rehearsals. It took him three days to recover from the flight. When he finally attended a work-through in the rehearsal studio, he arrived in a wheelchair, pale and fragile, unable to speak. Afterward, he recovered his voice, at least long enough to give the company his detailed notes. He had notes for himself as well—an incisive list of cuts and changes to the lyrics throughout the score.

In addition to the one-legged tango, I developed a stop-time arrangement for a chilling tap dance that Ann Reinking choreographed, featuring the yellow shoes that the townspeople couldn't resist purchasing. Rehearsals for this number were usually scheduled at the beginning of the day.

Ann would invariably appear five minutes late, apologizing breathlessly, unrecognizable with no makeup and tangled wet hair. For the first half hour of rehearsal, she would crouch on a stool near the piano, intently doing her face and hair, while her assistant reviewed the previous day's choreography with the cast. One day, she forgot her little mirror. I was at the piano, working on the arrangement. Pausing from her efforts, she looked at me, her gorgeous blue eyes now ringed with their customary eyeliner, lips red, cheeks rouged, her long hair brushed and held in a crisp ballet dancer's bun. She asked me, with throaty sincerity, "Do I look like Ann Reinking yet?"

Terrence McNally, I can't imagine why, invited his friend Renée Fleming, the acclaimed operatic soprano, to our first full run-through in the rehearsal studio. She was in town, appearing in *Otello* at the Chicago Lyric Opera. I guess she needed entertainment on a slow afternoon.

Chita, already nervous about running the show for the first time, went temporarily insane at the thought of having one of the world's finest singers sitting ten feet away from her. Visibly upset, she grabbed me in the hallway and dragged me into a large janitorial broom closet, on the verge of tears, talking *rapidamente* about how unfair this was, and how could they let this happen, and what was I going to do about it? The stage manager called "Places!" for the run-through. Chita abruptly stopped talking. I wondered if she would refuse to rehearse. Suddenly resolute, she ran out of the broom closet and into the rehearsal room, where she stood directly in front of the surprised soprano. With a determined grin, Chita kicked her seventy-eight-year-old right leg high over her head and said, "Bet you can't do that, Renée!"

Then she went to her place to start the run-through.

•   •   •

IN 2008, THE PRODUCTION OF *THE VISIT* AT THE SIGNATURE THEATRE IN Washington, D.C., was the first job I took after being diagnosed with Parkinson's. The two-year run of *Curtains* was coming to a close, and I was determined to keep working. The stars this time were Chita Rivera and George Hearn. George's beautiful voice was a revelation, highlighting the richness of the score, and his scenes with Chita had great humor, which the piece sorely needed.

I was keeping my diagnosis a secret, or so I thought. Rehearsals were excruciating.

My eggs were all in one basket. I had no backup plan. As a music director, I had to be able to conduct, play, and arrange. I had made my career and my reputation by being unimpeachably reliable: the one who no one ever worried about, who never missed performances, who was never late. The thought of being the weak link was unacceptable to me.

Parkinson's was making me weak.

Everyone with Parkinson's fields a different set of symptoms, specially tailored just for them. I did not have the visibly shaking hand that is often a clear giveaway. The slight tremor in my left hand remained almost unnoticeable, except when I got nervous. My major symptoms were stiffness in my legs and arms, and a general slowing down. It was difficult to stand up straight, difficult to hold my head up. My left arm now consistently didn't swing when I walked.

The neurologist had started me on some medication, which did seem to help, but not for long periods of time and not reliably. I eventually realized that the timing and the content of my meals had a significant effect on the efficacy of the medication.

I needed help with almost everything—carrying scores, getting coffee. I discovered that it is quite easy, in New York City, to get bright young people who are interested in the theater to do practically anything, no matter how menial, just for the privilege of being in a professional rehearsal room. I had remarkable luck with assistants—a cheerful string of talented, underpaid young artists—each discreet and kind and helpful. I dispensed information on a need-to-know basis, convinced that secrecy was the best route.

Ordinary activities had become humiliating ordeals. Putting on a jacket was awkward. I tried to get dressed in places where nobody could see me, a near impossibility in most rehearsal halls. My assistants became masters of the unobtrusive assist. Buttons were a daunting challenge. Pedro stocked my closet with shirts he'd had tailored to appear buttoned but which were actually held together by Velcro.

The neurologist was making me increasingly uneasy. He was insistent that I audition his grandniece. He mentioned other patients of his by name, people in musical theater, people I knew. I could only assume that he was being equally careless with my name.

At the top of my urgent to-do list, I added: FIND A DIFFERENT NEUROLOGIST.

MY FIRST REACTION TO THE DIAGNOSIS HAD BEEN NUMB SHOCK, ACCOMPANIED by a chilling despair that I was not up to the challenges of living with this disease. Everyone, at some point, has to face something seemingly unbearable, I told myself. I had lived forty-five years without any significant health problems. Be grateful.

What I had skipped, I realized later, was an acknowledgment of the acute sadness I felt, and also the anger I was feeling that this had happened to me. I had jumped right to my usual knee-jerk optimism, which quickly became an impossibly false place to live.

I had always felt lucky that my passion was also my career. But where does that leave you when your passion is being taken from you, brain cell by brain cell?

Pedro was suddenly my caretaker, which I couldn't bear. This was not the relationship we had imagined. It was a complete reversal of our usual roles. I lay awake in bed at night, worrying. Would he continue to be attracted to me? Would he have second thoughts about our relationship, now that it had changed so much?

In fact, he didn't hesitate for an instant, embracing this new aspect of our life together with a steady resolve that took me a long time to accept. The thought of facing Parkinson's alone was terrifying to me. I continued to think that he must be just as scared, looking at his own future with my Parkinson's.

Ah, Wolf, indeed.

WE DID ONE READING OF *THE VISIT* IN WHICH JASON DANIELEY, WHO HAD PLAYED the teenage son in the first reading, was now old enough to play the part of the Schoolmaster.

Two weeks later, Marin and Jason and I were performing on a college campus in Morristown, Tennessee. As I played the piano, I heard the mistakes I was making, the missed notes, the lack of finesse. The joy of our show had always been that we listened to each other, discovering new details in the familiar material. This performance had none of that. My playing had dipped below an acceptable level. It wasn't fair to Marin and Jason. Or the audience.

The three of us convened as usual, in our pajamas, in my hotel room, later that night. We chatted. Marin and Jason were each holding a glass of wine. It seemed like the right time.

I gathered my courage.

"I have something to tell you," I said.

They looked at me, surprised.

I couldn't say it.

Marin's eyes filled with tears.

She reached over and held my hand.

"Just say it," she said.

Why was it so hard to say?

"I have Parkinson's," I said. "I don't think I can play your show anymore. Not the way I want to play it."

They responded with deep compassion. They had known something was wrong, of course, but hadn't wanted to pry, as I was clearly not ready to open up. I asked Marin and Jason to keep my secret. I was far from ready to tell the Broadway directors, producers, and composers upon which my career depended. We talked and talked. And cried. And, eventually, laughed. They hugged me goodnight and returned to their room.

By this time, I had a new neurologist, the remarkably empathetic Dr. Alessandro Di Rocco, who had no relatives in show business and refrained from mentioning his other patients by name. Tall and handsome, with a long, expressive face, he was at the cutting edge of scientists looking for a cure for Parkinson's.

Dr. Di Rocco's long-term approach was for me to take as little medication as possible—just enough to make life bearable. The side effects from the drugs are unpleasant, and the more you take, the more extreme those side effects become. He also told me that the drugs, eventually, would lose their effectiveness and that the best way to postpone that was to take as little medication as I could, for as long as I was able. I was getting by, but I had stopped playing the piano. And, reluctantly, I was only accepting jobs as a music supervisor or as an arranger—jobs that meant I didn't have to conduct.

Playing the piano was my identity. A childhood spent in practice rooms had created in me a lifelong need for the simple act of making music. Accompanying singers was a skill I had been developing my whole life. Making music with another person was the closest thing I had to a religion.

I was grateful for the supervising jobs, but the thought of never conducting another Broadway musical, never standing in that privileged vortex, caught between worlds—listening, leading, following—was deeply depressing.

Who was I, really, without these treasured gifts?

IN 2011, THE ACTORS FUND PRESENTED A ONE-NIGHT-ONLY BENEFIT
performance of *The Visit* at the Ambassador Theatre on Broadway.
The concert, starring Chita Rivera and John Cullum, was a few days
after Thanksgiving.

The night before Thanksgiving was snowy and slushy, and in the
tangled web of benefit rehearsals leading into the long holiday weekend, I clumsily lost my bottle of pills in a taxicab. It was eight at night;
Dr. Di Rocco's office had closed long before; no pharmacy would
give me medication without a prescription. I remember feeling the
precious drugs in my system wearing off as I was desperately calling
the Taxi and Limousine Commission; trying to find my pills; calling
the doctor's office and getting a recording; calling the pharmacies,
and getting nowhere.

It was sleeting, and I was huddled inside an ATM lobby. My phone
was dying. My shoes were soaking wet. Looking back, I realize I could
have tried going to an emergency room for a stopgap supply of pills,
but I was new at this, and it didn't occur to me. Maybe I could hang on
through the long weekend, I thought, then deal with getting replace-
ment medication on Monday. Laboriously, I got myself home. When
Pedro returned to the apartment, I avoided telling him the full extent
of the problem. I was afraid to admit, even to him, how compromised
I had become. I said I'd had a bad day and went to bed.

I was keeping other things from Pedro. Since I had stopped conducting, I no longer received a weekly salary through the Musicians'
Union, which was how I had always maintained my health insurance.
Six months earlier, my union insurance had ended. I was paying out-
of-pocket for unbelievably expensive medication and a top-flight doctor,
burning recklessly through our savings. Pedro never suspected anything because this was something I would never do. I had never been
late with a bill payment in my life, but now our finances were a disaster.

I have since learned that Parkinson's can affect "executive func-tion" in the brain—how we manage time and plan, how we make decisions based on our experiences, how we multitask. I was failing at all this and didn't know why. When I stalled before making a decision, or I put off making an important phone call, I knew I was making things worse, but I couldn't break the pattern.

Everything conspired against me that weekend. I was in a high-pressure position of responsibility, completely unmedicated and exposed. I wasn't conducting the concert, but I was supervising all the music, and those one-night events are a constant barrage of deci-sions to make, notes to give, problems to solve, and egos to assuage. I could barely get to the rehearsals. My arms were heavy, and it was hard to stand up. My head drooped. Walking was painful and slow. It was my first glimpse behind the curtain. The first demonstration since my diagnosis of what my Parkinson's was really capable of when left untreated.

It was terrifying.

Pedro and I took the train to a friend's house in New Jersey for a large Thanksgiving dinner party. It was a laborious trip, and when we arrived, I was exhausted. I sat helplessly in a chair by the fire, unable to participate in conversations unless people made the special effort of kneeling down to be at my eye level. It felt like a sneak preview of life as a ninety-eight-year-old. Pedro told me on the train home how shocked our friends had been at my decline. In the cold white light of the New Jersey Transit train car, he looked worried and tired.

How long could he bear this?

The final rehearsals for the benefit were a nightmare. I sat in the cold, chaotic theater avoiding interaction with anybody, giving notes through my assistant. During one lull in the turmoil, John Kander and I were alone for a few minutes. He looked at me, his eyes filled with concern. He couldn't bring himself to ask about what I so clearly didn't want to tell. Why couldn't I face the music? It would have been so natural to open up to him at that moment, but I just couldn't. We sat there, desolate.

I can't remember the performance. I skipped the party and went home.

PEDRO ACCOMPANIED ME TO SEE DR. DI ROCCO. AFTER I TOLD THE DOCTOR WHAT had happened, he asked Pedro to leave the office. I didn't know why. When we were alone, Dr. Di Rocco sat across from me and asked, clearly, if I had been trying to commit suicide that weekend.

I was stunned. It was a lot to take in.

He explained, carefully, just how dangerous it was to suddenly go off my various medications, each of which involved crucial balances in the chemistry of my brain.

I thought about what he had asked me before I answered. There had certainly been times, in the five years since my diagnosis, when life had seemed unbearable. There were times when I had said to Pedro that maybe jumping off the George Washington Bridge would be preferable to going through the long, slow decline of Parkinson's. I assumed he knew that I wasn't serious.

Or was I serious?

I knew I wasn't handling my diagnosis well. It seemed like there were two of me. When I wasn't medicated, I was miserable, and my despair included the fear that the medication would never work again, that I would be forever trapped in this helpless condition. When I was medicated, with the full use of my body, able to stand up straight and walk freely, my sense of well-being was joined by a feeling that this time the healthy condition might last and that I wouldn't slide back into immobility. Each day was not just a physical, but also an emotional, roller-coaster ride.

Being trapped in the grip of a progressive, degenerative disease is not something that anybody can prepare for. Why wouldn't I think about suicide? It seemed to me like a perfectly logical subject for thought.

But did I want to end my life?

When I thought about Pedro, I did not want to end my life. When I was making music and able to forget, even for a few moments, about the disease, I did not want to end my life. When I made a suggestion, in rehearsal, that improved a moment, when I gave an actor a thought that clarified a lyric, when I took a composer's melody and created harmony for a choir to sing, I did not want to end my life.

"No," I said to the doctor. "I did not try to commit suicide. But I understand why you would think that I might have."

He was quiet. He looked directly into my eyes, searching.

He invited Pedro back into the office. Taking out a notepad, he started diagramming medications and schedules. He designed a new protocol for me, mapping out a pattern of slowly elevating dosages, stretched out over many weeks. Because I had gone completely unmedicated for almost six days, he was being careful to reintroduce the familiar drugs, and to introduce some new, unfamiliar drugs, slowly, one by one, into my daily medication schedule.

"You are a person who lives through his work," he said. "It's going to take some time, but I'm going to give you your life back."

His words were comforting, but I didn't know if I had the strength.

In a disastrous piece of timing, I was supposed to start rehearsals for a revival of *Porgy and Bess* the following week.

I held on to Pedro's arm, and we walked slowly out of the doctor's office.

Chapter Twenty-Nine

2014

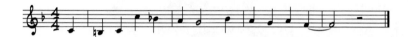

{**B**}y putting one foot in front of the other, I kept going. Supervising rehearsals as my medication slowly built back up was agony. For the first time in my charmed career, I had accepted a Broadway job that I didn't want. The less said about *Porgy and Bess*, the better, but it served its purpose. I had health insurance again, and our finances stabilized. I confessed to Pedro about the difficulties I was having managing our money. He was furious with me. We added it to the growing list of problems we hadn't fully discussed.

The following spring, when the phone rang with an offer to conduct *The Visit* at the Williamstown Theatre Festival, I decided that it was finally time to talk honestly with my collaborators about my health. I had stretched my silence to the breaking point.

I began with John Kander.

"I have Parkinson's," I said, over slices of Sara Lee pound cake.

"I know," he said kindly.

One by one, over lunches and coffees, in rehearsal rooms or at the piano, I said to my colleagues and my friends the dreaded words.

"I have Parkinson's," I said to David Hyde Pierce and Debra Monk, over mugs of tea at my kitchen table. They had come over, long after *Curtains* closed, to rehearse "Show People" for a benefit performance.

After the hugs and tears, David said, "We knew something was wrong, of course. But when you looked uncomfortable or in pain, I just assumed it was my singing."

"Oh, please!" said Deb. "Actors are so self-centered. As long as I got my cues from you, which I always did, you could have been upside-down drunk in a wheelchair, and I wouldn't have noticed."

Nothing bad ever came from revealing the truth about myself. Only good.

It was shocking to realize how much energy I had expended trying to cover my symptoms, how many rehearsals I had spent worrying if people knew I was compromised. So much time wasted, despairing over being found out.

The fear had been more paralyzing than the disease.

AFTER SIX MONTHS ON DR. DI ROCCO'S NEW MEDICATION SCHEDULE, I FELT significantly better. I was more alert. My body wasn't as stiff. I was walking for exercise, and, to my astonishment, I was playing the piano again. I even thought I might be able to conduct a show eight times a week. The offer from Williamstown provided the perfect opportunity to try. Pedro agreed. I made sure I had a strong assistant, and I accepted the job.

The ability to play the piano again was a gift for which I hadn't dared hope. Feeling my technique leaching away had been soul-destroying. Now, as my coordination was returning, I felt as if my most essential self, frozen and immobile, was thawing. It was a surprising feeling—coming back to life.

An offer came to do *Sondheim on Sondheim* again, this time with the Boston Pops. They asked if I would play the nine-foot concert grand piano with the orchestra. Instinctively, I said yes, and then immediately regretted it. Pedro insisted that I stick to my commitment. The experience turned out to be the thrill of a lifetime. Two performances at Symphony Hall in Boston, and then, even better, a performance at Tanglewood, in the huge open-air "shed," playing my arrangements with that glorious orchestra, Stephen Sondheim happily in attendance.

I called it my "Fuck You, Parkinson's" performance.

THE STARS OF *THE VISIT* IN WILLIAMSTOWN WERE CHITA RIVERA AND ROGER Rees. Thirty-two years before, in 1982, I had seen Roger as the title character in *Nicholas Nickleby* on Broadway. Doddy and I watched all eight-and-a-half hours of the play on one unforgettable day. The tickets were a hundred dollars each, which seemed outrageous at the time, but we scrounged the money together, and after seeing Roger and the rest of the Royal Shakespeare Company give everything they had that day, we had to admit it was worth every penny.

Roger hadn't had good luck with Broadway musicals. On *The Red Shoes*, a calamitous bomb, he was fired during previews, along with the director, the lyricist, and two other actors.

Two weeks before our rehearsals began, I started working with Roger on his music for *The Visit*. Charming and self-effacing, he confessed to me that he was terrified of singing. He couldn't understand why he had been cast in the part. I adjusted the keys to suit his voice, but at our next session, he was still apprehensive. He paced fretfully around my living room, then sat down next to me, wondering out loud if he should attempt the role.

Life is so strange, I thought. One of my lifelong heroes is sitting two feet away from me, in genuine distress, asking me for career advice? Years before, in London, I had seen him in a dazzling one-man show that included some Shakespearean monologues. I suggested to Roger that he recite a familiar speech by Shakespeare and then immediately try to sing with that same confidence.

"What a piece of work is a man . . ." he began.

The speech was riveting, of course. He spoke it directly to me. His voice was warm and relaxed, and he used it like a painter to highlight words, shade feelings, and make connections between thoughts. As he finished, I played the introduction to one of his songs, hoping for a miraculous transformation. *If this works*, I thought, *I will have invented a new technique*. True, it's a technique that I could only use on certain legendary stars of the Royal Shakespeare Company, but hey!—if Judi Dench ever wants to come over to rehearse a revival of *Mame*, I'll know just what to do.

When Roger sang, it was definitely better, though not quite the magic trick I was looking for. He sang with a bit more conviction and he finally relaxed a little. I kept using this technique during rehearsals, and he steadily improved.

Williamstown turned out to be the perfect place to continue developing *The Visit*. The bucolic college campus created an atmosphere of clearheaded concentration. An old friend of mine joined the company, and we rented a comfortable house with a pool—my idea of heaven. Like being back in summer stock, except cleaner and nicer and we were all adults.

A new director, John Doyle, and a new choreographer, Graciela Daniele, brought a stylized perspective to the piece. John edited the script down to the bone so that it could be played in one act. Graciela even threw out the showstopping tango, asking me to create, instead, a "Mazurka" for Claire to dance with the actress portraying Claire's younger self. We placed their *pas de deux* after Chita sang "Love and Love Alone," a mordant Kander & Ebb ballad, and it proved to be the highlight of the show—an emotional breakthrough for Claire that hadn't existed in previous versions.

I was nervous about conducting the orchestra. I decided that rather than stand for the entire show, as I had always done, I would sit on a stool. To my relief, it worked. I could still control the musicians, and it was less physically taxing.

Again, a producer announced *The Visit* for Broadway.

Again, I crossed my fingers.

Chapter Thirty

2014

{I} had never been to a gay wedding before attending my own.

The entire summer that I was in the Berkshires working on *The Visit*, Pedro was at our house in the Catskills, planning our wedding. There had been no dramatic proposal. Nobody knelt.

We were driving back to New York, and out of nowhere, Pedro asked if I thought we should get married on our property or at some other venue.

"Are you proposing to me?" I asked.

He nodded.

"Well, let's do it at our place," I said.

Our twentieth anniversary was coming up.

We had been through a lot.

After my diagnosis, I had been so desperate not to stop working that . . . I never stopped working. I was home less and less. I took our relationship for granted. While I was buried in my own whirl of fear, we grew apart without ever acknowledging that problems were mounting. The terror that I carried around about Parkinson's infected everything. Finally, after the truth came out about our finances, Pedro insisted that we see a couples counselor.

"I'm not comfortable with that," I said.

"I really don't care," said Pedro.

"Well, can we talk about it?" I asked.

"No," he said. "This is nonnegotiable."

I had never seen him so determined.

I agreed to go to counseling.

Her office was in the Village. I was filled with apprehension. I had never been in therapy. Pedro was more experienced. I didn't like the thought of airing our problems to a third party, and I resented Pedro for forcing me to go through this. We sat silently in the tiny waiting area outside her office. The distance between us felt enormous.

Joan, the therapist, turned out to be frighteningly good at her job. Zaftig and funny and intuitive, she had a disarming way of asking one of us a simple question, listening to the answer, and then analyzing that answer for the rest of the session, mining it for revelations, letting it lead us to what needed to be examined. After a few sessions, I started to understand how essential it was that we talk about our relationship, and how it had changed, and how we had changed in the eighteen years we had been together.

It was harrowing. There was more than just my fear of the disease. I had made serious mistakes. Many things had gone undiscussed over the years. One by one, those carefully suppressed issues appeared in that Greenwich Village office, marching out on cue. I found the process agonizing, and we said things to each other that I would never have been able to recover from in previous relationships. But Pedro was different from anybody I had known and worth fighting for, no matter how difficult the struggle.

At one session, Joan asked me to characterize Parkinson's.

"A cunning thief," I said. "Everything I care most about is being stolen from me."

"Not everything," she said, looking at Pedro. "And do you see how much it hurts him to hear you say that?" she asked me.

I saw her point.

She asked me how I felt when I couldn't work.

"Like it's the end of the world," I said.

"And where does that leave him?" she asked.

She forced me to confront how I had almost destroyed myself and our relationship when I had secretly allowed my insurance to lapse and then gone off my medication.

She asked if I felt worthless.

I had to acknowledge how much of my identity was tied up in my work. Without work, who was I?

Yes, I had felt worthless. And I had treated Pedro as if he were worthless, too.

I may not have been conscious of it, she said, but contrary to what I might have told Dr. Di Rocco, I *had* been trying to kill myself that slushy weekend. And I had almost succeeded.

Eventually, the simple act of talking about the problems, the mistakes we'd made, robbed them of their power over us.

DURING ONE SESSION, I MENTIONED MY FRIEND CHRIS NICHOLSON. HE HAD come into my thoughts unexpectedly.

"Who the hell is Chris Nicholson?" asked Pedro.

"My friend from North Country School who died in a climbing accident when I was at Exeter."

"In almost twenty years together, you have never ever mentioned him," said Pedro.

He was right. I hadn't mentioned him. And I realized that in all the time since his death, I had never mourned him. Never taken the time to acknowledge how his death had made me feel. How it made the world seem randomly cruel and unknowable.

Why was I like this? What had made me so detached, so unfeeling, that I hadn't taken the time to grieve the loss of my friend?

Something shifted that day. I took a long walk, by myself, from Joan's Greenwich Village office up through Midtown and then up Central Park West. I thought about my friend from so long ago. How we had talked and explored together. I thought about the night we had slept nestled in leaves, held in the roots of a birch tree. Images came flooding back. Just taking the time to bathe in the recollections, to linger over details long forgotten, seemed luxurious and new. I found myself asking him questions and finally acknowledging the loss I felt in my own life, knowing that he was gone.

I had formed a protective shell, like an egg about to emerge from a chicken. The shell was meant to protect me from sadness and fear. But it had gotten so hard, so impenetrable, that allowing someone else inside that shell, all the way inside, had become the hardest thing of all.

I finally felt ready to crack it open.

Our wedding was the best day of both our lives.

We held the ceremony on the lawn of our house over a warm Labor Day weekend. I was responsible only for the music. The thought of a rock band or a DJ made me physically ill. I hired a swanky eleven-piece society swing band that played tunes from the thirties and forties. Pedro handled everything else. We put up a big white tent, with tables and chairs for 125 friends and family members. People traveled from all around the country, many of whom we hadn't seen in years. They parked on the main road and walked down our long, winding driveway, through the forest, to our house. Arriving in twos and threes, their eyes wide with amazement at the sight of the little house in the clearing, the tent, the orchestra, the flowers . . . They all seemed radiantly happy to be there.

Kathleen McNenny, wife of Boyd Gaines, married us. Scott Ellis's twins were our ring bearers. Arden, my friend from Surflight, flew in from California. Stro and Debra Monk kept a watchful eye on the forest, convinced that there might be bears. Liz Callaway, my pal from *Merrily We Roll Along*, sang "My Heart Is So Full of You" at the ceremony. Our friend Rebecca Luker gave her lustrous soprano to a Cuban song. Marin and Jason, and many others, sang at the reception. David Hyde Pierce and Lynn Ahrens wrote poems.

John Kander dispensed sage advice. Even the weather behaved, waiting until just after the ceremony had finished before providing a cooling shower.

Pedro had planned every detail so thoroughly that he actually enjoyed himself the entire day. There was a table stocked with flavored waters, herbal teas, and lemonades, so nobody fainted in the heat. The food was simple and delicious. We had the Rolls-Royce of porta-potties, a large, multi-roomed affair with a generator, parked discreetly in a field of ferns. As the only air-conditioned spot on the property, it proved very popular.

I put on the suit Pedro had chosen for me to wear. Cellists played Bach and Saint-Saëns as we walked on the grass with our two "best women" and four flower girls. We processed slowly around the house to the front lawn, where our guests were seated. At one point, Pedro, walking ahead of me, tripped over a tent stake.

"*Cojones!*" he swore audibly.

The Spanish-speaking side of the guests giggled.

He looked so handsome, standing across from me, glowing with the joy of the day. Kind and patient. Caustically funny. Wise and sweet and honest and strong.

The time came for our vows. We had each prepared a personal statement. They would be followed by identical vows, which Kathleen had typed out for us so we wouldn't mess them up.

"My love for you is unconditional and absolute," Pedro said as part of his statement. "There is no illness or circumstance that could ever diminish that." Then he read the vow: "I love you, and you are my closest friend. Will you let me share the rest of my life with you?"

"I will," I said.

"I look at you, Pedro, and I know I'm the luckiest person in the world," I said, as part of my statement. "You are the family I choose. You are the kind face I want to come home to every night." I looked at the vow. Kathleen had mistakenly typed: "I love you, and you are my *closet* friend . . ."

I couldn't pretend I hadn't seen it.

Turning to our guests, I said, "It says here, 'I love you, and you are my closet friend,' and I am NOT going to say that!"

I never imagined that I would get a big laugh at my wedding.

I waited for the laughter to crest before continuing. "I love you, and you are my *dearest* friend. Will you let me share the rest of my life with you?"

I picked up the ring that Pedro had chosen for me to give to him.

IN 2003, ELEVEN YEARS EARLIER, ON A BRIDGE OVER THE ARNO, IN FLORENCE, WE had exchanged a different set of rings.

Pedro was spending the summer in Italy, singing in an opera program. I was between shows, so I joined him. On one of our last days there, we drove to Florence. We explored the ancient city, ate gelato, and meandered through museums. Near the cathedral, we found an old jewelry store. Dignified and un-touristy, the store had been in the same family for centuries. We spotted two rings we loved. Hammered gold, like something out of Middle-earth. On a whim, we bought them.

When I started to put mine on, Pedro wisely stopped me, demanding a more meaningful experience. We walked through the ancient streets, waiting for a spot to reveal itself, eventually finding ourselves drawn to the *Ponte Santa Trinita*, a bridge with a perfect view of the *Ponte Vecchio*. We put the rings on each other's fingers, told each other how much we loved each other, and asked a passing German tourist to take our picture.

As we got into position, Pedro murmured, "If I'd known I was getting married today, I would have blow-dried my hair."

ON OUR REAL WEDDING DAY, WE REMOVED THOSE ITALIAN RINGS. DURING THE ceremony, we planted a magnolia tree. We had asked our parents to bring soil with them from their homes. My mother brought dirt from Pasadena, to which my father added compost from North Country

School. Pedro's parents brought sod from their yard in Bethesda and, incredibly, a vial of sand from Cuba. Our four parents sprinkled their ancestral offerings on the tree's roots. Our nephews added the rest of the dirt, which the flower girls watered. We buried our old rings at the foot of the magnolia, and we put new rings—rings that carried the power of the Supreme Court's recognition of the fundamental right to marry—on each other's fingers.

My father made a funny, moving, politically insightful toast. The orchestra struck up an Irving Berlin medley, and Pedro and I danced to "Cheek to Cheek." He held me in his arms, and we floated around the dance floor.

We danced with our mothers. Then, in the spirit of the day, it seemed right to ask our fathers to dance with us. They acquiesced. While Pedro and his father did a sly rhumba, my father danced with me square-dance style, and he swung his partner 'round and 'round. I thought of the two of us, side by side in his car, twenty-seven years before. Who could ever have imagined, then, a day like this one?

There were many firsts that weekend.

Our two families met for the first time, and nothing too alarming happened.

The man who built our house brought his young son to the ceremony. It was the first wedding, of any kind, that the boy had attended. I hope that he remembers it as I will, not as a gay wedding, but as a wedding—a day filled to the brim with love.

While we were setting up the tables in the tent, I looked over and saw my parents. They were adjusting one of the tablecloths and discussing the place settings. I watched as my mother showed my father exactly how Pedro wanted the silverware laid out. They were smiling. I caught my sister's eye and nodded discreetly at them. She looked at them, then back at me, her eyes shining. At her wedding, three decades before, they had been unable to speak to each other. Seeing them together now, after so much time, wrenched my heart open.

The happy Cincinnati family of my childhood was a distant memory. There had been such a spark between them. Secrets they had shared. The years between then and now stretched like a rope bridge between two cliffs. The small red house may have been gone, bull-dozed into oblivion, but here we were, the four of us. Still standing.

The ancient ache was still there, but as I watched them, I felt it dissolving. Years of suppressed hurt gently lifted, cleansed by the pure water of this gathering.

Look at them, I thought, fussing over the table settings for their son's wedding to a man. A beautiful man who continued to shake me when I needed shaking. I looked across the lawn at Pedro, and I thought something I never would have predicted. I thanked the universe for giving me Parkinson's. Without the calamity of the disease, I realized, we would never have had the honest, painful discussions that had saved our relationship and brought us to this blessed day.

Chapter Thirty-One

2015

{During *The Visit*'s fifteen-and-a-half-year journey to Broadway, everything had changed. I had been healthy, received a crippling diagnosis, wrapped it in a shroud of secrecy, and fallen almost completely apart. And I had, with help, turned my life around, revealed the dreaded secret, and married the love of my life.

I still had Parkinson's, but somehow, I felt the capacity to be happy again. At one of my visits to Dr. Di Rocco, I described each day as "a chemistry experiment." I explained that as a freelance musician, I rarely had a string of identical days in a row, so I was always fine-tuning my treatment—adjusting the timing of my medication, as well as how much and what to eat. Dr. Di Rocco listened and gave me a sad smile.

"I think you have finally accepted that you have Parkinson's," he said.

What a strange accomplishment, I thought. But, it seemed, a necessary one.

TO BE IN AN ORCHESTRA PIT, FACING CHITA RIVERA IS, TO ME, THE DEFINITION OF happiness. Chita's voice had long ago become part of my chromosomal makeup, as evidenced by the well-worn recordings of *Bye Bye*

Birdie and *West Side Story* in my parents' cabinet. Conducting *The Visit* on Broadway, I occasionally had to pinch myself, in case the sight of her before me was just the colorful dream of a ten-year-old boy still stuck on a farm. Watching her focus and her concentration as she worked on that part, year after year, was extraordinary. And I had the best seat in the house.

I witnessed the effortless way she led the company. How she looked for positive responses to whatever challenges the day brought, and how her dressing room door was always open (except for the ten minutes right before each performance, which was her sacred, private time). I observed the mischievous fun she had onstage, watching the actors around her. I could also see the look in her eyes as she and the rest of the company, shortly after we opened, became aware that something terrible was happening to Roger Rees.

It started oddly: He couldn't find his dressing room. Then, on stage, speeches he'd rattled off perfectly a hundred times were suddenly garbled nonsense. Sometimes, when he was singing, he would stop mid-song. I would call out the lyrics as I kept the music going, and sometimes he could get back on board, but sometimes he couldn't.

Audiences wondered if he had been drinking. Backstage, the stage managers posted signs pointing the way to Roger's dressing room. The company became experts at helping him, showing him where to move, sometimes taking his arm to guide him. They discovered ways to salvage scenes when he dropped his lines.

Making those strange weeks even more peculiar were nights when Roger was his old self.

He was suffering from a particularly awful form of brain cancer known as glioblastoma. Determined to perform, he struggled on.

Watching one of the great classical actors of our time spewing gibberish onstage was one of the most upsetting things I'd ever experienced. But I understood his desperate desire to keep working. We define ourselves, in the theater, by our work. Foolishly, we feel ashamed when we are unemployed. We cling to each job as if it will be our last. And if something is threatening our ability to perform . . . well, I knew exactly how he felt.

One matinée, he finally called in sick. His understudy, Tom Nelis, went on and performed flawlessly. Roger was never able to come to the theater again. Tom finished the run.

I visited Roger once, near the end of his life, in his apartment on Central Park West. His husband made sure that Roger's final days were surrounded by friends and flowers and laughter. He was barely conscious. Three weeks later, he left us.

Beverley Randolph's powerful light was extinguished by breast cancer soon after *Curtains* closed. She was fifty-nine. After a valiant three-year battle, Marin Mazzie's radiant spirit was stolen by ovarian cancer. She was fifty-seven. Dear Rebecca Luker succumbed to the quick ravages of ALS. She was fifty-nine. I found these losses to be unbearable. Tidal waves of grief washed over me at unexpected moments.

As someone raised without religion, I have found my spiritual fulfillment in the collaborative power of people gathered in a rehearsal room, working together to tell a story. The solace of community—learned on an organic farm, nurtured in the theater—is everything to me.

Sometimes, I envision the friends I've lost all doing a show together. I imagine an exuberant opening night—no critics allowed. Peter Neufeld and Robert Whitehead are producing, along with Hal Prince and Ruth Mitchell. Ushers greet the audience, making sure that Doddy is seated well away from Grandma and Grandpa. Grandmommy and Granddaddy have seats on the aisle, so that Granddaddy, who has gotten so short, can see. MAC and Beverley are in the wings, calling cues. Barbara Cook and Zoe Caldwell are in the dressing room, practicing their duet. The stage fills with faces that I know and love. They sing together with passion and clarity and joy. I take comfort in the thought that one day, when it's my time, I'll join them. Someone has to give them their cutoffs.

Postlude : 2015

At the podium, conducting *Curtains*, after being diagnosed with Parkinson's, I had thought, *Maybe this is the last show I will conduct on Broadway.* As sad as that made me, I knew I had managed to have exactly the career I wanted—varied and creative, with collaborators I loved and respected. To end it with as blissful an experience as *Curtains* felt like a privilege, no matter what dark uncertainties the future might hold.

But miraculously, here I am again, baton in hand, score open, musicians assembled, actors in the wings, an audience gathered. I have been given another chance. And there is a new element.

Conducting *The Visit*, after confronting my fear of Parkinson's, has been life-changing. It has taken me decades of working in musical theater to be ready to learn one more lesson. Just as Dorothy Gale, returning from Oz, sees home through fresh eyes, I, too, discover something that has been there all along.

I find I can dedicate each performance to the opportunity to conduct *this* show, on *this* night, with *these* musicians, and *these* actors, for *this* audience.

I am not trying to re-create last night's performance.

I am here. Now. Listening.

Making music in the present tense.

It doesn't sound like a major realization. It may well be something that other conductors have always been able to do. For me, it is revelatory.

I can feel its effect on the musicians. The pit at the Lyceum Theatre becomes a place of ardently attentive music-making. Because of it, every performance of *The Visit* is a gift to be treasured.

THE REVIEWS ARE MIXED; AUDIENCES ARE SPARSE. *THE VISIT* RECEIVES FIVE TONY nominations. The producers are humbled, honored, hopeful. It's so disappointingly familiar. Have I really spent fifteen years working on this show, only to end up here again?

The Tony Awards have returned to Radio City Music Hall. We will be performing "Love and Love Alone" and then the "Mazurka." Margery greets me with an odd look in her eyes. Her salt-and-pepper hair is now mostly salt. "Follow me," she says, somewhat shamefacedly.

Curiously, instead of escorting me to the pit, we take an elevator up to an area I have never seen. Apparently, the backstage is so crowded that the only space the Tony Award producers could find for the conductors is a men's room on the seventh floor.

A camera has been hung on the bathroom wall, next to a mirror. A small video screen by the sink shows the stage. An X is taped to the bathroom floor. Standing on the X, we listen to the recorded orchestra track on headphones. When we conduct, we must blindly hope that our arms are visible in the video shot that the distant actors are watching.

Other music directors—friends of mine, all in tuxes—stand awkwardly in the men's room. Todd, my assistant from *She Loves Me*, is there to pretend to conduct the number from *An American in Paris*. We laugh. If ever we needed confirmation of the low regard with which "the business" views the artists who conduct their musicals, this is it. I look at the drab tiles on the bathroom walls, the harsh fluorescent lights. Thirty-four years of working as a professional music director have led me here. Zoe Caldwell's words come zinging back to me: "Yet another opportunity for abject humiliation."

Chita looks tiny on the Radio City Music Hall stage. We lose all five of the awards for which we were nominated. I feel nauseous.

I keep thinking about the ridiculous amount of time I have spent preparing this undesired show.

And it occurs to me that maybe my stay in this particular world has run its course. It's been a fantastic ride—the crushing disappointments balanced by so many dreams come thrillingly true. But is it, now, time for *me* to pass the baton to a younger musician, to relinquish my cherished position on the podium, and to take a step in another, as yet unknown, direction?

Todd and I somehow take the wrong elevator when we leave the men's bathroom/conducting area. We end up in a long, unfamiliar corridor lined with doors. I half expect to see a white rabbit in the distance ahead of us.

One of the doors flies open, and a riotous throng of colorfully costumed children comes tumbling toward us. They are running, giddy with post-performance energy, squealing and laughing, pulling phones and video games out of their embroidered silk tunics and sarongs. Seconds later, another door opens and a parade of handsome sailors appears, striding briskly in their crisp uniforms, headed for the stage. *The King and I* collides with *On the Town*, and the two groups meld into a ragtag dance of precision and chaos, white and gold and green and pink and red.

I have every reason to despair. *The Visit* soon closes, having played a mere twelve weeks on Broadway. Once again, I will be starting over. But this time, I feel held. By Pedro, my new husband. And by the misfits and oddballs that keep us company. Who knows what the future might bring?

Broadway is a complex Wonderland. But I'm where I always dreamed of being.

Part of a community in which I can be myself.

I can be the president of the Athletic Losers Group.

I can be as gay as Cole Porter.

I can be a conductor with a degenerative brain disease.

Facing the music has set me free.

Chapter Titles

For those of you who may have been wondering what the musical phrases at the beginning of each chapter represent, here are the corresponding lyrics.

Prelude: 2007
"Another op'nin', another show . . ." *Kiss Me Kate*; Music and lyrics by Cole Porter

Chapter One: 1967
"Why, oh why, oh why-o . . ." "Ohio," *Wonderful Town*; Music by Leonard Bernstein, lyrics by Betty Comden and Adolph Green

Chapter Two: 1970
"A whole new world . . ."; *Aladdin*; Music by Alan Menken, lyrics by Tim Rice

Chapter Three: 1972
"Chicks and ducks and geese better scurry . . ."; "The Surrey with the Fringe on Top," *Oklahoma!* Music by Richard Rodgers, lyrics by Oscar Hammerstein II

Chapter Four: 1974
"I'd like to be a lion tamer, sequins and tights and silk top hats . . ." *The Magic Show*; Music and lyrics by Stephen Schwartz

Interlude: 2007
"There's a special kind of people known as 'show people' . . ." *Curtains*; Music by John Kander, lyrics by Fred Ebb

Chapter Five: 1975
"Try to remember the kind of September . . ." *The Fantasticks*; Music by Harvey Schmidt, lyrics by Tom Jones

Chapter Six: 1976
"One singular sensation, every little move she makes . . ." *A Chorus Line*; Music by Marvin Hamlisch, lyrics by Ed Kleban

Chapter Seven: 1980
"There's no business like show business, like no business I know . . ." *Annie Get Your Gun*; Music and lyrics by Irving Berlin

Chapter Eight: 1980
"I don't know how to love him . . ." *Jesus Christ Superstar*; Music by Andrew Lloyd Webber, lyrics by Tim Rice

Chapter Nine: 1981
"Light the candles, get the ice out, roll the rug up, it's today . . ." *Mame*; Music and lyrics by Jerry Herman

Chapter Ten: 1981
"It started out like a song . . ." "Good Thing Going," *Merrily We Roll Along*; Music and lyrics by Stephen Sondheim

Chapter Eleven: 1981
"Give my regards to Broadway . . ." *Little Johnny Jones*; Music and lyrics by George M. Cohan

Chapter Twelve: 1981
"It's our time, breathe it in . . ." *Merrily We Roll Along*; Music and lyrics by Stephen Sondheim

Chapter Thirteen: 1981
"Behold the hills of tomorrow . . ." *Merrily We Roll Along*; Music and lyrics by Stephen Sondheim

Chapter Fourteen: 1982
"Look for a sky of blue . . ." *Little Mary Sunshine*; Music and lyrics by Rick Besoyan

Interlude: 2007
"We're off to see the wizard . . ." *The Wizard of Oz*; Music by Harold Arlen, lyrics by E.Y. Harburg

Chapter Fifteen: 1984
"Only make believe I love you . . ." *Show Boat*; Music by Jerome Kern, lyrics by Oscar Hammerstein II

Chapter Sixteen: 1990
"You know what we'll do? What? We'll do a revue. What? *What?* We'll do a revue of our own . . ." "Opening Doors," *Merrily We Roll Along*; Music and lyrics by Stephen Sondheim

Chapter Seventeen: 1991
"Gather around, I've got a story to tell . . ." "Ring Them Bells," *And the World Goes 'Round*; Music by John Kander, lyrics by Fred Ebb

Chapter Eighteen: 1993
"She loves me. And to my amazement . . ." *She Loves Me*; Music by Jerry Bock, lyrics by Sheldon Harnick

Chapter Nineteen: 1994
"Maria. I just met a girl named Maria . . ." *West Side Story*; Music by Leonard Bernstein, lyrics by Stephen Sondheim

Chapter Twenty: 1995
"Down by the sea lived a lonesome oyster, every day getting sadder and moister . . ." "The Tale of the Oyster"; Music and lyrics by Cole Porter

Interlude: 2007
"I could while away the hours, conferrin' with the flowers, consultin' with the rain . . ." "If I Only Had a Brain," *The Wizard of Oz*; Music by Harold Arlen, lyrics by E.Y. Harburg

Chapter Twenty-One: 1997
"Here I go again . . ." "Willing to Ride," *Steel Pier*; Music by John Kander, lyrics by Fred Ebb

Chapter Twenty-Two: 1998
"Climb every mountain, ford every stream . . ." *The Sound of Music*; Music by Richard Rodgers, lyrics by Oscar Hammerstein II

Chapter Twenty-Three: 1998
"Crime of the century! Crime of the century! Giving the world a thrill . . ." *Ragtime*; Music by Stephen Flaherty, lyrics by Lynn Ahrens

Chapter Twenty-Four: 2000
"Sunrise, sunset, sunrise, sunset . . ." *Fiddler on the Roof*; Music by Jerry Bock, lyrics by Sheldon Harnick

Chapter Twenty-Five: 2007
"Put on your Sunday clothes when you feel down and out . . ." *Hello, Dolly!*; Music and lyrics by Jerry Herman

Chapter Twenty-Six: 2008
"I'm so happy, I'm afraid I'll die here in your arms . . ." *Passion*; Music and lyrics by Stephen Sondheim

Chapter Twenty-Seven: 2010
"Goodnight, my someone, good night, my love . . ." *The Music Man*; Music and lyrics by Meredith Willson

Chapter Twenty-Eight: 2011
"When you're young, feeling oh so strong . . ." "Love and Love Alone," *The Visit*; Music by John Kander, lyrics by Fred Ebb

Chapter Twenty-Nine: 2014
"Our days are tied to curtains, they rise, and they fall . . ." "Show People," *Curtains*; Music by John Kander, lyrics by Fred Ebb

Chapter Thirty: 2014
"I'm gettin' married in the mornin' . . ." *My Fair Lady*; Music by Frederick Loewe, lyrics by Alan Jay Lerner

Chapter Thirty-One: 2014
"An English teacher, an English teacher . . ." *Bye Bye Birdie*; Music by Charles Strouse, lyrics by Lee Adams

Postlude: 2015
"Getting to know you, getting to know all about you . . ." *The King and I*; Music by Richard Rodgers, lyrics by Oscar Hammerstein II

Musicals the Phillips Exeter Academy Library Should Have in its Record Collection

by David Loud
November 7, 1975

110 in the Shade

1776

A Chorus Line

*A Funny Thing Happened
on the Way to the Forum*

A Little Night Music

Annie Get Your Gun

Anyone Can Whistle

Anything Goes

Applause

Bells Are Ringing

The Boys from Syracuse

Brigadoon

Bye Bye Birdie

Cabaret

Call Me Madam

Camelot

Candide

Carousel

Chicago

Company

Do Re Mi

Don't Bother Me, I Can't Cope

The Fantasticks

Fiddler on the Roof

Finian's Rainbow

Fiorello!

Flower Drum Song

Follies

Funny Girl

Gentlemen Prefer Blondes

George M

Godspell

Goodtime Charley

Grease

Guys and Dolls

Gypsy

Hair

Hello, Dolly!

How to Succeed in Business
Without Really Trying

I Do! I Do!

Irene

Jaques Brel Is Alive and Well
and Living in Paris

Jesus Christ Superstar

The King and I

Kismet

Kiss Me Kate

Lady in the Dark

The Magic Show

Mame

The Me Nobody Knows

The Music Man

My Fair Lady

No, No, Nannette

Oklahoma!

Once Upon a Mattress

Pacific Overtures

Pal Joey

Pippin

Porgy and Bess

Raisin

The Robber Bridegroom

Seesaw

Shenandoah

Show Boat

The Sound of Music

South Pacific

St. Louis Woman

Sweet Charity

The Threepenny Opera

The Wiz

West Side Story

Where's Charley?

You're a Good Man,
Charlie Brown

Acknowledgments

This book was born because I was asked to deliver a commencement address to the graduating class of 2016 at North Country School. The remarkably persuasive Judith Regan was in attendance, and she kindly approached me with the idea of writing a book, based on the speech I had just given. I must have looked like I wasn't taking her suggestion seriously because she also took the trouble to find and explain to my husband, Pedro, that her interest was genuine and that she was, in fact, a successful publisher with her own imprint: Regan Arts. A week later, Judith and I met at her impressively chic downtown Manhattan office, and I've been writing and rewriting ever since.

I would like to thank my first listeners and readers, Patty Ben Peterson, David Garrison, Mana Allen, Randy Graff, Michele Ragusa, Tom Richter, Valerie Wright, Martha Thomas, Amber Edwards, Erin Dilly, Sam Davis, Lynn Ahrens, David Hyde Pierce, John Kander, Roger Loud, and John Berendt for their frank criticism and unwavering support as I wandered down wrong roads and dead ends, and my musical theater history students at Manhattan School of Music for listening, over the years, to my chapters on *She Loves Me*, *Ragtime*, *Merrily We Roll Along*, *Sondheim on Sondheim*, and *The Scottsboro Boys*, and in particular, my student Madeline Bergeron for enthusiastically shepherding me into the world of social media.

Heartfelt thanks to Jane Labanz for her unstintingly generous grammatical suggestions, Kathryn Blessington for her editorial clarity, Vanessa Lemonides for her eagle-eyed fact-checking, and Alexis Gargagliano for her powerful editing and her willingness to repeatedly ask me hard questions.

I am especially grateful to Stephen Sondheim for allowing me to use two lyrics of his that were cut from *Merrily We Roll Along,* and to Don Rand for granting me permission to include his lyrics for the final chorale from his oratorio, *Little Red Riding Hood.*

Finally, I wanted to express my gratitude to the extraordinary musical assistants who made it possible for me to keep working as a music director while I was struggling with the effects of Parkinson's: Neil Douglas Reilly, Haley Bennett, Harrison Beck, Hannah Bernard, Nehemiah Luckett, and the young intern himself, Aaron Fischer.

A Note About the Author

David Loud is currently teaching in the musical theater program at Manhattan School of Music, a program that he helped found in 2016.